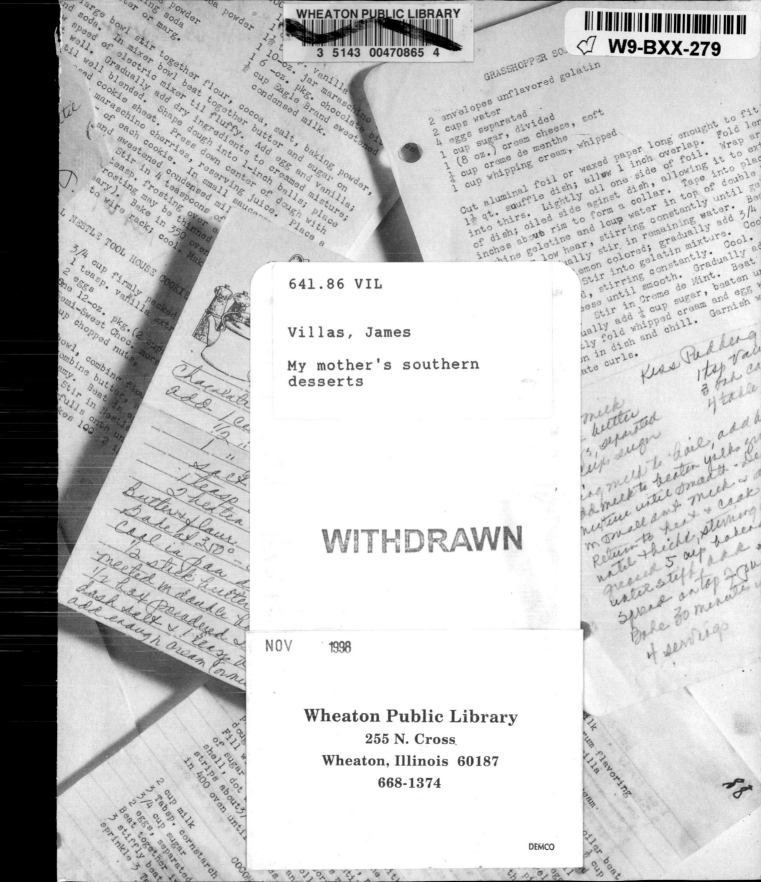

My Mother's
Southern Desserts

OTHER BOOKS BY JAMES VILLAS

My Mother's Southern Desserts

JAMES VILLAS

with

MARTHA PEARL VILLAS

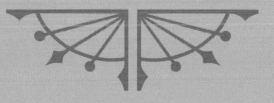

William Morrow and Company, Inc.
New York

Copyright © 1998 by James Villas
Photography copyright © 1998 by Dennis Gottlieb

Photography by Dennis Gottlieb
Food styling by Fred Thompson
Prop styling by Randi Barritt

It is the policy of William Morrow and Company, and its imprints and affiliates, recognizing the importance of preserving what has been written, to print the books we publish on acid-free paper, and we exert our best efforts to that end.

Library of Congress Cataloging-in-Publication Data

Villas, James.
My mother's southern desserts / by James Villas with
Martha Pearl Villas.—1st ed.
p.   cm.
Includes index.
ISBN 0-688-15695-9
1.   Desserts.   2.   Cookery, American—Southern style.   I.   Villas,
Martha Pearl.   II.   Title.
TX773.V544   1998
641.8'6—dc21   97-51399
CIP

Printed in the United States of America

First Edition

1 2 3 4 5 6 7 8 9 10

BOOK DESIGN BY JEANNETTE JACOBS

www.williammorrow.com

To Lady Mary Homi

Acknowledgments

Once again, a joyful toast of Jack Daniel's with a splash of branch to our loyal editor at William Morrow, Pam Hoenig, who, from the start, has encouraged, prodded, questioned, consoled, made invaluable suggestions, and even developed a fine Rebel sweet tooth. Our thanks also to fellow Southerner Fred Thompson and to Dennis Gottlieb for making the desserts in this book look as wonderful as they taste.

Contents

Introduction

"Jimmy, I'm not going to tell you again to quit eating that icing," I remember Mother carping many, many years ago as I dipped my finger once more into the luscious caramel frosting and licked it clean. "If you keep that up, there's not gonna be enough left for Paw Paw's birthday cake—and you're gonna be sick as a dog. Now stop it this minute!"

And with that stern directive, she pushed the bowl to the back of the counter where I couldn't reach it, finished positioning the three cake layers precisely on the large crystal plate, spooned a big glob of frosting on the top, and, using an icing spatula, began very slowly and methodically to spread the brownish, glistening mixture toward the edges of the cake. Another glob, more careful daubing, and then, gathering smaller amounts of the frosting on the spatula, she let me (awkwardly) ice parts of the sides before taking over again and rendering a texture that was smooth as silk. Standing back, she studied the masterpiece as intently as an artist would a canvas, made a few decorative strokes here and there, and, forgetting momentarily her scolding as she handed me back the coated spatula, uttered proudly, "Now that's a pretty cake."

Although I have endless childhood memories of cooking with Mother while growing up in Charlotte, North Carolina, none are so vivid as those connected with the staggering array of Southern desserts produced for every conceivable special occasion of the year. How well I recall the sensation of first mixing with my hands the thick, aromatic, fruit-and-nut-studded batter for her many Christmas fruitcakes and helping her assemble the ingredients for a rich Valentine's Day Nesselrode Pie or summertime Mixed Berry Crumble. At Halloween, it would intrigue me how Mother would temper egg yolks (a technique I wouldn't master for years) while preparing my Unca' Nalle's favorite Butterscotch Pudding, and when she'd make Benne Cookies, Jimbo Treats, Pecan Diamonds, and Lord knows what other distinctive confections to pack into her "friendship" boxes and holiday tins for shut-ins, or to thank someone for a kind gesture, or to congratulate a mother on the birth of a new baby, I could almost count on the summons, "Come on, son, and help me fix these." For Mother's wondrous Snowflake Coconut Cake baked specially for christening receptions, it was always my duty to drain the milk from the coconut, crack the shell with a hammer, and pry out the fresh meat; for her Thanksgiving Huguenot Torte, she'd let me beat the sherried cream to be spread on top; and when she and Daddy would decide to celebrate the Fourth of July or Labor Day by throwing an elaborate ice cream social for friends and neighbors, guess who got stuck with peeling and cutting up the peaches and cranking the ice cream churn—the reward being the privilege of licking every last morsel of that velvety frozen nectar off the dasher?

Although the Southern passion for rich, dramatic desserts is legendary, my mother's involvement with sweets as the ultimate emblem of social and culinary celebration has, for the past sixty or so years, bordered on obsession. Of course most Southern ladies do take great pride in the desserts they prepare for Christmas, Thanksgiving, Easter, birthdays, and other major traditional holidays and events, and rest assured that many of Mother's relatives and friends provide stiff competition when it comes to turning out a monumental pound cake, a more than respectable pecan or sweet potato pie, and a classic fruit cobbler. Few, on the other hand, still place the same serious emphasis as Mother does on observing Father's Day, the Kentucky Derby, graduations, and even funerals with a special Buttermilk Pie, or spicy Persimmon Pudding, or stunning Angel Bavarian; and few can boast such a vast (and colorful) repertory of venerable creations for specific occasions, like Mother's complex Hummingbird Cake, her Dubie Slump, and her creamy Coconut Igloos. I think it's safe to say that you can name the circumstance and Mother has just the right dessert with which to celebrate, honor, commemorate, or glorify it. "I know we eat too many sweets in the South," she confesses, "but that's part of our tradition, and, like my mama and her mama before, if I couldn't find legitimate reasons to celebrate with a beautiful cake or mousse or fruit crisp, I'd invent excuses."

And over all these years, legitimate reasons have included not only the more obvious celebratory picnics, backyard cookouts, fund-raising barbecues, church suppers, and ice cream socials but also the many bridge luncheons, book club meetings, Charity League workshops, morning coffees, and afternoon teas that play as important a role in Mother's life in Charlotte as the festive cocktail parties and formal dinners she still loves to host as much today as when I was an adolescent. Actually, I guess that Mother enjoys nothing better than her "get-togethers with the girls," all of whom share her love of cooking in general and her infatuation with desserts in particular. Whether they're just socializing or engaged in serious work projects, the friends never abandon for long the topic of Southern cakes, pies, and puddings, discussing which ones they've served or tasted recently, praising or criticizing brutally any cobblers or brown Bettys or soufflés that have appeared in the paper, in magazines, or in new cookbooks, and, to be sure, exchanging ideas and one recipe after the next. Only rarely have I had the opportunity to witness one of these sessions, but even if I have detected more than a little jealousy when the subjects of perfect fruitcakes, mud pies, fruit flummeries, and gingerbreads are genteelly debated, I've never failed to be impressed that these ladies are not only contributing fresh dimension to Mother's (and each other's) dessert legacy but constantly enriching an aspect of our Southern culinary heritage that must be preserved.

Which, of course, is the reason I decided to write this book under the steady guidance, ardent supervision, and suspicious eye of Mother every step of the way. As usual, it was push-and-tug from beginning to end as I waded through the multitude of dessert recipes casually jotted down in her disorganized, sacred black "receipt" book, tried to decipher and interpret scant directions on cards and napkins and ragged sheets of paper, and quizzed and questioned and antagonized her in the effort to produce recipes that would be clear, precise, and fully complete. To wit, her directions for making Hummingbird Cake:

"Mix everything together—bake till done—frost with cream cheese icing." Period.

"But, Missy," I protest in utter frustration as we begin the batter, "shouldn't the dry ingredients be combined separately before adding liquid and stirring in the fruit and nuts?"

"Why, of course they should!" she huffs impatiently, mixing and moistening the ingredients so quickly and deftly that I lose track of exactly what she's doing. "Everybody knows that—or at least every *Southern* cook knows."

"And you don't even say what temperature to bake it at," I continue, not having noticed that she put the oven on ten minutes ago.

"Three hundred and fifty degrees," she mutters, greasing three cake pans with her fingers. "Hummingbirds are always cooked at three hundred and fifty degrees. People who don't know that shouldn't be making Hummingbird Cake."

"And this frosting," I persist. "Why can't it be made with granulated instead of confectioners' sugar?"

She glares at me, then pops me on the rear. "Jimmy, for Lord's sake, didn't I teach you anything about baking? If you want a lumpy icing, go ahead . . . just go ahead and use regular sugar and the icing will be dense and heavy as lard. Honestly, son!"

We do argue and cajole and rib each other in endless ways that often startle those with no sense of humor or awareness of our extremely close bond, but, as a result, I not only have learned more from her about authentic Southern desserts than I'd ever glean from any cookbook but have slowly come to recognize her incredible instinct for dealing so readily with subtle ingredient and flavor combinations, dough and batter textures, creamed mixtures and frostings, variable baking temperatures, and all the other dessert complexities that can intimidate even the most confident home cooks. As you can see from most of the recipes in this book, Mother makes it all seem so simple, and the truth is, it *is* all relatively simple if you just follow her (that is, my) directions and keep a cool head. "I've never understood why some people shy away from making fancy cakes and soufflés, delicate custards and puddings, and plain old cobblers," I've heard her exclaim over and over to equally talented cooks (fellow Southerner Craig Claiborne included). "I say just use common sense, practice as much as possible, and try . . . to have fun!"

Although the recipes in this book are divided according to various celebrations and observances that Mother generally equates with certain desserts, this does not necessarily imply that she always prepares a specific dish only for a specific occasion. Obviously, she does not make holiday fruitcakes or hand-dipped Santa Claus candies for summer picnics and cookouts, nor would she ever dream of serving Strawberry Shortcake or homemade ice cream except at warm-weather events. However, she's very flexible when it comes to year-round favorites like Lemon Cheese Cake, Apple Dumplings, Chocolate-Almond Bavarian, and virtually all cookies and coffee cakes, and while it's a veritable ritual for her to make Praline Ice Cream Pie for New Year's and Satan Chocolate Pound Cake for Halloween, should someone (like me) express a craving at any time for such a specialty, she's only too happy to oblige. "I have my own particular ideas about what desserts to serve when," she clarifies, "but so long as people are aware of the seasons and really try hard to use fresh ingredients, there's no reason on earth why most of my desserts can't be adapted to many different occasions. Just use your imagination."

Red Devil Cake, Crème de Menthe Pie, Big Puddin's Fruit Ice Cream, Blackberry Fool, Coconut Igloos, Secession Brown Betty, Sassy Shortbread, Bridal Snowballs, Pussycat Syllabub—some of the (dead serious) names of Mother's desserts almost drip with Southern mystery and quaintness, and to call them by any other titles would, to use one of her regular expressions, "make the fur fly." What's important is that these confections couldn't be any more personal and distinctive, symbols of Mother's long and productive life devoted in such great part to bringing joy and happiness to others the only way she knows how. If ever the cliché "labor of love" had more apt meaning, it would certainly have to apply to Mother's involvement with all the sweets that come out of her Southern kitchen, desserts that are so warmly satisfying, different, and, yes, lots of fun to make.

TRADITIONAL HOLIDAY CELEBRATIONS & OBSERVANCES

Christmas

&

New Year's

The Holiday White Fruitcake

The Original "Prize Cake"

Patsy Ann's Orange Slice Cake

Sacrifice Jam Cake

Resolution Cranberry-Orange Spice Cake

Cinnamon-Walnut Coffee Cake

Hootie's Eggnog-Walnut Pie

Sugar Bowl Praline Ice Cream Pie

Tidewater Trifle

Coconut Igloos

Bourbon Cream Mold with Shaved Chocolate

Christmas Ambrosia

Santa Claus Hand-Dipped Candy Balls

Christmas Whiskey Pecans

For Mother, Christmas is a nonstop religious, social, and culinary ritual that hasn't changed one iota since I was a child. In her home, the season begins immediately after Thanksgiving with the making of the first fruitcakes and extends to after New Year's (often to Twelfth Night), and I truly don't know which is more elaborate, the house decorations (both a large *and* a small lighted Christmas tree, all sorts of wreaths, figurines, and ornaments, exquisite handmade table skirts and cloths, a tiny snow village on the mantelpiece, etc.) or the incredible array of desserts and confections expected by both children and adults.

Stacked in colorful tins are aromatic cakes, six or seven varieties of cookies, Whiskey Pecans, large coffee cakes, and hand-dipped candy balls, all intended to feed the steady flow of family and friends who stop in "to visit" and to play some role in all the holiday lunches, dinners, afternoon teas, and cocktail parties that Mother loves to host. It seems that she is forever preparing desserts when she's not entertaining—a Prize Cake for some church benefit, an elegant Bourbon Cream Mold or Eggnog-Walnut Pie for a midday bridge game with the ladies, a sumptuous Tidewater Trifle or big crystal bowl of Ambrosia for Christmas Eve dinner, and, of course, all types of sweets to be given as presents or taken to shut-ins. Often we cook together, and while I'm usually exhausted after a morning of mixing, rolling, baking, frosting, shaving, and decorating, Mother is just getting her second wind and is ready to continue till she's assured that there are "plenty of Christmas goodies in the house."

Christmas Eve dinner and Christmas breakfast and dinner are royal productions at home, but no more so than Mother's festive New Year's Eve dinner and, next day, the Sugar Bowl blast where neighbors, while watching the game, traditionally are served her meringue-topped Praline Ice Cream Pie and whatever cakes and cookies might be left over from Christmas. After this, you'd think that she would let up baking for a while, only to have her remind me that "Valentine's Day is just around the corner."

THE HOLIDAY WHITE FRUITCAKE

In My Mother's Southern Kitchen, I wrote at some length about the luscious dark heirloom fruitcakes that Mother bakes every year between Thanksgiving and Christmas and the role this ritual has played in our family for generations. Here I present her much less involved but equally remarkable white fruitcake (i.e., a cake with no dark fruits, spices, or crystallized citrus peels) intended for everyday eating and as a gift to special friends. Suffice it that if you're still under the sad illusion that all fruitcakes by nature are wretched, wait till you taste this moist, sapid, boozy masterpiece that has become one of Mother's most celebrated signature desserts. Stored in airtight containers and sprinkled periodically with a little bourbon or rum, the cakes just get better and better with age.

2 cups (4 sticks) butter, softened
3 cups granulated sugar
14 large eggs
5 cups all-purpose flour
2 teaspoons baking powder
1½ cups light rum or bourbon, plus more for soaking
2 teaspoons pure vanilla extract
2 teaspoons pure almond extract
2 teaspoons pure lemon extract
2½ pounds crystallized pineapple, coarsely chopped
2½ pounds crystallized cherries, about 8 whole cherries reserved and remainder coarsely chopped
2¼ pounds pecans, chopped

Grease one 10 × 4-inch tube pan and two 8 × 4½ × 2½-inch loaf pans and set aside.

In a large mixing bowl, cream the butter and sugar together with an electric mixer till light and fluffy, then add the eggs one at a time, beating constantly. Sift 3 cups of the flour and the baking powder into the mixture and blend thoroughly. Add 1 cup of the rum or bourbon and the extracts and blend thoroughly. Mix the chopped fruit and pecans with the remaining 2 cups flour in another large mixing bowl and fold them well into the creamed mixture.

Preheat the oven to 250°F and place a small pan of water in the bottom of the oven to provide moisture.

Scrape the batter evenly into the prepared pans, arrange the reserved cherries in a decorative manner over the tops, and bake till a cake tester or straw inserted in the center comes out clean, about 3 hours. Pour the remaining ½ cup rum or bourbon over the tops of the cakes and let them cool completely in the pans. Wrap each cake securely in cheesecloth soaked in rum or bourbon and store them in airtight containers for at least 3 weeks before cutting.

YIELD 1 large 5- to 6-pound cake; two 2½-pound cakes

THE ORIGINAL "PRIZE CAKE"

After Emma Rylander Lane of Clayton, Alabama, created and won a first prize for this sensational cake in the late nineteenth century, for years locals called it simply Prize Cake. Then, as the cake's fame spread throughout the South and beyond, it gradually became known to some as Lane Cake, though many, like my Georgia grandmother and great-grandmother, always referred to it by the original name—and Mother still does. In any case, the distinctive cake is now a Christmas tradition and, in Mother's home, as treasured as her fruitcakes.

For the cake

2 cups granulated sugar
1 cup (2 sticks) butter, softened
2 teaspoons pure vanilla extract
3 cups all-purpose flour
1 tablespoon baking powder
1 teaspoon salt
1 cup milk
7 large egg whites (yolks reserved), beaten to stiff peaks (see Sweet Note)

For the filling

½ cup (1 stick) butter
7 large egg yolks
1 cup granulated sugar
1 cup chopped pecans
1 cup seedless dark raisins
½ cup fresh (see Sweet Note on page 17) or frozen grated coconut
½ teaspoon pure vanilla extract
½ cup bourbon

Preheat the oven to 375°F. Grease and flour two 9-inch square cake pans and set aside.

To make the cake, combine the sugar, butter, and vanilla in a large mixing bowl and beat with an electric mixer till light and fluffy. Sift the flour, baking powder, and salt into another bowl and, alternately with the milk, gradually beat this into the sugar mixture. Carefully fold in the egg whites, then scrape equal amounts of the batter into the prepared pans and bake till a cake tester or straw inserted in the center comes out clean, about 25 minutes. Turn the cakes out onto a wire rack and let cool.

To make the filling, melt the butter in the top of a double boiler over simmering (not boiling) water. Meanwhile, in a large mixing bowl, beat together the egg yolks and sugar. Gradually add to the butter, stirring constantly till the mixture is thick enough to coat the back of a spoon. Remove the pan from the heat, stir in the pecans, raisins, coconut, vanilla, and bourbon, and let cool.

*P*lace the first cake layer on a cake plate and spread about one third of the filling over the top. Add the second cake layer and spread the remaining filling over the top and around the sides. Cover the cake and let stand overnight for the flavors to meld before cutting.

YIELD One 2-layer 9-inch cake; at least 8 servings

Martha's Sweet Note

*W*hen beating egg whites or cream, both the bowl and beaters must be completely dry, since even a trace of moisture can ruin their texture.

PATSY ANN'S ORANGE SLICE CAKE

This unusual firm Christmas cake is the pride of Mother's first cousin, Patsy Ann White, who, for as long as anybody can remember, has never failed to show up at the house on Christmas Eve bearing never a whole but a half-cake to share with the family. When Mother first told me about the cake, I sort of snickered over the orange slice candy; then, when she produced one herself, I tasted it and understood immediately why everyone loves it so much.

For the cake

1 pound orange slice candy, chopped
1 pound pitted dates, chopped
2 cups chopped pecans or walnuts
1 tablespoon grated orange rind
4 cups all-purpose flour
1 cup (2 sticks) butter, softened
2 cups granulated sugar
4 large eggs
½ cup buttermilk (see Sweet Note)
1 teaspoon baking soda
1 tablespoon pure vanilla extract
½ teaspoon salt
3½ ounces frozen grated coconut, thawed

For the glaze
½ cup fresh orange juice
½ cup confectioners' sugar, sifted

Preheat the oven to 275°F. Grease and flour a 10-inch tube pan, tapping out any excess flour, and set aside.

To make the cake, combine the candy, dates, nuts, orange rind, and 2 cups of the flour in a large mixing bowl, mix well, and set aside. In another large mixing bowl, cream the butter and sugar together with an electric mixer till smooth, then add the eggs one at a time, beating well after each addition. In a small bowl, combine the buttermilk, baking soda, vanilla, and salt, mix well, and add alternately with the remaining 2 cups flour to the creamed mixture, beating till well blended. Add the candy mixture plus the coconut to the mixture and, using your hands, mix till well blended. Scrape the batter into the prepared pan, place the pan on the middle shelf of the oven with a separate shallow pan of water on the bottom shelf, and bake till a cake tester or straw inserted in the center comes out clean, about 3 hours.

continued

Meanwhile, to make the glaze, combine the orange juice and sugar in a small bowl and stir till well blended.

Remove the cake from the oven and, while it is still hot, spoon the glaze slowly over the top till absorbed by the cake. Let the cake cool completely, then cover with plastic wrap and chill overnight before removing from the pan.

YIELD One 10-inch tube cake; 10 to 12 servings

Martha's Sweet Note

To substitute whole milk for buttermilk in baking, add 1 teaspoon of white vinegar per quart of whole milk and let it stand for about 10 minutes.

SACRIFICE JAM CAKE

Spicy jam cake has always been one of the many ceremonial cakes that Mother makes for Christmas, but the modifier in the name came about only recently when, over Christmas Eve dinner, I heard her exclaim to guests, "I'll have you know that I have to sacrifice two whole cups of my homemade jam for this cake to turn out right." And since every summer I go through the laborious task of helping Mother put up all her fruit jams and preserves, I can assure you that using some of them in a cake is indeed a sacrifice! I've discovered that high-grade commercial jams make a very respectable cake, but for truly glorious results, nothing equals the flavor and texture of homemade (including some found at country farm stands—but don't tell Mother I said so!).

1 cup (2 sticks) butter, softened
1 cup granulated sugar
4 large eggs, separated
1 teaspoon pure vanilla extract
3 cups all-purpose flour
2 teaspoons baking soda
2 teaspoons ground cinnamon
2 teaspoons ground allspice
1 teaspoon ground cloves
1 teaspoon ground nutmeg
1 cup buttermilk (see Sweet Note on page 10)
1 cup seedless blackberry jam
1 cup seedless raspberry jam

Preheat the oven to 325°F. Grease a 10-inch tube pan and set aside.

In a large mixing bowl, cream the butter and sugar together with an electric mixer till smooth, then add the egg yolks and vanilla and beat till well blended. In a medium-size mixing bowl, combine the flour, baking soda, and spices. Add the dry ingredients alternately with the buttermilk to the creamed mixture, beating well after each addition. Stir the two jams into the batter and mix well. Wash and dry the mixer beaters, then, in a medium-size mixing bowl, beat the egg whites till stiff but not dry peaks form. With a rubber spatula, fold the whites gently into the batter. Scrape the batter into the prepared pan and bake for 30 minutes.

Increase the oven temperature to 350°F and continue baking till a cake tester or straw inserted in the center comes out clean, about 40 minutes longer. Let the cake cool for 10 minutes, then turn it out onto a wire rack to cool completely. Serve the cake plain or iced with Seven-Minute Frosting (page 252).

YIELD One 10-inch tube cake; 12 to 15 servings

RESOLUTION CRANBERRY-ORANGE SPICE CAKE

*M*other's ritual celebration of New Year's Day began many years ago when my father would invite friends and colleagues over to the house to watch the football games on TV and she would come up with a traditional Southern buffet to feed everybody. Today, Daddy roots for his favorite teams from on high, but come every January 1, Mother still religiously has fans to the house, serves them whiskey sours, fills the serving bowls and platters with hog jowls, "lucky" black-eyed peas, collard greens, and corn bread, and cuts her beloved cranberry and orange Resolution spice cake.

½ cup (1 stick) butter, softened
1 cup granulated sugar
1 large egg
1¾ cups all-purpose flour
1 teaspoon baking soda
1 teaspoon ground cinnamon
½ teaspoon ground cloves
¼ teaspoon salt
1 cup seedless dark raisins
½ cup coarsely chopped walnuts
One 14-ounce jar cranberry-orange relish (available in most supermarkets)

*P*reheat the oven to 350°F. Grease and flour a 10-inch tube pan, tapping off some excess flour, and set aside.

*I*n a large mixing bowl, cream the butter and sugar together with an electric mixer till smooth, then add the egg and beat till well blended. In another bowl, combine the flour, baking soda, cinnamon, cloves, and salt, mix well, and stir into the creamed mixture. Stir in the raisins and walnuts, mixing well. Stir in the relish and mix thoroughly. Scrape the batter into the prepared pan and bake till a cake tester or straw inserted into the center comes out clean, about 1 hour. Transfer the cake to a cake plate and let cool.

YIELD One 10-inch tube cake; 8 to 10 servings

Martha's Sweet Note

Since even lightly salted butter will make cakes (and some cookies) stick to the pan, I make it a general practice to grease baking pans, tins, and sheets with vegetable shortening.

CINNAMON-WALNUT COFFEE CAKE

Although this traditional, versatile coffee cake is a wonderful addition to any festive breakfast or brunch buffet, Mother makes it frequently both for bereavements and, decorated with colorful ribbons, as a gift for special friends— especially during the Christmas holidays. What's particularly appealing about this coffee cake is that it freezes beautifully (up to two or three months) and can be reheated in no time. As with most coffee cakes, I personally love to run a wedge of this one quickly under the broiler and eat it topped with homemade fruit preserves for breakfast.

2½ cups all-purpose flour
1¼ cups granulated sugar
1 tablespoon baking powder
1 teaspoon salt
1 cup milk
¼ cup Crisco shortening
1½ teaspoons pure vanilla extract
2 large eggs
1½ cups coarsely chopped walnuts
1 teaspoon ground cinnamon
2 tablespoons butter, cut into pieces

Preheat the oven to 350°F. Butter a 10-inch round baking pan and set aside.

Into a large mixing bowl, sift together 2 cups of the flour, 1 cup of the sugar, the baking powder, and salt. Add the milk, Crisco, and vanilla and beat for 3 minutes with an electric mixer. Add the eggs and beat 2 minutes longer, then scrape the batter into the prepared pan. Distribute the walnuts evenly over the top.

In a medium-size mixing bowl, combine the remaining ½ cup flour and ¼ cup sugar with the cinnamon, then add the butter and work it in with your fingertips till the mixture resembles coarse meal. Distribute the mixture evenly over the walnuts and bake the cake till a cake tester or straw inserted in the center comes out clean, about 45 minutes. Let the coffee cake cool slightly, transfer to a round serving dish, and cut into wedges.

YIELD One 10-inch coffee cake; 8 to 10 servings

 Martha's Sweet Note

Don't ask me to give all the reasons I use only Crisco shortening. All I know is that the few times I've tried (at Jimmy's instigation) other (cheaper) brands, the baking results have never been exactly right. Crisco always allows the dough for piecrusts to maintain the same texture no matter the baking temperature, resulting in a tender, flaky crust.

HOOTIE'S EGGNOG-WALNUT PIE

Since the walnuts are in the crust instead of the filling, this glorious pie developed by Mother and my sister, Hootie, is one of the most distinctive I've ever tasted. Because of its eggnog flavor, I like to serve it at Thanksgiving or Christmas, while Mother's favorite occasion seems to be one of her guild or Charity League meetings, book club sessions, or bridge games. You can substitute bourbon for the rum with interesting results, but, heretical as it may sound coming from Southerners, I tend to agree with Mother that in cooking, rum holds its flavor better than our more beloved distilled spirit.

Dough for one 9-inch Basic Pie Shell (page 243)
¼ cup crushed walnuts
1 envelope unflavored gelatin
¾ cup milk
3 large eggs, separated
½ cup granulated sugar
¼ teaspoon ground nutmeg
⅛ teaspoon salt
1 teaspoon pure rum extract
1 teaspoon pure vanilla extract
½ cup heavy cream

Preheat the oven to 425°F. Grease a 9-inch pie plate and set aside.

To prepare the pie shell, roll out the dough on a lightly floured work surface to generously fit a greased 9-inch pie plate. Sprinkle the walnuts over the dough, press them into the dough, and fit the dough into the prepared pie plate, trimming off any excess and crimping the edges. Bake till lightly browned, about 13 minutes, then let cool completely.

To make the filling, soften the gelatin in ¼ cup of the milk in a small bowl and set aside. In the top of a double boiler over simmering water, combine the egg yolks, ¼ cup of the sugar, the nutmeg, salt, and the remaining ¼ cup milk and stir till the mixture thickens and coats the back of a spoon. Add the softened gelatin and stir well till the gelatin is completely dissolved. Remove from the heat and let cool, then stir in the rum and vanilla extracts till well blended.

In a small bowl, whip the heavy cream with an electric mixer till stiff peaks form. Set aside and thoroughly wash and dry the beaters. In a medium-size mixing bowl, beat the egg whites with the mixer till stiff peaks form, then gradually beat in the remaining ¼ cup sugar, and, using a rubber spatula, fold the whites into the gelatin mixture. Fold the whipped cream thoroughly into the mixture, then scrape the mixture into the prepared pie shell. Chill the pie well before serving.

YIELD **One 9-inch pie; 6 to 8 servings**

SUGAR BOWL PRALINE ICE CREAM PIE

*I*t doesn't matter that this unusual, incredibly sensuous pie should, by its very nature, be served during the warm months. Years ago, while Mother and Daddy were attending the Sugar Bowl game in New Orleans, she was utterly smitten when a local friend served the pie at a luncheon on the verandah. Naturally, she wasted no time getting the recipe, and from that day on, and despite the generally cold weather in North Carolina at New Year's, the pie has remained fixed in her mind as a specialty to celebrate the Sugar Bowl. To prevent the frozen filling from melting completely, be sure to serve the pie just as soon as the meringue has browned—with the sauce passed on the side.

½ cup firmly packed dark brown sugar
½ cup heavy cream
2 tablespoons butter, softened
1 cup chopped pecans
1½ teaspoons pure vanilla extract
1½ quarts vanilla ice cream
1 prebaked 9-inch Basic Pie Shell (page 243)
3 large egg whites
¼ teaspoon cream of tartar
⅓ cup granulated sugar
Brandy Sauce (page 259)

*I*n a medium-size, heavy skillet, heat and stir the brown sugar over moderate heat till it just begins to melt, 10 to 12 minutes. Gradually blend in the heavy cream, cook till smooth, 2 to 3 minutes, and remove from the heat. Stir in the butter, pecans, and 1 teaspoon of the vanilla till well blended, then let the praline mixture cool.

*P*lace the ice cream in a large mixing bowl, stir just to soften, and quickly fold in the praline mixture. Scrape the mixture into the pie shell and freeze for at least 4 hours.

*P*reheat the oven to 475°F.

*J*ust before serving, place the egg whites, the remaining ½ teaspoon vanilla, and the cream of tartar in a medium-size mixing bowl and beat with an electric mixer till soft peaks form. Gradually add the sugar and beat till stiff peaks form. Spread the meringue on top of the frozen ice cream, making sure to seal the edges, and bake till lightly browned on top, about 4 minutes. Serve the brandy sauce on the side.

YIELD One 9-inch pie; 6 to 8 servings

TIDEWATER TRIFLE

Perhaps reflecting her British-Southern heritage, Mother loves nothing more than a great trifle, and she spent years searching for the perfect recipe till a friend from Tidewater Virginia explained how her English mother used to make hers. Once Mother had mastered the technique, the trifle became a major feature at her elaborate New Year's Eve dinner, and when, just recently, one of my friends, Lowell Judson, presented her with a crystal footed trifle bowl, you would have thought he'd given her gold ingots. If you don't own a genuine trifle bowl (available in finer kitchen supply shops), a simple large glass one works fine.

¼ pound macaroons
One 13 × 9-inch Sponge Cake (page 239)
1 cup apricot jam
3 cups sweet sherry
2 tablespoons plus 1 teaspoon brandy
1 cup Boiled Custard (page 142)
1 pint heavy cream
1 teaspoon pure vanilla extract
2 teaspoons granulated sugar
2 ounces slivered almonds
Maraschino cherries for garnish

Arrange the macaroons over the bottom of a trifle bowl. Cut the sponge cake into thin slices, then spread each slice with jam and arrange the slices evenly over the macaroons. Pour the sherry and 2 tablespoons of the brandy over the top and let the layers soak for about 1 hour.

Pour the custard evenly over the soaked layers. In a medium-size mixing bowl, beat the cream with an electric mixer till thick (*not* stiff, or it won't pipe correctly), then add the vanilla, sugar, and the remaining teaspoon of brandy and beat till well blended. Scrape the whipped cream into a pastry bag and pipe over the top of the trifle in a decorative manner. Garnish the top with the almonds and cherries and chill the trifle for about 2 hours before serving with a large spoon.

YIELD 8 to 10 servings

COCONUT IGLOOS

This is one of Mother's oldest creations and one that she's been serving both at bridge parties and at her New Year's Day dinner (with barbecued pork ribs, collard greens, and, of course, hoppin' John for good luck) since I was a child. Bags of plain, crisp butter cookies are available almost everywhere, but you can substitute any simple, unflavored cookie so long as it's not too soft (the fruit mixture softens the cookies while they stand and meld). You really must use fresh coconut in this recipe.

½ cup (1 stick) butter, softened
1 cup granulated sugar
One 20-ounce can crushed pineapple, well drained
1 cup seedless dark raisins, finely chopped
1 cup finely chopped hazelnuts
Two 8-ounce bags butter cookies (30 cookies each)
1 pint heavy cream
1 cup grated fresh coconut (see Sweet Note)

In a large mixing bowl, cream the butter and sugar together with an electric mixer till light and fluffy, then add the pineapple, raisins, and nuts and mix till well blended. Spread a little fruit mixture over one butter cookie, top with another cookie, spread fruit on top of the second cookie, and finish with a third cookie. (Use 3 cookies for each igloo.) Repeat the procedure till all the cookies and fruit mixture are used up, place on a platter, cover with plastic wrap, and let the igloos stand at room temperature for at least 8 hours.

Wash and dry the mixer beaters, then, in a medium-size mixing bowl, beat the cream till stiff peaks form. Spread the whipped cream lightly on the top and sides of each igloo, and sprinkle the coconut over the tops.

YIELD 20 igloos

 Martha's Sweet Note

To remove fresh coconut meat easily from the shell after draining the milk (using an ice pick or screwdriver), preheat the oven to 400°F and bake the shell for about 15 minutes. While it is still hot, split the shell with a hammer. The meat should come out easily and cleanly, but if it doesn't, pry it from the shell with a small, heavy knife and remove any brown skin with a vegetable peeler.

BOURBON CREAM MOLD WITH SHAVED CHOCOLATE

When members of our family who live out of town come to deliver Christmas presents, Mother always marks the occasion by serving a fairly elaborate midday lunch that traditionally features this beautiful cream mold decorated with shaved chocolate. And why so little bourbon in the recipe? "Because the children wouldn't touch the dessert if there was too much whiskey," she explains almost regretfully—meaning you can feel free to adjust according to taste. For the right light texture, Mother always uses a whisk instead of an electric mixer when beating these ingredients.

1½ envelopes unflavored gelatin
¼ cup water
1 cup confectioners' sugar, sifted
3 large egg yolks
1½ cups milk, scalded (see Sweet Note)
2 teaspoons pure vanilla extract
1 tablespoon bourbon
1½ cups heavy cream, whipped to stiff peaks
Chocolate curls for garnish (see Sweet Note on page 127)

In a small bowl, sprinkle the gelatin over the water and set aside to soften.

In the top of a double boiler, whisk the confectioners' sugar and egg yolks together till creamy, then stir in the milk and vanilla till well blended. Place over briskly simmering (not boiling) water and cook, stirring constantly, till the mixture thickens and coats the back of a spoon, 2 to 3 minutes. Remove from the heat and stir in the softened gelatin, then return to the heat and stir just till the gelatin is completely dissolved. Strain the mixture through a sieve into a large mixing bowl, add the bourbon, stir well, and let cool completely. Fold in the whipped cream, then scrape the mixture into a 1-quart mold and chill till firm, about 2 hours. Loosen the sides of the mold with a hot knife and gently unmold onto a chilled crystal serving plate. Garnish the top with chocolate curls and serve.

YIELD 6 servings

Martha's Sweet Note

When scalding milk in a saucepan, stir constantly over moderate heat to prevent a film from forming. Never allow the milk to come to a boil, and remove the pan from the heat the moment steam begins to rise.

CHRISTMAS AMBROSIA

*I*f ever Mother were a purist about her vast repertory of classic Southern desserts, ambrosia would be at the top of the list as one specialty that defies modification in any shape or form. "People who add grapefruit, pineapple, grapes, bananas, and Lord knows what else to ambrosia simply don't understand ambrosia," she lectures sternly, forever convinced that it's the simplicity of this subtle combination of orange and coconut traditionally served at Christmas that makes it the perfect foil to fruitcake, elaborate pies, rich cookies, and other aggressive Yuletide treats. I've never once known Mother to make ambrosia except at Christmas— served, of course, in one of her finest cut-crystal bowls. Here fresh coconut and orange juice are obligatory.

6 large oranges
½ cup granulated sugar
2 cups grated fresh coconut (see Sweet Note on page 17)
¼ cup fresh orange juice

*P*eel the oranges, cutting away all the white pith, then carefully remove the orange sections from the membranes that surround them and discard any seeds. Arrange a layer of orange sections in the bottom of a large crystal bowl and sprinkle a little of the sugar and coconut on top. Repeat the layers till the ingredients are used up, ending with a layer of coconut. Drizzle the orange juice over the top, cover the bowl with plastic wrap, and chill well before serving in crystal compote dishes.

YIELD 6 servings

SANTA CLAUS HAND-DIPPED CANDY BALLS

*W*hen my father's Swedish mother died and the wife of one of his printing customers brought this candy to the bereavement, Mother wasted no time jotting down the recipe and making her typical adjustments. Eventually, she began including the candy in her Christmas gift tins, and the rest is history. As you can tell from the list of ingredients, Mother varies not only the extract flavorings (rum, sherry, maple, vanilla, etc.) but also the style of chocolate (sweet, semisweet, or bittersweet) and the nuts (pecans, walnuts, or almonds). Improbable as it may sound, she also puts out bowls of this candy at holiday cocktail parties after hearing guests plead, "But, Martha Pearl, where is your Santa Claus candy?" In case you forgot, Southerners love sweets with their booze.

½ cup (1 stick) butter, softened
One 14-ounce can condensed milk
Two 1-pound boxes confectioners' sugar, sifted
2 cups finely chopped pecans
1 teaspoon extract flavoring
½ pound chocolate
½ block paraffin
About 100 pecan or walnut halves

*I*n a large mixing bowl, combine the butter, condensed milk, and confectioners' sugar and mix well with a wooden spoon. Add the chopped pecans and flavoring, cover with plastic wrap, and chill till very firm, at least 2 hours.

*I*n a small, heavy saucepan, melt the chocolate and paraffin together over low heat, stirring.

*U*sing your hands, roll the chilled butter mixture into small balls about the size of medium marbles and, stabbing each with a toothpick, dip the balls into the chocolate to coat well. Place the balls on waxed paper and, before the chocolate hardens, press a nut half into the top of each ball. Let the balls cool completely and store in an airtight container.

YIELD About 100 balls

 *Martha's Sweet Note*

*W*hen dipping candies in chocolate and paraffin, keep the mixture warm in the top of a double boiler over hot water so that it doesn't harden.

CHRISTMAS WHISKEY PECANS

*D*uring the Christmas holidays, there are never less than three glass bowls of these boozy pecans that Mother began making decades ago and that literally taste like Christmas to me. And, of course, the same pecans turn up at cocktail parties anytime between Thanksgiving and New Year's. Since the pecans freeze so beautifully in freezer bags, I usually have some on hand year-round. A warning: They are utterly addictive.

1 cup granulated sugar
½ cup evaporated milk
¼ teaspoon salt
2 tablespoons bourbon
3 cups pecan halves

*I*n a large, heavy saucepan, combine the sugar and evaporated milk and bring to a low boil over moderate heat, stirring constantly, till the syrup registers 240°F on a candy thermometer or forms a soft ball when a small glob is dropped into ½ cup of cold water. Remove the pan from the heat, add the salt, bourbon, and pecans, and stir till the nuts are thoroughly coated with the syrup. Pour the pecans out onto waxed paper and let them cool completely before storing.

YIELD 3 cups pecans

 *Martha's Sweet Note*

*T*o test for the soft ball stage without a candy thermometer, drop a small amount of the hot syrup into ½ cup of cold water and roll the glob between your thumb and index finger; if done, a soft ball will form.

Valentine's Day, St. Patrick's Day & Kentucky Derby

Mocha Velvet Cake

Derby Whiskey Cake with Praline Glaze

Cupid's Nesselrode Pie

Boozy Mud Pie

St. Pat's Crème de Menthe Pie

Cuddin' Berta's Georgia Kiss Pudding

Orange Bavarian Surprise

Chilled Grasshopper Soufflé

Apple-Bourbon Fritters

The Delta Queen's Pralines

Ever the romantic, Mother has celebrated Valentine's Day with a big party for friends and neighbors as long as I can remember, an informal, casual get-together where she pulls out her special red-and-white tablecloths, colorful cupid decorations, and delicate cordial glasses with which guests toast one another's happiness while tucking into a rich Nesselrode Pie, Kiss Pudding, and heaven knows what other sweet treats that Mother considers appropriate. I always kid her that she watches too many soap operas (she's a loyal fanatic about two programs in particular), to which she counters bluntly, "That's one way I stay young . . . and hopeful!"

Mother's St. Pat's Day and Kentucky Derby celebrations might not involve as many people as the Valentine's Day party, but observe these two occasions she does every single year. At the first, she serves a classic sit-down corned beef and cabbage dinner highlighted by either her greenish Crème de Menthe Pie or Grasshopper Soufflé and, believe me, the beer flows. For the much more casual Derby brunch, there's always a big Whiskey Cake on the buffet, but the most fun comes when everybody (except the children) gathers in the kitchen to help Mother fry up batches of Apple Fritters spiked with bourbon. Mother doesn't know exactly when or how this fritter tradition began (possibly because my Unca' Nalle from South Carolina was a nut about horse racing and apple fritters), but I can easily recall when the Derby was first telecast and how we all sat in front of that primitive oval black-and-white tube cheering the horses on and nibbling on these wonderful fritters eaten with our fingers.

MOCHA VELVET CAKE

*E*very year, Mother seems to come up with at least one new cake to serve at her Valentine's Day party for family and neighbors, and this beauty is the most recent one. It's a fairly complex recipe that underwent a number of changes before she pronounced it perfect, so don't tamper too much with the ingredients or technique. A fine brandy can be substituted for the rum if necessary, but don't try to use strong brewed coffee instead of the instant in the icing— it's just not intense enough. Mother decorates this cake with a single red rosebud smack in the center.

For the custard
5 ounces bittersweet baking chocolate
½ cup milk
1 cup granulated sugar
1 large egg, separated

For the cake
½ cup (1 stick) butter, softened
1 cup firmly packed light brown sugar
2 large eggs, separated
2 cups cake flour (see Sweet Note), sifted
1 teaspoon baking soda
½ teaspoon salt
¾ cup milk
1 teaspoon pure vanilla extract
1 large egg white

For the frosting
1 cup (2 sticks) butter, softened
2 tablespoons instant coffee granules, dissolved in ¼ cup boiling water
½ teaspoon salt
2½ cups confectioners' sugar, sifted
2 teaspoons dark rum

*T*o make the custard, combine the chocolate and milk in a small, heavy saucepan and stir over low heat till the chocolate is melted and the mixture smooth. Add the granulated sugar and egg yolk and cook, stirring constantly, till the custard is thick and smooth, about 3 minutes. Remove the pan from the heat and let cool.

*P*reheat the oven to 375°F. Evenly grease and flour two 9-inch round cake pans, tapping out any excess flour, and set aside.

*T*o make the cake, cream the butter and brown sugar together in a large mixing bowl with an electric mixer till smooth, then add the egg yolks and beat till well blended. In another bowl, combine the flour, baking soda, and salt, mix well, and alternately beat this mixture and the milk into the creamed mixture. Add the vanilla and stir till well blended, then add the custard to the batter and stir till well blended.

*W*ash and dry the beaters. In a medium-size mixing bowl, beat the 4 egg whites with the electric mixer till stiff peaks form, then fold gently into the cake batter with a rubber spatula. Scrape the batter into the prepared cake pans and bake till a cake tester or straw inserted in the center comes out clean, 25 to 30 minutes. Transfer the cakes to wire racks to cool in their pans.

*T*o make the frosting, beat the butter, coffee mixture, and salt together in a large mixing bowl, then gradually beat in the confectioners' sugar till well blended, about 3 minutes. Add the rum and beat till the frosting is well blended and spreadable.

*U*nmold one of the cake layers on a cake plate and, with a knife, spread the frosting smoothly over the top of it. Place the other cake layer on top of it and spread the remaining frosting over the top and sides.

YIELD One 2-layer 9-inch cake; 8 to 10 servings

Martha's Sweet Note

Cake flour gives cakes such as angel food a lighter texture than all-purpose flour, but if a recipe calls for cake flour and you don't have any, you can sift and resift all-purpose flour eight to ten times and get the same results.

DERBY WHISKEY CAKE WITH PRALINE GLAZE

*K*entucky Derby parties in North Carolina? You can bet your bottom dollar there's one at Mother's place, complete with mint juleps, multiple hors d'oeuvres, burgoo, hot buttermilk biscuits, and this ceremonial whiskey cake with a dark praline glaze—all consumed on small tables in front of two TVs as everybody bets on the races. "I know lots of people in Charlotte who give Derby parties," huffs Mother, "and as for whiskey cake, I'll put mine up against any made by those folks over there in Louisville." I concur.

For the cake

1 cup seedless dark raisins
½ cup bourbon
1 cup (2 sticks) butter, softened
2¼ cups granulated sugar
5 large eggs
3¼ cups all-purpose flour
1 teaspoon baking powder
½ teaspoon baking soda
1½ teaspoons ground nutmeg
1 cup buttermilk (see Sweet Note on page 10)
2 cups coarsely chopped pecans

For the glaze

½ cup firmly packed dark brown sugar
¼ cup granulated sugar
½ cup (½ stick) butter
¼ cup heavy cream
½ cup pecan halves

*I*n a small bowl, combine the raisins and bourbon, mix well, cover, and refrigerate for at least 1 hour.

*P*reheat the oven to 325°F. Grease and flour a 10-inch tube pan, tapping out any excess flour and set aside.

*T*o make the cake, cream the butter and granulated sugar together in a large mixing bowl with an electric mixer till light and fluffy, then add the eggs one at a time, beating well after each addition till the mixture is smooth. In another bowl, combine the flour, baking powder, baking soda, and nutmeg and mix well. Add the dry ingredients to the creamed mixture alternately with the buttermilk, beginning and ending with the dry ingredients and mixing well with a wooden spoon after each addition. Fold in the pecans and the soaked raisins and any unabsorbed bourbon. Scrape the batter into the prepared pan and bake till a cake tester or straw inserted in the center comes out clean, about 1½ hours. Let the cake cool in the pan for 10 minutes, then invert it onto a wire rack set over a large plate.

*T*o make the glaze, combine the two sugars, butter, and cream in a small, heavy saucepan and stir constantly over low heat till the mixture reaches the soft ball stage (240°F on a candy thermometer—see Sweet Note on page 21). Remove the pan from the heat and stir in the pecans, then drizzle the glaze evenly over the cake. Cool the cake completely before serving.

YIELD One 10-inch tube cake; 8 to 10 servings

CUPID'S NESSELRODE PIE

*E*ver since Mother was introduced to nesselrode pie some forty years ago at a New York restaurant called The Lobster and got the recipe from the Southern owner, this rich, colorful dessert has been a staple at her annual Valentine's Day celebration, when special red-and-white tablecloths and paper flowers are used to decorate the house. Since she can no longer find acceptable nesselrode fruit mixture in jars (which infuriates her), she simply buys extra candied fruits in the fall when making fruitcakes and stores them to dice for nesselrode pie later on. The pie, with tiny valentines on sticks stuck in the top, is always served on crystal plates with small glasses of cordial to sip.

2 tablespoons light rum
¼ cup diced mixed candied fruits (cherries, pineapple, and citron, orange, and lemon peel)
2 envelopes unflavored gelatin
⅔ cup granulated sugar
½ teaspoon salt
2 cups cold milk
3 large eggs, separated
1 cup heavy cream
1 prebaked 9-inch Basic Pie Shell (page 243)
Candied fruits for garnish (optional)

*I*n a small bowl, sprinkle the rum over the candied fruits and set aside.

*I*n the top of a double boiler over simmering water, combine the gelatin, half of the sugar, and the salt, then gradually stir in the milk and cook till the ingredients are well dissolved, stirring.

*I*n a medium-size mixing bowl, beat the egg yolks with a fork and gradually add the gelatin mixture, stirring constantly. Return the mixture to the double boiler and continue to cook over simmering water, stirring, till it is thickened and coats a spoon. Remove the pan from the boiler and let cool. When cooled, add the soaked fruits with rum and stir well.

*I*n a medium-size mixing bowl, whip the heavy cream with an electric mixer till peaks form. Set aside and thoroughly wash and dry the beaters. In a large mixing bowl, beat the egg whites with the mixer till stiff peaks form, then gradually add the remaining sugar. Carefully fold the whites into the gelatin mixture. Fold in the whipped cream, then pour the mixture into the pie shell and chill till firm. Garnish the top with the optional candied fruits.

YIELD One 9-inch pie; 6 servings

Martha's Sweet Note

Although in all these many years I've never once encountered a health problem using uncooked eggs in various desserts, I'm certainly aware of today's potential dangers of salmonella and other harmful bacteria and do take precautions. The AA-graded eggs I use are the freshest I can find (cartons should be stamped with an expiration date), but even then, I'm careful to always keep my eggs well refrigerated. (People—and I've known a few—who allow eggs to sit in the carton or a basket on the counter are just asking for trouble.) Even if, to ensure the best cooking results, a recipe calls for eggs to be at room temperature, I never allow mine to drop below the slightly chilled stage—especially in summertime.

BOOZY MUD PIE

To hear my mother and Craig Claiborne discuss (i.e., argue about) mud pie is a lesson in polite but slightly heated Southern diplomacy. Craig insists that the rich pie originated in Mississippi ("Mississippi mud" and all that) and never contained either spirits or nuts. Mother holds that various members of her family in Georgia were making mud pies with brandies, liqueurs, and bourbon in the nineteenth century and that no respectable Carolinian would even bother with a recipe that didn't include pecans. Whatever, the pie is, in all truth, little more than a giant, gummy, wonderful brownie served in wedges, and Mother considers it never more appropriate than at a Valentine's Day celebration—the top decorated with little candy hearts and cupids. "There's something so . . . sexy about the pie," she quips modestly. Needless to say, I find mud pies also ideal for picnics and cookouts.

½ cup (1 stick) butter, cut into pieces
3 ounces bittersweet chocolate, broken into pieces
2 tablespoons brandy
1 tablespoon coffee liqueur
3 large eggs
2 tablespoons light corn syrup
1½ cups granulated sugar
1 teaspoon pure vanilla extract
½ cup chopped pecans
1 unbaked 9-inch Basic Pie Shell (page 243)

Preheat the oven to 350°F.

In a large, heavy saucepan, combine the butter, chocolate, brandy, and liqueur and stir gently over low heat till the chocolate is melted. Remove the pan from the heat. In a medium-size bowl, beat the eggs with an electric mixer till frothy, then add the corn syrup, sugar, and vanilla and beat till well blended. Gradually pour this mixture into the chocolate mixture, stirring constantly, then add the pecans and stir till well blended. Scrape the filling into the pie shell and bake till set and slightly crunchy on top, about 35 minutes. Let cool completely before cutting into wedges.

YIELD One 9-inch pie; 6 to 8 servings

Martha's Sweet Note

To keep a piecrust from becoming soggy during baking, I often dust the bottom beforehand with a few graham or plain cracker crumbs.

ST. PAT'S CRÈME DE MENTHE PIE

This pie is a Southern classic, and of all Mother's gelatin dessert recipes, none is in greater demand than this version made with chocolate wafers, which is the annual highlight of her highly festive St. Patrick's Day shindig, "when even we staunch Episcopalians become Irish Catholics for the day." Mother says it's overkill, but I do like to shave ice-cold chocolate over the top of my crème de menthe pie.

2 cups crushed chocolate wafer crumbs
½ cup granulated sugar
½ cup (1 stick) butter, melted
1½ teaspoons unflavored gelatin
⅓ cup half-and-half
4 large egg yolks, beaten
¼ cup crème de cacao liqueur
¼ cup crème de menthe liqueur
1 cup heavy cream, whipped to stiff peaks

Preheat the oven to 450°F. Butter a 9-inch pie plate and set aside.

In a medium-size mixing bowl, combine 1½ cups of the wafer crumbs, ¼ cup of the sugar, and the butter and stir till well blended. Pat the crumb mixture evenly over the bottom and sides of the prepared pie plate. Bake the crust for 5 minutes; let cool.

Meanwhile, in a small saucepan, soften the gelatin in the half-and-half, then stir steadily over low heat to dissolve the gelatin completely. Set aside.

In a large mixing bowl, combine the remaining ¼ cup sugar and the egg yolks and beat with an electric mixer till frothy. Stirring well, add the gelatin mixture and liqueurs. Chill till the mixture is slightly thickened, about 30 minutes. With a rubber spatula, fold in the whipped cream, then scrape the filling into the prepared crust and chill till fully firm, about 1 hour. Sprinkle the remaining ½ cup wafer crumbs evenly over the top.

YIELD One 9-inch pie; 6 to 8 servings

CUDDIN' BERTA'S GEORGIA KISS PUDDING

*M*y maternal grandmother Maw Maw's first cousin, whom everybody called Cuddin' Berta, lived in a huge Colonial house in Monticello, Georgia, and every summer it was simply taken for granted that Maw Maw, Paw Paw, and their daughters, Martha Pearl and Jane, would pile into the old Ford and drive down from Charlotte to visit Cuddin' Berta for a long weekend. "Naturally, the big meal of the day (at noon sharp) was consumed on the spacious old porch," Mother remembers, "and Cuddin' Berta prided herself as much on her tangy kiss pudding as her fluffy corn bread." Apparently, kiss pudding has always been a Georgia specialty, and Mother continues to make it for birthdays and wedding receptions, as well as for her Valentine's Day party. And the origins of the quaint name? "Well, we've never really known, but Cuddin' Berta used to say it must have something to do with the way the pudding makes your lips pucker."

6 cups milk
3 tablespoons butter
2½ cups granulated sugar
5 large eggs, separated
5 tablespoons cornstarch
2 teaspoons grated lemon rind
⅓ cup fresh lemon juice
½ teaspoon ground cinnamon
1 teaspoon pure vanilla extract

*P*reheat the oven to 350°F. Grease a large baking dish and set aside.

*I*n a large, heavy saucepan, bring 5 cups of the milk to a boil, then add the butter and 2¼ cups of the sugar, stir till well blended, and remove the pan from the heat. In a medium-size mixing bowl, whisk the egg yolks together and gradually add about ½ cup of the hot milk mixture to the yolks, whisking constantly. Pour the yolks into the milk mixture in the saucepan, whisking constantly. In a small bowl, dissolve the cornstarch in the remaining cup of milk, add it to the hot milk mixture, and stir well. Return the saucepan to moderate heat and cook till the mixture thickens, stirring constantly. Remove the pan from the heat, add the lemon rind, lemon juice, cinnamon, and vanilla, and stir well. Pour the mixture into the prepared baking dish.

*I*n a large mixing bowl, beat the egg whites with an electric mixer till almost stiff, then gradually add the remaining ¼ cup sugar, beating till the whites form stiff peaks. Spread the meringue over the top of the pudding, making sure to seal the edges, and bake till the top is nicely browned, about 30 minutes. Serve the pudding warm.

YIELD About 6 servings

Martha's Sweet Note

*S*ee SWEET NOTE *on page 31 regarding the use of uncooked egg whites.*

ORANGE BAVARIAN SURPRISE

Like many Southern cooks, Mother loves and is especially adept at making fanciful molded desserts like this spiffy Bavarian created to "upgrade" ordinary ambrosia and sometimes served at her Valentine's Day celebration. The "surprise" is the crushed macaroons, which not only simulate the flavor of coconut in ambrosia but also add a delightful slight crunch to the otherwise smooth mold.

1 envelope unflavored gelatin
¾ cup water
½ cup granulated sugar
¼ teaspoon salt
2 large eggs, separated
One 6-ounce can frozen orange juice concentrate, thawed
¼ cup crushed coconut macaroons
1 cup heavy cream, whipped to stiff peaks
2 cups chilled fresh orange sections

In a small bowl, sprinkle the gelatin over ¼ cup of the water, let soften for 3 minutes, and pour into a large, heavy, nonreactive saucepan. Add ¼ cup of the sugar and the salt and stir. In another small bowl, whisk together the egg yolks and the remaining ½ cup water till frothy, then add to the gelatin mixture and stir over low heat till the gelatin dissolves completely and the mixture thickens slightly, 4 to 5 minutes. Remove from the heat, add the orange juice concentrate and macaroons, and stir till the mixture is thick.

In a medium-size mixing bowl, beat the egg whites with an electric mixer till soft peaks form, then gradually add the remaining ¼ cup sugar, beating till stiff peaks form. Fold the whites into the gelatin mixture, then fold in the whipped cream, scrape the mixture into a 5-cup mold, and chill till firm, about 6 hours. Serve the Bavarian with orange sections on the side of each portion.

YIELD 6 to 8 servings

Martha's Sweet Note

See SWEET NOTE on page 31 regarding the use of uncooked egg whites.

CHILLED GRASSHOPPER SOUFFLÉ

Since Mother's birthday almost coincides with St. Patrick's Day, she thinks nothing of inviting friends over for corned beef and cabbage, preparing soda bread and her elaborate grasshopper soufflé, and, as she puts it, "killing two birds with one stone." Then, of course, she just sits back and waits for the same friends to invite her for more birthday fun. "It's almost embarrassing to admit, but sometimes my birthday is celebrated three or four times—and I love every minute of it, since there are always so many different dishes to taste."

2 envelopes unflavored gelatin
2 cups water
4 large eggs, separated
1 cup granulated sugar
One 8-ounce package cream cheese, softened
¼ cup crème de menthe liqueur
1 cup heavy cream, whipped to stiff peaks
Chocolate curls (see Sweet Note on page 127) for garnish

To prepare the soufflé dish, cut a sheet of aluminum foil or waxed paper long enough to fit around a 1½-quart soufflé dish, allowing a 1-inch overlap, and fold lengthwise into thirds. Lightly oil one side of the foil or paper and wrap it around the dish (oiled side against dish), allowing it to extend 3 inches above the rim to form a collar. Tape the collar into place.

In the top of a double boiler set over simmering (not boiling) water, combine the gelatin and 1 cup of the water and cook till the gelatin dissolves completely, stirring. Gradually stir in the remaining cup of water. In a bowl, whisk the egg yolks together till thick, then gradually add ¾ cup of the sugar, whisking well. Stir the egg mixture into the gelatin mixture and cook over the simmering water till thickened, stirring constantly. Remove from the heat and let cool.

In a large mixing bowl, beat the cream cheese with an electric mixer till smooth, then gradually add the egg yolk mixture and beat till well blended. Stir in the crème de menthe. Wash and dry the mixer beaters. In another large mixing bowl, beat the egg whites till foamy, then gradually add the remaining ¼ cup sugar and beat till stiff peaks form. Gently fold the whites plus the whipped cream into the yolk mixture. Scrape the mixture into the prepared soufflé dish and chill till the soufflé is firmly set, at least 2 hours. Remove the collar from the dish and garnish the top of the soufflé with chocolate curls before serving.

YIELD 6 to 8 servings

Martha's Sweet Note

See SWEET NOTE *on page 31 regarding the use of uncooked egg whites.*

APPLE-BOURBON FRITTERS

Some years, Mother decides to celebrate the Kentucky Derby by inviting just a few neighbors over for a very casual, informal brunch, and when she does, most attention centers on frying up big batches of these fritters, intended to be eaten with fingers and washed down with mint juleps. Ditto for Halloween in the fall, when the fritters might be the last item to be placed on a more festive dessert buffet and when whiskey sours, old-fashioneds, and bourbon and branch keep spirits high. How these people drink booze with all these sweets still mystifies me, but, as at cocktail parties, it's a Southern tradition—and that's that!

1 cup granulated sugar
¼ cup bourbon
½ teaspoon ground cinnamon
6 medium-size Granny Smith apples, cored, peeled, and cut into
    ¼-inch-thick rings
1 cup all-purpose flour
½ teaspoon salt
1 cup water
2 teaspoons vegetable oil
2 large egg whites, beaten till frothy
Vegetable oil for deep-frying
Confectioners' sugar for dusting

In a large, shallow baking dish, combine the sugar, bourbon, and cinnamon and stir till well blended. Add the apple rings and let macerate for 1 hour, turning once.

To make the batter, sift together the flour and salt into a medium-size mixing bowl, add the water, and mix with a wooden spoon till pasty. Stirring steadily, add the 2 teaspoons oil gradually, then add the egg whites and stir gently till well blended and smooth. (Do not overmix.) Cover with plastic wrap and set aside till ready to use.

When ready to make the fritters, heat 2 inches of vegetable oil to 350°F in a deep fryer or deep, heavy skillet. In batches, dip each apple ring into the prepared batter and fry it in the oil, turning, till golden and puffed, about 5 minutes in all. Drain the fritters on a brown paper bag and sift confectioners' sugar over the top. Serve as soon as possible.

YIELD 6 to 8 servings

THE DELTA QUEEN'S PRALINES

*D*ibby Smoot, an old-fashioned Southern belle if I ever met one, was a real character, and since she was a North Carolina transplant from Mississippi, we all called her the Delta Queen till she finally sipped her last cocktail just recently. "Martha Pearl, I'm getting thirsty," she would announce around four o'clock in the afternoon during one of her "socials," a directive that would send Mother to the bar for Dibby's favorite Early Times bourbon. "And you might as well bring out a few of those pralines I brought over." Now, you must understand that Dibby had absolutely no use for classic Louisiana pralines, convinced that since the batter was never beaten like hers, the texture was all wrong. At first, we balked at this heresy, but then the more Mother tried Dibby's "beaten pralines," the more raves she got when she served them at her Valentine's Day party. The main difference is that these pralines are lighter and more delicate.

2 cups firmly packed dark brown sugar
2 cups granulated sugar
¼ cup (½ stick) butter
1 cup evaporated milk
1 cup milk
¼ teaspoon salt
1½ teaspoons pure vanilla or maple extract (or a combination of both)
3 tablespoons light corn syrup
2 cups coarsely chopped pecans

*I*n a large, heavy saucepan, combine all the ingredients except the pecans and mix till well blended. Cook, stirring, over moderate heat till the mixture registers 240°F on a candy thermometer or forms a soft ball when a glob is dropped into ½ cup cold water (see Sweet Note on page 21). Cool the mixture slightly, then beat with a wooden spoon till creamy. Add the pecans and stir till well blended and smooth. Drop the batter by the teaspoon onto waxed paper and let the pralines cool completely before serving or storing.

YIELD About 3½ dozen pralines

Mother's Day

&

Easter

The Great $100 Chocolate Cake

Sunshine Chiffon Cake with Orange Butter Frosting

Scripture Cake

Easter Moravian Sugar Cake

Mother's Day Boston Cream Pie

Minty Lemon Mousse

Pineapple Dessert Soufflé

Blueberry Flummery

n the South, families have traditionally observed Mother's Day by wearing a red flower (usually a rose) if your mother is alive and a white one if she's deceased. Practicing the age-old custom gradually diminishes, however, once the children have grown up and other family members pass on—everywhere, that is, except in Mother's home. No, indeed, for, to Mother, it's still as important to celebrate this special Sunday when you're eighty as when you're twenty. If, therefore, children and grandchildren happen to be around to come by the house around noon for a slice of her Boston Cream Pie, fine; if not, she invites a group of old church friends and neighbors to share with her the ritual pie—plus, maybe, a little Pineapple Soufflé—and a few glasses of sherry. It's all very nostalgic, civilized, and heartwarming.

Since Mother is very active in her church altar guild, much of Holy Week leading up to Easter involves not only certain religious duties but also various working lunches and socials where she's expected to contribute all sorts of dishes. Primary among these are such appropriate desserts as her spicy Scripture Cake, based on ingredients found in the Bible, though some years she might surprise a Lenten study group by serving her sumptuous version of a $100 Chocolate Cake. Easter Day itself is something of a continuous celebration that begins with early church (8:00 A.M.) followed by an elaborate Southern family breakfast featuring Mother's ritual Moravian Sugar Cake. Lunch can be rather fancy or modest, depending on whether or not she's invited friends and neighbors, but when I'm home, she goes all out for Easter dinner by preparing my favorite shrimp toast and small curried meat custards called hobotee, maybe a majestic baked country ham stuffed with greens, and, since the very first blueberries are usually in the market, her elegant Blueberry Flummery.

THE GREAT $100 CHOCOLATE CAKE

*Y*ears ago, when the local paper sponsored a cake cook-off with a first prize of $100, one of Mother's best friends submitted this chocolate cake recipe and walked away the winner. All would have been well and good, of course, except that when the recipe was printed, Mother saw that the "sheet cake" (i.e., a cake baked in a large, shallow, rectangular sheet pan) was basically the same as the one she'd been making for years. Did I not detect just a bit of jealousy and envy? "That's absurd," she countered. "Yes, it's a very good chocolate cake, but if I had the time to fool with those cook-offs, I have cake recipes that are much more original and could probably win five hundred dollars!"

For the cake

½ cup (1 stick) butter, softened
2 cups granulated sugar
4 ounces unsweetened chocolate, melted
2 large eggs
2 cups cake flour (see Sweet Note on page 27)
2 teaspoons baking powder
1½ cups milk
2 teaspoons pure vanilla extract
1 cup chopped pecans

For the frosting

½ cup (1 stick) butter, softened
2 cups confectioners' sugar, sifted
2 ounces unsweetened baking chocolate, melted
1 large egg
1 teaspoon pure vanilla extract
1 teaspoon fresh lemon juice
Dash of salt
1 cup chopped pecans

*P*reheat the oven to 350°F. Grease and flour a large sheet pan, tapping out any excess flour, and set aside.

*T*o make the cake, combine the butter and granulated sugar in a large mixing bowl and cream together with an electric mixer till light and fluffy, then add the melted chocolate and eggs and beat till well blended. In a small bowl, combine the flour and baking powder, mix well, and beat into the creamed mixture alternately with the milk. Add the vanilla and pecans and stir with a wooden spoon till well blended. Scrape the batter into the prepared sheet pan and bake till a cake tester or straw inserted in the center comes out clean, about 35 minutes. Let the cake cool completely in the pan.

*T*o make the frosting, combine all the ingredients in a large mixing bowl and beat with the electric mixer till well blended and spreadable. Frost the top of the cake with a knife, cut the cake into squares, and serve right from the pan.

YIELD 1 sheet cake; 8 to 10 servings

Martha's Sweet Note

A good cake tester is a wise (and cheap) investment since it is more reliable than a toothpick and far more practical than pulling straws out of a broom.

SUNSHINE CHIFFON CAKE WITH ORANGE BUTTER FROSTING

Mother has made this elegant cake for many a bridal reception, but she also considers it perfect for either her popular Mother's Day luncheon or more formal Easter dinner. In addition, the cake is very good with a simple Seven-Minute Frosting (page 252). For lightness, cake flour should be used here.

8 large eggs, separated
1⅓ cups granulated sugar
1 teaspoon grated orange rind
½ cup fresh orange juice
1 cup cake flour (see Sweet Note on page 27)
1 teaspoon cream of tartar
½ teaspoon salt
Orange Butter Frosting (page 254)

Preheat the oven to 325°F.

In a large mixing bowl, beat the egg yolks with an electric mixer till frothy, then gradually add ⅔ cup of the granulated sugar, beating till thick. In a small bowl, combine the orange rind and juice and add to the yolk mixture alternately with the flour, beating till well blended.

Wash and dry the beaters. In another large mixing bowl, combine the egg whites, cream of tartar, and salt and beat till soft peaks form, then gradually add the remaining ⅔ cup granulated sugar and beat till stiff peaks form. Gently fold the egg whites into the yolk mixture, scrape the batter into an ungreased 10-inch tube pan, and bake till a cake tester or straw inserted in the center comes out clean, about 1 hour and 10 minutes. Let the cake cool in the pan for 10 minutes, then invert onto a wire rack to cool completely.

Frost the top and sides of the cake with the orange frosting, and let the cake stand for at least 1 hour before serving.

YIELD   One 10-inch tube cake; 10 to 12 servings

Martha's Sweet Note

Whether to use a tube (or angel food) or Bundt pan for cakes is really a matter of choice, since the only basic difference is the weight and design (a Bundt pan is heavier, with scalloped sides). Generally, I use a tube pan for light cakes and a Bundt pan for heavier ones.

SCRIPTURE CAKE

*B*eing a devout Episcopalian, Mother has always been fascinated by food ingredients mentioned in the Bible, many of which she's used to create any number of desserts intended to celebrate religious holidays. This spicy Scripture cake she makes for Easter is a good example, and when she serves it, she never fails to relate certain biblical facts and stories about dates, raisins, almonds, eggs, and all the spices used in ancient dishes. This is also a very good cake to serve with afternoon tea or at bridge parties.

½ cup (1 stick) butter, softened
1½ cups granulated sugar
2 large eggs
1½ cups unsweetened applesauce
1½ cups all-purpose flour
1½ teaspoons baking soda
¼ teaspoon salt
1½ teaspoons ground cinnamon
½ teaspoon ground nutmeg
½ teaspoon ground cloves
½ teaspoon ground allspice
1 cup seedless dark raisins
1 cup coarsely chopped pitted dates
1 cup chopped almonds

*P*reheat the oven to 275°F. Grease and flour a 10-inch tube or Bundt pan, tapping out any excess flour, and set aside.

*I*n a large mixing bowl, cream the butter and sugar together with an electric mixer till smooth, then add the eggs one at a time, beating well after each addition. Add the applesauce and stir till well blended. In a small bowl, combine the flour, baking soda, salt, and spices and stir till well blended. Add the dry ingredients to the cream mixture and stir till well blended, then stir in the raisins, dates, and almonds till well blended. Scrape the batter into the prepared pan and bake till a cake tester or straw inserted in the center comes out clean, 2 to 2½ hours. Let the cake cool for about 10 minutes, then turn out onto a wire rack to cool completely.

YIELD One 10-inch tube or Bundt cake; at least 8 servings

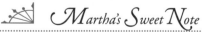 *Martha's Sweet Note*

*W*hen using dried fruits, raisins, and nuts in baking, I always dust them with flour before mixing into the batter to prevent them from sinking to the bottom.

EASTER MORAVIAN SUGAR CAKE

For over a century, the sugar cake made by the Moravians in Winston-Salem, North Carolina, has been a much-sought-after regional specialty, and for years it was Mother's habit every Easter to buy a large cake at the Moravian church in Charlotte and share it at breakfast with my sister and her family. Then, when the cakes became scarce due to reduced production at the bakery in Winston, she simply got the original recipe from one of her many connections and began making the cake herself. Since the dough must be subjected to lengthy risings, the procedure is time-consuming and a little risky, but, as Mother says, "It's worth every second of work and inconvenience, since there's no cake like it." Do follow the directions to the letter. This cake freezes very well.

2 medium-size red potatoes, peeled and quartered
3 cups water
One 1-ounce package active dry yeast
1½ cups plus ½ teaspoon granulated sugar
¼ cup warm water
1 cup Crisco shortening
½ teaspoon salt
3 large eggs
7 cups all-purpose flour
1 cup (2 sticks) cold butter, cut into ⅛-inch pieces
2 cups firmly packed dark brown sugar
Ground cinnamon to taste

Grease two 9 × 13-inch baking pans and set aside.

Place the potatoes in a saucepan with the 3 cups water and bring to a boil, then reduce the heat to moderate and cook till very tender, about 20 minutes. Drain 2 cups of the water into a bowl and discard the remaining water. Beat and mash the potatoes with an electric mixer till smooth to measure 1 cup and set aside.

In a small bowl, combine the yeast and ½ teaspoon of the sugar in the ¼ cup warm water and set aside till the mixture is bubbly, about 5 minutes. In a large mixing bowl, combine the potato water, mashed potatoes, the remaining 1½ cups sugar, the Crisco, and salt and beat in the eggs one at a time with an electric mixer. Gradually add 3 cups of the flour and beat till smooth. Gradually add 3 more cups of the flour, beating well, then cover the bowl with a tea towel and let the dough rise in a warm place till doubled in bulk, about 1½ hours. Punch the dough down and stir in the remaining cup of flour. Spread the dough evenly in the prepared pans, cover, and let rise again till spongy, about 45 minutes.

Preheat the oven to 375°F.

In rows, press the cold butter pieces into the dough about 1½ inches apart and top each butter piece with about 1 teaspoon of the brown sugar. Sprinkle cinnamon over the entire surface and bake the cake till firm, about 20 minutes. Cut the cake into squares, making sure that at least one "piddle" of butter and sugar is in each square. Serve the cake warm or cold.

YIELD Two 9 × 13-inch cakes; seventy 2-inch squares

MOTHER'S DAY BOSTON CREAM PIE

*W*ho says that Mother's Day is no longer to be formally celebrated just because the children have grown up and left the nest? Not my mother, who, some years ago, began the tradition of inviting older friends to the house on this special Sunday for a mid-day "social," pinning a red or white flower on the ladies, and serving her very special Boston cream pie with glasses of sherry while everybody brings everybody else up to date on their children's (and grand-children's) activities. "Even some of the husbands now show up," Mother says proudly, "and, believe me, since this pie takes such time and effort, it's the only time of year I make it." And despite the pie's name, Mother continues to stubbornly insist that it's really an old-fashioned *Southern* pie that migrated north at some point.

For the cake layers

2 large eggs, separated
1½ cups granulated sugar
2¼ cups all-purpose flour, sifted
2 teaspoons baking powder
1 teaspoon salt
⅓ cup vegetable oil
1 cup milk
1½ teaspoons pure vanilla extract

For the filling

⅓ cup granulated sugar
3 tablespoons all-purpose flour
¼ teaspoon salt
1¼ cups milk
1 large egg, beaten
1 tablespoon butter
1 teaspoon pure vanilla extract

For the glaze

1½ ounces unsweetened baking chocolate
2 tablespoons butter
1½ cups confectioners' sugar, sifted
1 teaspoon pure vanilla extract
Boiling water

*P*reheat the oven to 350°F. Flour two 9-inch round cake pans, tapping out any excess flour, and set aside.

*T*o make the cake layers, place the egg whites in a medium-size mixing bowl and beat with an electric mixer till soft peaks form, then gradually add ½ cup of the sugar, beating till very stiff peaks form. In a large mixing bowl, combine the flour, the remaining 1 cup sugar, the baking powder, and salt and mix well. Add the oil, ½ cup of the milk, and the vanilla and beat well, scraping the sides of the bowl from time to time. Add the remaining ½ cup milk and the egg yolks and beat well, then gently fold in the egg whites with a rubber spatula. Divide the batter evenly between the two prepared pans and bake till a cake tester or straw inserted in the center comes out clean, about 25 minutes. Let the cakes cool for about 10 minutes, turn out onto a wire rack, and let cool completely.

*T*o make the filling, combine the sugar, flour, and salt in a small, heavy saucepan, gradually add the milk, and stir till well blended. Over moderate heat, cook till the mixture thickens and comes to a boil, stirring constantly. Very gradually stir a little of the hot mixture into the beaten egg, then return the egg mixture to the pan and stir till the mixture boils. Remove from the heat, add the butter and vanilla, and mix till well blended. Cover the pan with waxed paper and let cool (do not stir).

*T*o make the glaze, melt the chocolate and butter together in a small, heavy saucepan over low heat, stirring constantly. Remove from the heat, add the confectioners' sugar and vanilla, and stir till the mixture is crumbly. Add 3 tablespoons of boiling water and blend well. Gradually add about 2 more teaspoons of boiling water and stir to form a medium glaze of pouring consistency. Keep the glaze hot over low heat.

*S*pread the cream filling evenly between the two cake layers, then pour the hot glaze over the top, spreading it evenly over the top and sides. Let the pie cool completely before serving.

YIELD One 2-layer 9-inch pie; 6 to 8 servings

Martha's Sweet Note

One of the trickiest maneuvers in cooking many desserts is the proper tempering of hot mixtures containing eggs so that the eggs don't curdle when exposed to excessively high temperatures. When directions in a recipe call for tempering beaten eggs (especially yolks) with a hot liquid, my technique is to add gradually a few tablespoons of the liquid to the eggs, whisking very briskly and constantly, till you have about ½ cup of mixture, then to pour the tempered mixture back into the hot liquid, still whisking constantly.

MINTY LEMON MOUSSE

With Mother's passion for lemon, this versatile, zesty mousse shows up year-round on buffets for every occasion, from wedding receptions to Easter luncheon to small bereavements. For variation, you can also prepare the mousse with orange juice and the grated rind of one large orange, in which case the top of the mold should be sprinkled with about half a cup of chopped toasted almonds in place of the mint leaves, plus grated orange rind.

2 envelopes unflavored gelatin
½ cup water
24 ladyfingers, split in half and bases trimmed straight
8 large eggs, separated
1 cup granulated sugar
Grated rind of 3 small lemons
½ cup fresh lemon juice
1 cup heavy cream
2 teaspoons confectioners' sugar, sifted
¼ teaspoon pure vanilla extract
7 fresh mint leaves for garnish

In a small bowl, sprinkle the gelatin over the water and let soften. Line the bottom and sides of a 9-inch springform pan with the ladyfinger halves and set aside.

In the top of a double boiler, beat the egg yolks with an electric mixer till frothy, then gradually add the granulated sugar, beating constantly. Stir in about three quarters of the lemon rind and the lemon juice, place the pan over gently simmering (not boiling) water, and cook till the custard thickens, stirring constantly. Add the gelatin mixture and stir till it is completely dissolved. Pour the mixture into a bowl and let cool completely.

Wash and dry the mixer beaters. Beat the egg whites in a large mixing bowl till stiff peaks form; fold them into the lemon mixture. Scrape the mixture into the mold and chill till firm, 4 to 6 hours.

In a medium-size mixing bowl, whip the cream and confectioners' sugar together with a whisk (*do not* use an electric mixer) till thick and stir in the vanilla. Unmold the mousse onto a crystal plate, spread the whipped cream evenly over the top, and garnish the top with the remaining grated lemon rind and the mint leaves.

YIELD 8 to 10 servings

Martha's Sweet Notes

See SWEET NOTE on page 31 regarding the use of uncooked egg whites.

So that ladyfingers used to line a baking dish or tart pan will stand up evenly, trim the tips off the bases.

PINEAPPLE DESSERT SOUFFLÉ

Mother usually serves her suave Boston cream pie at the Mother's Day luncheon she organizes every year for friends who no longer have much family, but when she knows the guests will all be older ladies, she might well substitute this fairly light and refreshing soufflé—"perfect for fragile digestive systems," she explains. This is a good example of a typical Southern "soufflé," meaning virtually any dish (savory or sweet, cooked or uncooked) that is leavened with egg whites.

2 envelopes unflavored gelatin
½ cup cold water
6 large eggs, separated
2 tablespoons grated lemon rind
¼ cup fresh lemon juice
1 cup granulated sugar
½ teaspoon salt
1⅓ cups canned crushed pineapple, drained
1 cup heavy cream, whipped to stiff peaks
Canned pineapple chunks for garnish
Fresh mint leaves for garnish

Lightly grease a 6-cup ring mold and set aside.

In a small bowl, sprinkle the gelatin over the water to soften and set aside.

In the top of a double boiler, whisk the egg yolks together till frothy, then stir in the lemon rind, lemon juice, sugar, and salt and cook over simmering (not boiling) water, stirring constantly, till the mixture thickens. Remove from the heat and add the gelatin mixture, stirring till it is completely dissolved. Add the crushed pineapple, mixing well, and set aside to cool till slightly thickened, about 30 minutes.

In a large mixing bowl, beat the egg whites with an electric mixer till stiff but not dry peaks form, then fold the whites and whipped cream into the egg yolk mixture. Scrape the mixture into the prepared ring mold, cover with plastic wrap, and chill overnight. Unmold the soufflé onto a serving platter and garnish with pineapple chunks and mint leaves.

YIELD 6 to 8 servings

Martha's Sweet Note

See SWEET NOTE on page 31 regarding the use of uncooked egg whites.

BLUEBERRY FLUMMERY

Like trifles, syllabubs, and most other thickened puddings, Southern flummeries can be traced back in England almost to the Middle Ages, and, like many of their gustatory cousins, their name derives from a manner of speech (you still hear in the South, "Oh, you're so full of flummery," meaning excess flattery). Originally, flummeries probably contained no fruit, and the simple cream puddings would have been thickened with ground nuts, oatmeal, or isinglass (ancestor to gelatin). This is one of Mother's most delicate desserts, one that befits both her formal Easter dinner and her quaint bridge luncheons. Any fresh berries can be used to make the dessert, but if berries are not in season, thawed frozen ones (except strawberries) work remarkably well and need only to be heated with the sugar, not boiled. Some people stir whipped cream into the berries; Mother doesn't.

1 envelope unflavored gelatin
¼ cup plus 2 tablespoons water
1 quart (about 4 cups) fresh, ripe blueberries, stemmed, and rinsed
1¼ cups granulated sugar
Whipped cream for garnish

In a small saucepan, sprinkle the gelatin over ¼ cup of the water to soften and set aside.

In a large, heavy, nonreactive pot, combine the blueberries, sugar, and the remaining 2 tablespoons water and stir well to crush the berries slightly. Bring slowly to a boil, stirring constantly till the berries are softened and juicy, about 3 minutes, then remove from the heat. With a slotted spoon, remove about 1½ cups of the berries and set aside.

Over low heat, heat the gelatin mixture and stir till dissolved completely. Add the gelatin to the pot of berries and stir well, then strain the mixture through a fine sieve into a mixing bowl, pressing the pulp with a heavy spoon to extract as much juice as possible. Stir in the reserved berries, spoon the flummery into glass serving dishes, and chill for at least 1 hour. Serve with dollops of whipped cream on top.

YIELD 6 to 8 servings

Memorial Day
&
Father's Day

 think it truly offends Mother that people (Southerners included) aren't more seriously observant of both Memorial Day and Father's Day, a problem she quickly rectifies each year whether she's at home or visiting me on Long Island by initiating patriotic, flag-waving lunches and half-day barbecues to which almost every father she knows is invited. I've never fully understood whether her traditional Raisin Rum Cake and inimitable Lattice Apple Pie are supposed to be symbolic of the disappearance of cold weather or of the arrival of summer, but when I see her fix the first Cherry Cobbler, Buttermilk Pie, Rhubarb and Strawberry Parfait, or Dubie Slump of the season, I know without doubt that she's thinking of those desserts that were relished most by my daddy, granddaddy, and Unca' Nalle—and that I love equally as much.

RAISIN RUM CAKE

*I*f you ask me why Mother ever started serving her raisin rum cake every year to celebrate Memorial Day, I can't give a logical answer. If you ask why she corrupted traditional Southern rum cake by adding raisins, she's quick to explain, "If raisin rum ice cream is so good, it goes to reason that raisins would be great in this cake." In any case, our first barbecue of the season simply wouldn't be the same without this wonderful dessert, and people are forever asking for the recipe. The trick here is to keep the raisins in suspension, meaning they should never be macerated in rum beforehand and must be floured to keep them from sinking to the bottom during baking.

1 cup finely chopped almonds
1 cup seedless golden raisins
1½ cups all-purpose flour
1 cup (2 sticks) butter, softened
1½ cups granulated sugar
4 large eggs, separated
1 teaspoon pure vanilla extract
1 teaspoon pure almond extract
3 tablespoons light rum, or more, if desired

*P*reheat the oven to 325°F. Grease and flour a 10-inch springform pan, tapping out any excess flour. Sprinkle the nuts into the pan, press them evenly against the bottom and sides, and set the pan aside.

*I*n a small bowl, combine the raisins with ¼ cup of the flour, toss well to coat, and set aside.

*I*n a large mixing bowl, cream the butter and sugar together with an electric mixer till smooth, then add the egg yolks one at a time, beating after each addition. Add the extracts and rum and beat well, then add the remaining 1¼ cups flour gradually, beating till well blended. Wash and dry the mixer beaters, then beat the egg whites in a medium-size mixing bowl till stiff but not dry peaks form, and, with a rubber spatula, gently fold them into the batter. Add the raisins and stir till well blended. Scrape the batter into the prepared pan and bake till a cake tester or straw inserted in the center comes out clean, about 1½ hours. Let the cake cool for about 10 minutes, remove the sides of the pan, and let the cake cool completely before serving.

YIELD One 10-inch cake; 10 to 12 servings

THE ULTIMATE OLD-FASHIONED LATTICE APPLE PIE

*M*other is kindly open-minded to most suggestions about what constitutes any putatively authentic dish, but only those prepared for a thirty-minute diatribe would risk questioning this lattice apple pie recipe she's been using for over half a century—and that her relatives passed down to her. As far as Mother is concerned, there simply is no other way to make apple pie, a prejudice justified by the flavor and texture of this classic wonder. She is considerably more liberal about toppings for the pie, allowing for scoops of vanilla ice cream or dollops of freshly whipped cream, but also reminding that nothing is more Southern than thin slices of aged cheddar cheese allowed to melt slightly. Although familiar guests at our annual Memorial Day celebration almost demand this pie, Mother also makes it throughout the year for numerous other occasions.

Dough for 1 double unbaked 9- to 10-inch Basic Pie Shell (page 243)
6 Granny Smith or other tart apples, cored, peeled, and cut into small wedges
½ lemon, seeded
1 cup granulated sugar
1 teaspoon ground cinnamon
½ teaspoon ground nutmeg
¼ cup (½ stick) butter, cut into small pieces

*O*n a lightly floured surface, divide the dough in half. Roll out one half into a circle about ⅛ inch thick and fit it snugly across the bottom and up the sides of a 9-inch pie plate. Roll the other half of the dough into a rectangle about ⅛ inch thick, cut the dough into strips about ¼ inch wide, and set aside.

*P*lace the apple wedges in a large mixing bowl and squeeze the lemon half over the top of them. In a small bowl, combine the sugar, cinnamon, and nutmeg, mix well, and set aside.

*P*reheat the oven to 350°F.

*T*o assemble the pie, arrange the apple wedges overlapping one another evenly in the pie shell, sprinkle the sugar mixture over them all, and distribute the butter pieces evenly over the top. Starting in the middle of the pie and working out in either direction, lay half of the reserved strips of dough in one direction about ½ inch apart. In the other direction, carefully weave the remaining strips ½ inch apart over and under the first strips to make a lattice pattern. Trim the excess dough hanging over the edges and, if needed, reroll and cut into more strips. Crimp the edges of the pie together with a fork dipped in flour to seal the bottom and top layers of the dough.

*P*lace the pie on a wide sheet of aluminum foil (to catch drips), in middle of the oven and bake till the apples are tender and the crust golden brown, 30 to 35 minutes. Serve the pie warm.

YIELD One 9-inch pie; 8 servings

NALLE'S CHERRY BUTTERMILK PIE

If there were any of Mother's desserts that my Unca' Nalle Belliveau from South Carolina loved more than the butterscotch pie she always baked for his birthday, it was this cherry buttermilk pie that he begged her to make every year for Father's Day. This tangy pie couldn't be any more simple, and, for variety, I've found that you can very successfully substitute small red seedless grapes, blueberries, or blackberries—even raisins—for the cherries.

1½ cups granulated sugar
3 tablespoons all-purpose flour
⅛ teaspoon salt
3 large eggs, well beaten
2 tablespoons butter, melted
1½ cups buttermilk (see Sweet Note on page 10)
1 teaspoon pure vanilla extract
½ teaspoon pure almond extract
½ teaspoon grated lemon rind
1 cup pitted fresh or canned (drained) red cherries, cut in half
1 unbaked 9-inch Basic Pie Shell (page 243)
Ground cinnamon to taste

*P*reheat the oven to 350°F.

*I*n a large mixing bowl, combine the sugar, flour, and salt and mix till well blended. Using an electric mixer, gradually add the eggs, beating well, then beat in the butter, buttermilk, extracts, and lemon rind till well blended and smooth. Fold in the cherries. Scrape the mixture into the pie shell, sprinkle cinnamon over the top, and bake till the pie is firmly set, about 35 minutes. Let the pie cool on a wire rack and serve at room temperature or chilled.

YIELD One 9-inch pie; 6 to 8 servings

DUBIE SLUMP

*D*ubies, dubies, we got dubies!" the old lady hawked at the roadside stand on the way to our cottage at Ocean Isle Beach, North Carolina. Slowly, carefully, Mother inspected the huge dewberries, nodded her approval, turned to Daddy and me, and whispered, "I'll do a slump for everybody tonight." Dewberries are little more than big blackberries that grow wild on trailing vines, and while they're even sweeeeter than their smaller cousins, they're delicious cooked in cobblers, crisps, or, as in the Carolina Low Country, dumpling crusted slumps prepared in a heavy skillet on top of the stove. Dubies are scarce these days even in the South, but blackberries (or even raspberries) work just as well. Daddy loved this slump, which is probably why Mother still often makes it for the Father's Day dinner she prepares for my nephew, his family, and special friends.

1 cup all-purpose flour
1 cup granulated sugar
1 teaspoon baking powder
½ teaspoon baking soda
¼ teaspoon salt
¼ cup (½ stick) butter, melted
⅓ cup buttermilk (see Sweet Note on page 10)
6 cups fresh dewberries (or 5 cups fresh blackberries), rinsed
2 tablespoons water
1 tablespoon cornstarch
⅛ teaspoon ground cinnamon
Vanilla ice cream

*T*o make the dumplings, combine the flour, 3 tablespoons of the sugar, the baking powder, baking soda, and salt in a medium-size mixing bowl and stir till well blended. Drizzle the butter over the top and stir. Gradually add the buttermilk, stirring with a wooden spoon till the batter is just soft and still moist.

*I*n a medium-size, deep, cast-iron skillet, combine the dewberries, water, the remaining sugar, the cornstarch, and cinnamon and stir till well blended. Cover the skillet tightly and gradually bring the berries to a low boil. Uncover the skillet, reduce the heat to moderate, and drop rounded tablespoons of the batter over the berries till all the batter is used up. Cover the skillet again, reduce the heat slightly, and simmer till the dumplings have set, 15 to 20 minutes. Spoon portions of the slump into dessert bowls and top each with a large spoonful of ice cream.

YIELD 6 servings

HAROLD'S CHERRY COBBLER

I guess the only person who ever loved cherry cobbler more than I do was my father (Harold), and every year on Father's Day, it was almost a ritual for Daddy and Mother to invite a few members of his Senior Scholars group and their wives over to the house for a fried chicken dinner highlighted by this juicy cobbler topped with homemade vanilla ice cream. Why you don't see more cherry cobblers these days is beyond me, for there's truly no Southern dessert quite like it when prepared correctly. "I suppose most people don't want to go to the trouble of making the rich biscuit dough," Mother guesses, which I find ridiculous, since no dough could be simpler—and forget about making this cobbler if you're thinking about cheating with some bland, commercial biscuit or piecrust mix. Remember that the filling should be just bubbling and slightly juicy (I test it by wiggling a knife down through one of

For the filling
Two 16-ounce cans sour pitted cherries, drained and ⅓ cup
   of the juice reserved
1 cup granulated sugar
2 tablespoons cornstarch
1 teaspoon grated lemon rind
2 tablespoons fresh lemon juice
½ teaspoon ground cinnamon
¼ cup (½ stick) cold butter, cut into pieces

For the biscuit dough
2 cups all-purpose flour
2 tablespoons granulated sugar
2 teaspoons baking powder
1 teaspoon salt
6 tablespoons (¾ stick) cold butter
1 cup half-and-half

*P*reheat the oven to 425°F. Grease a 3-quart baking dish and set aside.

*T*o make the filling, combine the cherries, reserved cherry juice, sugar, cornstarch, lemon rind, lemon juice, and cinnamon in a large mixing bowl and stir till well blended. Pour the mixture into the prepared dish and dot with the butter pieces.

*T*o make the dough, combine the flour, sugar, baking powder, and salt in a medium-size mixing bowl and stir till well blended. Add the butter; cut it in with a pastry cutter or two knives till the mixture resembles coarse meal. Stir in the half-and-half and mix till the dough forms a ball. Place the ball on a floured surface and, with your fingers, press out the dough till it is large enough to cover the baking dish. Place the dough over the cherry filling, crimp the edges all around the dish, cut a few small vents in the top, and bake till the crust is golden brown and the filling is bubbly, about 30 minutes. Serve warm.

YIELD **About 8 servings**

the vents in the crust.
Scoops of vanilla ice cream
allowed to melt are the
classic topping, but the
cobbler is also delicious
with light brown sugar
sprinkled over the top.

 *Martha's Sweet Note*

Never overcook or use too much thickening agent in cobblers, since a genuine cobbler must have a little juice in the serving bowl. Bake only till the crust or topping is just golden brown—which means keeping a close eye on the cobbler during the last minutes of baking.

SAM'S BREAD PUDDING WITH BOURBON SAUCE

A couple of years ago when Mother and I were on a book tour in Houston for *My Mother's Southern Kitchen,* we were taken to Sam Segari's eclectic seafood restaurant one evening for dinner. Out came giant platters of sweet boiled Gulf shrimp, impeccably fried clam fritters, puffy stuffed flounder, and the most succulent crab cakes imaginable, but what really knocked Mother for a loop was Sam's bread pudding with a sublime bourbon sauce. "I always thought New Orleans had a lock on bread puddings," she informed Sam, "but . . . well, young man, you've simply got to send me this recipe as soon as possible." Suffice it to say that within two weeks she was taking the pudding to a church supper and, when spring arrived, proclaiming it "the best bread pudding in the South" at our big Memorial Day celebration on my deck. I must say it really does make a difference if you can use homemade country bread in this pudding.

For the pudding

10 slices day-old white bread, torn into pieces
1 quart milk, scalded (see Sweet Note on page 18)
1 cup heavy cream
4 large eggs, beaten
1 cup granulated sugar
1 teaspoon pure vanilla extract
1 teaspoon ground cinnamon
½ teaspoon ground nutmeg
½ cup (1 stick) butter, melted
½ cup seedless dark raisins
½ cup broken pecans

For the sauce

3 large egg yolks
1 cup granulated sugar
1 tablespoon pure vanilla extract
1 pint heavy cream
3 tablespoons bourbon

*P*reheat the oven to 350°F. Butter a 2-quart baking dish and set aside.

*T*o make the pudding, combine the bread, milk, and cream in a large mixing bowl and stir till well blended. In a medium-size mixing bowl, mix the eggs and sugar together till well blended, then stir into the bread mixture. Add the vanilla, cinnamon, and nutmeg and mix till well blended. Stir in the melted butter, raisins, and pecans. Scrape the mixture into the prepared baking dish, set the dish in a larger baking pan filled with warm water about 1 inch deep, and bake till a cake tester or straw inserted in the center comes out clean, about 1 hour. Remove the dish from the pan of water and let the pudding cool in the dish.

*T*o make the sauce, place the egg yolks in a medium-size, heavy saucepan and beat slightly. Add the sugar, vanilla, and cream, mix till well blended, and, stirring constantly, cook over moderate heat till the mixture comes to a boil. Immediately remove the pan from the heat and stir in the bourbon. Let the sauce cool slightly before spooning it over the pudding, served in deep bowls.

YIELD 8 servings

DADDY'S CHOCOLATE-ALMOND CHARLOTTE ROUSSE

Originally a fairly simple French molded, chilled cream pudding made with small sponge cakes, Charlotte Russe evolved in the South during the nineteenth century (the spelling changing to "Rousse") into an icebox cake lined with ladyfingers and eventually became the quintessential celebration dessert. Traditionally, the cake was flavored only with a little sherry, vanilla, and perhaps coffee, but at some point Mother began making her Rousse with chocolate and toasted almonds, creating a masterpiece that was always one of my daddy's special treats on Father's Day. Since the split ladyfingers tend to dry out very quickly, line the pan with them only after preparing the filling.

1 envelope unflavored gelatin
¼ cup cold water
3 ounces unsweetened baking chocolate
½ cup water
3 tablespoons sherry
4 large eggs, separated
¾ cup granulated sugar
1 teaspoon pure vanilla extract
1 cup heavy cream, whipped to stiff peaks
16 ladyfingers, split in half
¼ cup slivered almonds, toasted (see Sweet Note)

In a small bowl, sprinkle the gelatin over the ¼ cup cold water and let dissolve completely.

In a large, heavy saucepan over low heat, combine the chocolate and the ½ cup water and stir till the chocolate melts completely. Remove the pan from the heat, add the dissolved gelatin and the sherry, and stir till well blended. In a medium-size mixing bowl, beat the egg yolks with an electric mixer till frothy, then gradually add ½ cup of the sugar, beating till well blended. Stir in the vanilla, then gradually add this mixture to the chocolate mixture, stirring till smooth. Let cool.

Wash and dry the mixer beaters and, in a large mixing bowl, beat the egg whites till soft peaks form, then gradually add the remaining ¼ cup sugar and beat till stiff peaks form. Fold the egg whites into the cooled chocolate mixture, then fold in the whipped cream.

Line the bottom and sides of a 9-inch springform pan with about three quarters of the split ladyfingers and evenly fill with half the chocolate mixture. Arrange the remaining ladyfingers over the top, add the remaining chocolate mixture, and sprinkle the almonds over the top. Chill the Rousse for at least 3 hours before removing the sides of the pan and cutting the cake into wedges.

YIELD 12 to 14 servings

Martha's Sweet Notes

See SWEET NOTE on page 31 regarding the use of uncooked egg whites.

To toast nuts, preheat the oven to 300°F, spread the nuts across a baking sheet, and bake till slightly browned, about 10 minutes, stirring several times and watching them very carefully.

RHUBARB AND STRAWBERRY PARFAIT

Since my father loved the combination of rhubarb and fresh strawberries in any form, just as soon as both came into season in late spring or early summer, Mother would often begin planning a pie, tart, pudding, or this feathery parfait to serve at her Father's Day celebration. Do remember that overcooking rhubarb makes it stringy and tough, so simmer it only till it's soft, or you'll have trouble producing a smooth puree. When Mother serves the parfait at a formal dinner, she saves a few beautiful whole strawberries to garnish the top. Here there's no need to soften the gelatin.

2 pounds fresh rhubarb stalks
1 overflowing pint fresh, ripe strawberries, rinsed, hulled, and cut in half
1 cup granulated sugar
1½ envelopes unflavored gelatin
¼ teaspoon salt
½ teaspoon pure vanilla extract
3 large egg whites

Wash the rhubarb, trim off the leaves and bases, and cut the stalks into 3-inch lengths. Place the pieces in a large pot with enough water to cover, bring to a boil, reduce the heat to low, cover, and simmer just till soft, about 10 minutes. Drain the rhubarb and let cool.

In a blender or food processor, combine the rhubarb and strawberries (in batches if necessary) and reduce to a smooth puree. Transfer to a large, heavy, nonreactive saucepan, add the sugar, gelatin, and salt, and stir slowly over low heat till the gelatin has dissolved. Stir in the vanilla till well blended, then transfer the mixture to a large mixing bowl, cover with plastic wrap, and chill till slightly thickened, about 1 hour.

Add the egg whites and beat the mixture with an electric mixer till doubled in volume. Transfer to a large serving dish and chill for 2 hours before serving.

YIELD **8 servings**

Martha's Sweet Note

See SWEET NOTE on page 31 regarding the use of uncooked egg whites.

July Fourth

&

Labor Day

The One and Only Authentic Southern Strawberry Shortcake

Red Devil Cake

Grace's Four-Berry Pie

Ocean Isle Blueberry Cream Pie

Frank's Lemon Meringue Pie

Frozen Mud Pie with Chocolate Sauce

Confederate Peach Cobbler

Summertime Mixed Berry Crumble

Fresh Peach Crisp

Chewy Peanut–Chocolate Chip Drop Cookies

Caramel Chewies

Peanut Butter Blossoms

In the old days, when the entire family was alive and still together, both July Fourth and Labor Day were celebrated at our beach cottage in the coastal Carolina Low Country, and it still staggers my imagination to recall the multitude of spectacular desserts that Mother produced year after year for all the buffets and cookouts to which she and Daddy invited everybody but the chief of police. Today the feasts continue, only now, more often than not, Mother is at my home in East Hampton whipping up the same desserts for the same celebrations—when, that is, she's not putting up watermelon rind pickle and chowchow and pickled peaches and heaven knows how many fruit preserves.

Since these two holidays occur during the full bloom of summer, Mother naturally takes advantage of all the fresh bounty by making her Blueberry Cream Pie, Authentic Southern Strawberry Shortcake, and various peach desserts (despite the "inferior Yankee peaches"), but when the outdoor buffets are set up, guests can be somewhat dumbfounded to see also a quivering Lemon Meringue Pie, her colorful Red Devil Cake, and a tempting array of home-made cookies we make to accompany freshly churned ice cream. And when someone dares to exclaim in jestful horror over all the sweets, Mother casually comments, "Well, honey, this is the way we celebrate in the South, and remember, nobody's forcing you to eat every crumb on the plate"—which, of course, everybody does.

THE ONE AND ONLY AUTHENTIC SOUTHERN STRAWBERRY SHORTCAKE

*D*on't even start Mother talking about real Southern strawberry shortcake unless you're prepared for a heated two-hour discourse. Briefly, she abhors those little, overly sweet commercial sponge cakes used to make most shortcakes; she insists that the split biscuits (broken apart, *not* sliced) be buttered while still hot to add depth to the overall flavor; she cringes at just the mention of Cool Whip being substituted for fresh whipped cream; and the dessert must be served warm. Strawberry short-cake is sacred to Mother, and it continues to be the highlight of every July Fourth celebration we throw at her house or mine.

2 cups all-purpose flour
3 tablespoons granulated sugar
1 tablespoon baking powder
¼ teaspoon salt
½ cup (1 stick) butter, softened
1 large egg, beaten
⅔ cup half-and-half
Butter for spreading
4 cups fresh, ripe strawberries, rinsed, hulled, sliced in half, and sugared to taste
1 cup heavy cream, whipped to stiff peaks

*P*reheat the oven to 450°F.

*I*n a large mixing bowl, combine the flour, sugar, baking powder, and salt and mix well. Add the butter and, using a pastry cutter or two knives, cut the butter into the mixture till crumbly. In a small bowl, combine the egg and half-and-half and mix till well blended, then add to the flour mixture and stir till the mixture is thoroughly moist. Turn the dough out onto a floured surface and knead very briefly. With your hands, pat out the dough to about a ½-inch thickness, then, using a floured 3-inch biscuit cutter, cut out 6 biscuits. Place the biscuits on an ungreased baking sheet and bake on the upper rack of the oven till slightly brown on top, about 10 minutes.

*W*hile they're still hot, split open the biscuits, spread lightly with butter, and arrange close together on a crystal cake plate. Spoon the berries and cream onto the biscuits and serve while still warm.

YIELD 6 servings

RED DEVIL CAKE

*M*other still celebrates Halloween the way she did when I was a child (dressed up in every weird costume imaginable), and folks who drop in after dark can almost count on being served slices of her colorful red devil cake with the hot toddies. Notice that the sides of the cake are not frosted so that the red color can be seen, and if you really want to decorate the cake in Mother's style, you'll stick tiny candy pumpkins into the top. I've also found this to be a great cake for our July Fourth celebration—with fresh blueberries arranged around the base to carry out the patriotic color scheme.

½ cup (1 stick) butter, softened
1½ cups granulated sugar
2 large eggs
2 teaspoons red food coloring
1 teaspoon pure vanilla extract
¼ cup unsweetened cocoa powder
2 cups all-purpose flour
1 teaspoon baking soda
½ teaspoon salt
1 cup buttermilk (see Sweet Note on page 10)
Almond–Cream Cheese Frosting (see Carrot Cake, page 182)
½ cup sliced almonds, toasted (optional) (see Sweet Note on page 65)

*P*reheat the oven to 350°F. Grease and flour three 8-inch round cake pans, tapping out any excess flour, and set aside.

*I*n a large mixing bowl, cream the butter and sugar together with an electric mixer till smooth, then add the eggs one at a time, beating well after each addition. Add the food coloring and vanilla and beat till well blended. In a medium-size mixing bowl, combine the cocoa, flour, baking soda, and salt. Add the dry ingredients alternately with the buttermilk to the creamed mixture, beating well after each addition. Scrape the batter evenly into the three prepared pans and bake till a cake tester or straw inserted in the center comes out clean, about 25 minutes. Let the cakes cool in the pans for about 10 minutes, then turn them out onto a wire rack and let cool completely.

*P*lace one layer on a cake plate and spread one third of the frosting over the top. Repeat with the two remaining layers and the remaining frosting; do not frost the sides of the cake. If desired, garnish the top with the almonds.

YIELD One 3-layer 8-inch cake; 12 to 14 servings

GRACE'S FOUR-BERRY PIE

*W*hen I first introduced Mother to my friend Grace Martin from Jacksonville, North Carolina, and Grace concluded a Labor Day dinner with this sumptuous berry pie, all Mother wanted to know was how she got the crust so crisp. "The trick," Grace explained, "is ultrachilling the bottom crust in the freezer before it's given the initial baking"—a technique totally new to Mother (and to me). Also, Grace lines the bottom pastry with foil to prevent bulking as it bakes (another new trick that impressed Mother), and to keep the berries from liquefying too much, she uses tapioca. Needless to say, the two Tarheel cooks have been great friends ever since.

For the pastry

2 cups all-purpose flour
1 tablespoon granulated sugar
½ teaspoon salt
½ cup (1 stick) cold butter, cut into pieces
3 tablespoons cold Crisco shortening
5 tablespoons cold water

For the filling

1 pint fresh blueberries, stemmed
1 pint fresh strawberries, hulled and sliced in half
1 pint fresh blackberries, stemmed
1 pint fresh raspberries, stemmed
¾ cup granulated sugar
¼ cup quick-cooking tapioca

1 large egg, beaten
1 tablespoon granulated sugar

*T*o make the pastry, combine the flour, sugar, and salt in a large mixing bowl and stir till well blended, then cut in the butter, shortening, and water with a pastry cutter or two knives till the mixture resembles coarse meal. Gather the dough into two balls, flatten each slightly, wrap in plastic wrap, and chill for 1 hour.

*P*reheat the oven to 375°F.

*O*n a lightly floured surface, roll out one ball of dough to a circle about ⅛ inch thick, then press it into the bottom and up the sides of a 10-inch pie plate and place the plate in the freezer for 15 to 20 minutes. Fit a sheet of aluminum foil tightly over the chilled pastry, then bake till just golden, about 20 minutes. Let the crust cool. Meanwhile, roll out the other ball of dough into a rectangle about ¼ inch thick, cut it into ½-inch-wide strips, and set aside.

*T*o make the filling, combine the berries, sugar, and tapioca in a large mixing bowl, toss well, and let stand for about 15 minutes.

Spoon the mixture into the cooled piecrust (after removing the foil). Form a lattice pattern, interweaving the pastry strips over the filling, and crimp the edges to seal. Brush the strips and edges of the pie with the beaten egg, sprinkle the sugar over the top, and bake till the berries are soft and the pastry golden brown, about 40 minutes.

YIELD One 10-inch pie; 8 servings

OCEAN ISLE BLUEBERRY CREAM PIE

Mother and I concocted this delectable pie one summer day at our beach house in Ocean Isle, North Carolina, after visiting a blueberry farm and picking enough berries to eat, cook with, and freeze. Mother has never been crazy about blueberries, since she insists the flavor can't touch that of dewberries or blackberries, which is why she decided to add sour cream and nuts to give the pie "a little zip." Naturally, I disagree—at least partly. In any case, we now feature this chilled pie on our big July Fourth buffet, and guests wolf it down.

1 cup sour cream
5 tablespoons all-purpose flour
¾ cup granulated sugar
1 teaspoon pure vanilla extract
¼ teaspoon salt
1 large egg, beaten
2½ cups fresh blueberries, stemmed, rinsed, and patted dry
1 unbaked 9-inch Basic Pie Shell (page 243)
2 tablespoons butter, softened
¼ cup chopped nuts (pecans, walnuts, hazelnuts, or filberts)

Preheat the oven to 400°F.

In a large mixing bowl, combine the sour cream, 2 tablespoons of the flour, the sugar, vanilla, salt, and egg and beat with an electric mixer till smooth, about 5 minutes. Fold in the blueberries, then pour the filling into the pie shell and bake till the crust is firm, about 25 minutes.

Meanwhile, combine the remaining 3 tablespoons flour, the butter, and nuts in a bowl and mix with a wooden spoon till well blended. Remove the pie from the oven, spread the nut mixture over the top, and bake 10 minutes longer. Let the pie cool, then chill for about 1 hour before serving.

YIELD One 9-inch pie; 6 to 8 servings

FRANK'S LEMON MERINGUE PIE

*A*lthough this is the same glorious lemon meringue pie that Mother made when I was a child and that often highlights our big July Fourth buffet, today we call it "Frank's pie" for Frank Zachary, former editor in chief of *Town & Country*, who once begged Mother to make the pie for him while she was visiting me and then proceeded to devour it in a single sitting—with not the best consequences! One reason Mother's version is so superior to most other lemon meringue pies is that it's not made with condensed milk. Be sure to follow these directions to the letter.

1 cup plus 6 tablespoons granulated sugar
¼ cup cornstarch
¼ teaspoon salt
1½ cups boiling water
2 teaspoons grated lemon rind
⅓ cup fresh lemon juice
3 large eggs, separated
2 tablespoons butter
1 prebaked 9-inch Basic Pie Shell (page 243)

*P*reheat the oven to 325°F.

*I*n a medium-size, heavy saucepan, combine 1 cup of the sugar, the cornstarch, and salt and mix till well blended. Gradually add the boiling water, stirring constantly, and cook over moderate heat till the mixture thickens, stirring. Add the lemon rind and juice and stir. In a small bowl, beat the egg yolks till foamy, add a small amount of the hot lemon mixture to them, stirring constantly, and then pour the egg mixture into the lemon mixture in the saucepan, stirring. Add the butter and continue cooking, stirring, till the mixture is very thick, then pour into the baked pie shell.

*I*n a medium-size mixing bowl, beat the egg whites with an electric mixer till thickened. Gradually add the remaining 6 tablespoons sugar and beat till stiff peaks form. With a rubber spatula, cover the pie with the meringue, being careful to seal all the edges. With a spoon, make a few peaks in the meringue. Bake just till the top has browned slightly, about 10 minutes. Cool completely before serving.

YIELD One 9-inch pie; 6 servings

Martha's Sweet Notes

*S*ee SWEET NOTE *on page 31 regarding the use of uncooked egg whites.*

*W*hen *topping a pie with meringue, be sure to carefully spread the meringue all the way to the edges of the rim to prevent it from shrinking back toward the middle while baking.*

FROZEN MUD PIE WITH CHOCOLATE SAUCE

Rich mud pies have been made in the South (mainly in Mississippi) since the nineteenth century, and today there's not a serious cook who doesn't pride himself or herself on a given variation. What makes Mother's sacred version so distinct is the use of Oreo cookies instead of chocolate wafers (often difficult to find these days), ice cream, and peanuts, and never is the pie so popular as when she serves it "to our Yankee friends" at the big Labor Day bash we throw every year at my home on Long Island.

28 Oreo cookies, crushed
½ cup (1 stick) butter, melted
½ gallon coffee ice cream, softened a bit
1 cup granulated sugar
One 5-ounce can evaporated milk
4 ounces semisweet chocolate
6 tablespoons (¾ stick) butter, cut into pieces
1 cup heavy cream, whipped to stiff peaks
1 cup chopped peanuts

In a medium-size mixing bowl, combine the crushed cookies and melted butter and mix well. Spread the cookie mixture evenly over the bottom of a medium-size baking dish, spread the coffee ice cream on top of the cookie mixture, and place in the freezer for at least 2 hours.

In a medium-size, heavy saucepan, combine the sugar, evaporated milk, chocolate, and butter pieces and cook over moderate heat till the mixture is thickened, stirring constantly. Remove the pan from the heat and let cool completely.

Pour the chocolate sauce over the frozen ice cream and top with the whipped cream and peanuts. Cut the pie into squares and serve immediately.

YIELD 10 to 12 servings

CONFEDERATE PEACH COBBLER

If I were forced to identify the one dessert that best typifies Mother's art of Southern baking, it would certainly have to be this glorious peach cobbler that's been in our family for generations and that she prepares for every occasion from elaborate church suppers to Labor Day cookouts to informal weekend brunches. The cobbler is in such demand, in fact, that Mother freezes bag after bag of cut-up Elberta peaches (the sweet, juicy, ideal variety, in her opinion) so the dish can be made year-round. Since Southern peaches are now shipped (often, unfortunately, hard as rocks) to most areas of the country during the summer months, do try to find some soft ones if you want to see what a true Confederate peach cobbler is all about. Remember to poke this cobbler carefully while baking to make sure that a little juice remains on the bottom. Combine 2 pounds of fresh peaches and 4 cups of halved, ripe strawberries to make a strawberry-peach cobbler.

4 pounds fresh peaches, peeled (see Sweet Note), pitted, and cut into ½-inch-thick slices
⅔ cup plus 2 teaspoons granulated sugar
2 tablespoons butter, cut into small pieces
2 cups all-purpose flour
1 tablespoon baking powder
1 teaspoon salt
¼ cup cold Crisco shortening
1 cup heavy cream
Vanilla ice cream

*P*reheat the oven to 400°F.

*I*n a large mixing bowl, combine the peaches with ⅔ cup of the sugar and toss well. Spoon the fruit into a shallow 2-quart baking dish and dot with the butter.

*S*ift together the flour, baking powder, salt, and the remaining 2 teaspoons sugar into a large mixing bowl, then cut in the shortening with a pastry cutter or two knives till the mixture resembles coarse meal. Add the heavy cream and stir till the dough forms a ball. Turn the dough out onto a floured surface, roll out ¼ inch thick, and trim as necessary to fit the baking dish. Place the dough over the fruit, crimp the edges, and bake till the pastry is golden brown and the peaches are still slightly juicy, about 30 minutes. Let the cobbler cool for about 15 minutes and serve warm, topped with ice cream.

YIELD **6 servings**

Martha's Sweet Note

*T*o easily remove the peels of fresh peaches intended for cooking, dip the peaches briefly (15 seconds) in hot water, then rub off the peels. To keep the freshly cut flesh of peaches (and apples) from discoloring, sprinkle with fresh lemon juice.

SUMMERTIME MIXED BERRY CRUMBLE

*T*he moment the first fresh summer berries come into season, Mother almost goes berserk making pies, tarts, crumbles, fools, cobblers, and crisps for any and every occasion, and one of the most sensational is this three-berry crumble that might show up at weddings, graduation, or the July Fourth buffet. What's different about this crumble, of course, is that Mother uses oats instead of bread or cookie crumbs to attain an exceptionally crunchy and flavorful topping. We've also found that the crumble is just as delicious made with about four cups of chopped ripe but firm fresh peaches when the berries have disappeared from the market. Just be sure to use old-fashioned oats and not the quick variety.

½ cup old-fashioned rolled oats
½ cup finely ground almonds
¾ cup all-purpose flour
¾ cup firmly packed dark brown sugar
¾ cup (1½ sticks) cold butter, cut into pieces
1 pint fresh strawberries, hulled, rinsed, and patted dry
½ pint fresh blueberries, stemmed, rinsed, and patted dry
½ pint fresh raspberries, stemmed, rinsed, and patted dry
½ cup granulated sugar
2 tablespoons cornstarch

*P*reheat the oven to 350°F. Grease a 9-inch pie plate and set aside.

*I*n a large mixing bowl, combine the oats, almonds, flour, brown sugar, and butter and work the mixture together with your fingers till crumbly. Press half the crumb mixture against the bottom and sides of the prepared pie plate and set aside.

*I*n another large mixing bowl, combine the three berries, granulated sugar, and cornstarch and stir till well blended. Spoon the berry mixture into the pie plate, sprinkle the remaining crumb mixture evenly over the top, and bake till golden, about 30 minutes. Let the crumble cool slightly and serve warm.

YIELD **8 servings**

FRESH PEACH CRISP

*J*ust this past summer at my home in East Hampton, Mother worked and worked on this simple crisp for our July Fourth party, using local peaches and trying to produce something between a crumble and Brown Betty. Not once, however, was she completely satisfied with the texture of the topping—even though guests gobbled up every morsel of the crisp. Of course, the minute she returned to North Carolina and made the dessert with Southern Elberta peaches, she pronounced it "perfect—not too crisp, not too soft," and commenced to blame the previous failures on "those watery Northern peaches." All I can say is, take your chances.

1 cup all-purpose flour
½ cup granulated sugar
½ cup firmly packed light brown sugar
½ teaspoon salt
½ teaspoon ground cinnamon
½ cup (1 stick) cold butter, cut into pieces
4 cups peeled (see Sweet Note on page 76), pitted, and sliced fresh peaches
1 tablespoon fresh lemon juice
2 tablespoons water

*P*reheat the oven to 350°F. Grease a medium-size baking dish and set aside.

*I*n a medium-size mixing bowl, combine the flour, two sugars, salt, cinnamon, and butter and work the mixture together with your fingers till it resembles coarse meal. In another medium-size bowl, combine the peaches, lemon juice, and water, stir till well blended, and spoon the mixture into the prepared dish. Sprinkle the flour mixture over the peaches, cover with a sheet of aluminum foil, and bake for 15 minutes. Remove the foil and continue baking till the top is golden and crisp, another 35 to 45 minutes. Serve the crisp warm or at room temperature.

YIELD **6 to 8 servings**

CHEWY PEANUT–CHOCOLATE CHIP DROP COOKIES

Knowing my passion for any dessert combination of chocolate and peanut butter, as well as my insistence that chocolate chip cookies be ultrachewy, Mother spent ages perfecting these marvels. So why not simply use crunchy peanut butter and leave out the chopped peanuts? We tried that repeatedly once I got in on the act, and, though I can't explain why, it just doesn't produce the same chewy, miraculous results. Do note that the peanuts must be finely chopped for the texture to be exactly right, and, for Lord's sake, watch the cookies carefully to make sure they don't overcook. We serve the cookies at all events involving homemade ice cream—and especially at our outdoor Labor Day extravaganza.

½ cup (1 stick) butter, softened
½ cup smooth peanut butter
½ cup firmly packed light brown sugar
½ cup granulated sugar
2 large eggs
1½ cups all-purpose flour
1 teaspoon baking powder
½ teaspoon salt
One 6-ounce bag (1 cup) semisweet chocolate chips
¾ cup finely chopped peanuts
1 teaspoon pure vanilla extract

Preheat the oven to 350°F.

In a large mixing bowl, cream the butter and peanut butter together with an electric mixer till well blended. Add the two sugars and the eggs and continue beating till the mixture is well blended and smooth. Into a small mixing bowl, sift together the flour, baking powder, and salt and gradually beat this into the creamed mixture. Add the chocolate chips, peanuts, and vanilla and stir till well blended. Drop the batter by the tablespoon 2 inches apart onto ungreased baking sheets, and bake just till the cookies begin to brown lightly, about 10 minutes. Let the cookies cool for 10 minutes, then transfer them to a wire rack to cool completely.

YIELD About 30 cookies

 Martha's Sweet Note

A "baking sheet" refers either to a flat, single-sided cookie sheet or a shallow, four-sided jelly roll pan, and I do not necessarily use the two interchangeably. Since a cookie sheet allows heat to circulate freely, this is what I always use when I want cookies to be uniform and crisp.

CARAMEL CHEWIES

*E*veryone in our family loves caramel in any shape or form, which is why Mother developed these delightful, nutty chewies that she often takes to picnics and Labor Day parties instead of her standard chocolate brownies. "Just this past year, I took my fudge brownies to our big neighborhood Labor Day shindig, and do you know somebody had the gall to say, 'Oh, Martha Pearl, I was so looking forward to those wonderful, chewy caramel things you brought last year.'" These chewies, like most brownies, do harden very quickly, so, first, don't overcook them and, second, be sure to store them as soon as possible in a tightly closed tin. If they do get too hard, just use the old trick of dropping a piece of fresh bread into the tin from time to time.

½ cup (1 stick) butter, softened
2 cups firmly packed light brown sugar
2 large eggs
1 teaspoon pure vanilla extract
1 cup all-purpose flour
¼ teaspoon salt
1 cup chopped walnuts

*P*reheat the oven to 350°F. Grease a large rectangular baking pan and set aside.

*I*n a large mixing bowl, cream the butter and brown sugar together with an electric mixer, then add the eggs one at a time, beating till well blended. Add the vanilla, flour, and salt and beat till well blended. Add ½ cup of the walnuts and stir till well blended. Spread the batter fairly thin in the prepared baking pan and sprinkle the remaining ½ cup walnuts on top. Bake just till the cake is slightly firm, about 30 minutes, then cut into 48 chewies and let them cool completely in the pan.

YIELD 4 dozen chewies

PEANUT BUTTER BLOSSOMS

My sister, Hootie, used to make these cute blossoms exclusively for the children at birthday parties, but when Mother noticed that more adults than children were eating the cookies, she quickly adopted them to serve at our big July Fourth cookout. And I must say that if there were ever a cookie that is literally fun to make—for kids and grown-ups alike—this is it. Since I love any confection with peanut butter and chocolate, don't even ask if these blossoms taste wonderful.

1¾ cups all-purpose flour
½ teaspoon baking soda
½ teaspoon salt
½ cup Crisco shortening
½ cup granulated sugar
½ cup firmly packed light brown sugar
1 large egg
½ cup crunchy peanut butter
1 teaspoon pure vanilla extract
2 tablespoons milk
Granulated sugar for rolling
48 Hershey's Kisses, unwrapped

Preheat the oven to 350°F.

In a small mixing bowl, combine the flour, baking soda, and salt, mix well, and set aside. In a large mixing bowl, cream the Crisco and two sugars together with an electric mixer, then add the egg, peanut butter, and vanilla and beat till well blended. Add the dry ingredients alternately with the milk to the peanut butter mixture and beat till well blended. With your hands, roll rounded teaspoons of the dough into balls, roll each ball in sugar, and place on a large ungreased baking sheet about 1 inch apart. Bake for 12 minutes. Immediately after removing the cookies from the oven, press a Kiss into the middle of each till the edges crack slightly. Let the blossoms cool before serving.

YIELD 4 dozen blossoms

Halloween, Election Day & Thanksgiving

Satan Chocolate Pound Cake with
Chocolate-Marshmallow Frosting

Horse Pear Tart

Ballot-Box Black Bottom Pie

Real McCoy Southern Pecan Pie

Maw Maw's Sweet Potato Pie

Cajun Sweet Potato Pecan Pie

Huguenot Torte

Cranberry-Apple Cobbler

Unca' Nalle's Butterscotch Pudding

First Cousin Baked Apple Pudding

Mecklenburg County Persimmon Pudding

other loves Halloween like a child, possibly a throwback to her own youth when, unlike today, trick-or-treating kids were not plied with handfuls of cheap candy but offered small paper plates or cups of homemade cake, firm pudding, or colorful fresh cookies. "If stuff like candy corn existed back then," she says with a frown, "we didn't know about it." Halloween in those days was also an occasion for adult celebration, explanation of why Mother still decorates the house cleverly and invites people over (after dark) for chili, chunky applesauce, and one of her special desserts.

Election Day in the South (Southern politics being what they are) usually means a huge outdoor pork barbecue with mobs of people, held after most have voted. Mother and Daddy, however, always preferred a bit more intimate yet lively celebration with just close friends and plenty of good booze, finger food, and, of course, one or two of Mother's more outrageously rich pies. Today, she continues the tradition, and she can always count on hearing at least one arriving guest threaten jestfully, "I'll go back and vote a full Democrat ticket if you haven't made your Black Bottom Pie!"

As for Mother's desserts at our large, formal Thanksgiving dinner, all I can say is that no one would believe the spectacle who's not been there to witness the fruit cobbler and Southern Pecan Pie and Huguenot Torte and Persimmon Pudding and maybe a big bowl of Ambrosia displayed dramatically on the sideboard in the dining room. Thanksgiving in Mother's home is truly a Southern feast in the old extravagant tradition, a family meal that might easily last three hours and that (at least for Mother) would be an utter failure without at least four stunning desserts. "Everybody knows how much Southerners love sweets," she tries to explain, "and . . . well, you can never tell who's in the mood for sweet potato pie and who would like just a little pudding." And to really play it safe, she might well include a big plate of homemade cookies for the well-nourished children.

SATAN CHOCOLATE POUND CAKE WITH CHOCOLATE-MARSHMALLOW FROSTING

*M*other still makes a big to-do over Halloween (a big jack-o'-lantern, colorful paper decorations around the house, spooky figurines, etc.), and when neighbors drop by or trick-or-treaters show up, they're sure to be offered a thin slice of Mother's famous satan cake with its sinfully rich frosting. I'm the first to say that this cake represents a peak in Mother's baking art—truly the only chocolate cake I find hopelessly addictive. Just recently, when she produced the cake for a large dinner party at my house and forgot to give an elated guest a promised extra slice to take home, he drove back some fifteen miles to collect his special treat. Never satisfied completely with the pound cake, Mother keeps changing the amount of cocoa in the recipe—first two-thirds cup, then a quarter cup, now a half cup. I find the half-cup version ideal, but you might want to experiment.

1 cup (2 sticks) butter, softened
½ cup Crisco shortening
3 cups granulated sugar
5 large eggs
3 cups all-purpose flour
½ teaspoon baking powder
½ teaspoon salt
½ cup unsweetened cocoa powder
1 cup milk
1 teaspoon pure vanilla extract
Chocolate-Marshmallow Frosting (page 251)

*P*reheat the oven to 325°F. Grease and flour a 10-inch tube or Bundt pan, tapping out any excess flour, and set aside.

*C*ream the butter and Crisco together in a large mixing bowl with an electric mixer till light and fluffy. Add the sugar and continue beating till well blended. Add the eggs one at a time, beating after each addition till well blended. Into another bowl, sift together the flour, baking powder, salt, and cocoa and add alternately with the milk to the batter, beating well. Add the vanilla and beat till well blended. Pour the batter into the prepared pan and "spank" the bottom of the pan to distribute the batter evenly and eliminate any air bubbles. Bake 1 hour and 10 minutes, or till a straw or cake tester inserted in the center comes out clean, then let the cake cool completely in the pan before turning out onto a cake plate.

*W*ith a rubber spatula, spread the frosting liberally and evenly over the top and sides of the cake, let cool completely, and keep covered till ready to serve.

YIELD One 10-inch tube or Bundt cake; 12 servings

Martha's Sweet Note

*M*ost cakes freeze very well if wrapped tightly in aluminum foil and stored in large freezer bags. While some must be defrosted before serving, those containing lots of sugar and fat—like this pound cake—never freeze hard and can be cut immediately.

HORSE PEAR TART

When I was a child, I remember my uncle Robert would show up at the house in early fall lugging a big hemp sack of pears from his mother's farm that everybody called simply "horse pears." They were hard as rocks and inedible raw, but the preserves, pies, and tarts that Mother made from those yellowish, black-speckled pears were utterly incredible. Once in a blue moon these days, a friend or friend of a friend will tell Mother where she can find a few real horse pears, but generally she has to depend on Boscs or Anjous for this delectable glazed tart she sometimes makes for her Halloween celebration. Be warned that if you use eating pears such as Bartlett or Comice, or buy overripe pears, they will liquefy quickly and produce a mess.

7 ripe but firm Bosc or Anjou pears
3 tablespoons butter
2 tablespoons heavy cream
Grated rind of ½ small orange
½ cup granulated sugar
Ground cinnamon to taste
1 unbaked 10-inch Basic Tart Shell (page 243)
¾ cup apricot preserves
2 tablespoons water

Peel and remove the cores of three of the pears and coarsely chop. Heat 2 tablespoons of the butter in a medium-size, heavy, nonreactive skillet, add the chopped pears, cream, orange rind, ¼ cup of the sugar, and the cinnamon and cook over moderately low heat for 15 minutes, mashing the pears with a heavy fork into a rough puree. Let cool.

Preheat the oven to 375°F.

Peel and remove the cores of the four remaining pears and cut each one into very thin slices, dropping the slices into a bowl of cold water. Drain the slices on paper towels. Spoon the cooled puree evenly over the bottom of the tart shell and arrange circular layers of pear slices over the puree. Sprinkle the slices with the remaining ¼ cup sugar, dot with the remaining tablespoon of butter, sprinkle a little cinnamon over the top, and bake the tart till the crust is golden brown, about 40 minutes.

Meanwhile, combine the preserves and water in a small, heavy, nonreactive saucepan over low heat, stir till the preserves have melted, and strain into a small bowl, pressing the preserves with the back of a spoon.

When the pie is baked, brush the apricot glaze over the top and let the tart cool to room temperature.

YIELD One 10-inch tart; 8 servings

BALLOT-BOX BLACK BOTTOM PIE

I really have to laugh at the way some food writers think that black bottom pie is the greatest Southern dessert," huffs Mother. "Don't get me wrong: It's a delicious pie when made correctly, but to put it up against our pecan pies, and fruit cobblers, and congealed desserts. . . ." Well, as often happens, I disagree with Mother as much about the supremacy of this pie as about politics, not only because black bottom pie shows how complex Southern desserts can be but because it is indeed one of the most sensuous chocolate confections ever devised. Men, especially, love it, which I suppose is why Mother always fixes one for her big Election Day festivities. Traditionally, she serves the pie with ample glasses of sweet liqueur.

1 envelope unflavored gelatin
¼ cup cold water
1½ cups milk
4 large eggs, separated
1 cup granulated sugar
¼ teaspoon salt
1 tablespoon cornstarch
2 tablespoons dark rum
2 ounces unsweetened baking chocolate
1 teaspoon pure vanilla extract
1 baked 9-inch Chocolate Wafer Pie Shell (page 248)
1 cup heavy cream
¼ cup confectioners' sugar
1 ounce semisweet chocolate, coarsely grated

*I*n a small bowl, sprinkle the gelatin over the water and set aside to soften.

*I*n the top pan of a double boiler set over simmering (not boiling) water, scald the milk (see Sweet Note on page 18), then remove the pan from the water.

*I*n a small mixing bowl, whisk the egg yolks together, then add ½ cup of the granulated sugar, the salt, and cornstarch and whisk till well blended. Very gradually add about ½ cup of the hot milk to the yolk mixture, whisking constantly, then pour the yolk mixture into the hot milk, whisking constantly. Return the pan to the top of the double boiler and cook over simmering water till the mixture coats the back of a spoon, about 10 minutes. Remove the pan from the water, measure out 1 cup of the custard, and let cool till tepid, about 10 minutes. Add the dissolved gelatin to the remaining hot custard and stir till well blended. Add the rum, stir well, and chill while preparing chocolate mixture.

*I*n a small bowl set over a shallow saucepan of boiling water, melt the unsweetened chocolate. Remove the bowl from the heat and stir in the cup of tepid custard plus the vanilla. Mix till well blended and let cool to room temperature. Pour the cooled chocolate mixture into the baked pie shell, cover with plastic wrap, and chill till firm, about 1 hour.

*I*n a large mixing bowl, beat the egg whites with an electric mixer till stiff but not dry peaks form. Gradually beat in the remaining ½ cup granulated sugar, then fold the whites gently into the chilled custard. Scrape the custard over the chocolate mixture, covering evenly, and chill till firm, at least 2 hours.

*W*ash and dry the mixer beaters, then, in a medium-size mixing bowl, beat the cream and confectioners' sugar together till stiff peaks form. Spread the whipped cream evenly over the top of the pie and top with the grated chocolate.

YIELD One 9-inch pie; 8 servings

Martha's Sweet Note

*S*ee SWEET NOTE *on page 31 regarding the use of uncooked egg whites.*

REAL McCOY SOUTHERN PECAN PIE

*P*ecans are the only nut indigenous to the South, and while I well remember three giant trees soaring maybe fifty feet in the air in our backyard in Charlotte, by far the largest production (some one hundred million pounds per year) is in Georgia, where Mother was born. I've always suspected that the ancestor of pecan pie is England's treacle tart, an ultrasweet sugar-egg-syrup

4 large eggs
1 cup granulated sugar
1 cup light corn syrup
1½ teaspoons all-purpose flour
¼ teaspoon salt
1 teaspoon pure vanilla extract
¼ cup (½ stick) butter, melted
2 cups pecan halves
1 unbaked 9-inch Basic Pie Shell (page 243)
Whipped cream

*P*reheat the oven to 350°F.

*I*n a large mixing bowl, beat the eggs with an electric mixer till frothy, then add the sugar, corn syrup, flour, salt, and vanilla and

continued

confection to which we no doubt simply added our native nuts in Colonial times. In any case, Mother truthfully can't understand why people make such a production about her pie. "I mean, it's the same old pie I've been making for Thanksgiving since I was a young lady, and nothing could be simpler." Yeah, sure, but just let someone try to modify the sacred ingredients (like substituting maple syrup for corn syrup), or admit to using (often rancid) pecans bought in cellophane packages, or simply scatter the nuts over the top instead of incorporating them in the filling—well, the fur flies. The truth is that, unlike so many bastardized monstrosities you find around the country, Mother's pecan pie is indeed exemplary: neither gooey nor firm but somewhere in between; never too sweet, but certainly caramelized enough to satisfy any sweet tooth; and a crust that is perfectly golden brown but never in the least burned.

beat till well blended. Add the butter and pecans and stir till well blended. Scrape the mixture into the pie shell and bake till the filling is just soft in the center when the pie is gently shaken and the crust is golden brown, 50 to 60 minutes. Cool the pie completely on a wire rack and serve at room temperature or slightly chilled with dollops of whipped cream on top.

YIELD One 9-inch pie; 6 servings

Martha's Sweet Note

If you're really serious about producing genuine Southern pecan pie, you'll stock up on fresh pecans when they're in season, shell them, and freeze those you don't use in tightly sealed plastic bags (for up to about nine months).

MAW MAW'S SWEET POTATO PIE

The main reason this pie has been so popular in our family at Thanksgiving is simple: Maw Maw, my grandmother, hated pumpkin pie, so she always made sweet potato instead. "I never even tasted pumpkin pie till I was grown," Mother recalls. "Mama said pumpkin had a 'fainty' taste, and when Mama didn't like something, she refused to ever cook it— and that was that." When Mother was young, fall sweet potatoes were kept in the basement all winter, so, of course, she can't conceive of making this pie with the canned spuds. "And I don't care what anybody says: All sweet potatoes need doctoring with plenty of spices," she insists. I must say that once you've tried this exceptionally smooth, spicy, yummy pie, you too might forget all about pumpkin.

1½ cups boiled, peeled, and mashed sweet potatoes (from about 3 medium-size)
3 large eggs, slightly beaten
1 cup evaporated milk
½ cup dark corn syrup
½ cup firmly packed dark brown sugar
2 tablespoons butter, melted
1 teaspoon salt
1 teaspoon ground cinnamon
½ teaspoon ground nutmeg
¼ teaspoon ground ginger
½ cup chopped pecans
1 unbaked 9-inch Basic Pie Shell (page 243)

Preheat the oven to 400°F.

In a large mixing bowl, combine the mashed sweet potatoes, eggs, evaporated milk, corn syrup, brown sugar, butter, salt, and spices and beat with a wooden spoon till smooth and frothy. Stir in the pecans. Pour the mixture into the pie shell and bake for 15 minutes. Reduce the oven temperature to 350°F and continue baking till a cake tester or straw inserted in the center comes out clean, about 45 minutes. Let the pie cool before serving.

YIELD One 9-inch pie; 6 servings

CAJUN SWEET POTATO PECAN PIE

*M*other is staunch about what constitutes traditional Southern pecan pie, but after I introduced her to Paul Prudhomme when he was chef at Commander's Palace in New Orleans and she tasted this spicy Cajun version, it didn't take twenty minutes for her to jot down the ingredients and discuss with Paul how to make the pie for her next Thanksgiving feast. This is a fairly heavy pie, so make the serving portions small.

For the filling

3 medium-size sweet potatoes, boiled, peeled, and mashed
¼ cup firmly packed dark brown sugar
2 tablespoons granulated sugar
1 tablespoon butter
1 tablespoon pure vanilla extract
1 large egg
1 tablespoon heavy cream
¼ teaspoon ground cinnamon
Pinch of ground nutmeg
Pinch of ground allspice
1 unbaked 9-inch Basic Pie Shell (page 243)
½ cup chopped pecans

For the topping

¾ cup granulated sugar
2 large eggs
¾ cup dark corn syrup
1 tablespoon butter, melted
½ teaspoon salt
Ground cinnamon to taste
2 teaspoons pure vanilla extract
Whipped cream

*P*reheat the oven to 300°F.

*C*ombine the mashed sweet potatoes, both sugars, butter, vanilla, egg, cinnamon, nutmeg, and allspice in a large mixing bowl. Beat with an electric mixer till well blended and smooth. Scrape the mixture into the pie shell and sprinkle the pecans evenly over the top.

*I*n another large mixing bowl, prepare the topping. Combine the granulated sugar, eggs, corn syrup, melted butter, salt, cinnamon, and vanilla, stir till well blended and smooth, and scrape the mixture over the pecans. Bake till the pie is nicely browned, about 1½ hours. Let cool completely on a wire rack, and serve topped with whipped cream.

YIELD One 9-inch pie; 8 small servings

HUGUENOT TORTE

*F*or years we believed that Charleston's famous Huguenot torte could be traced back to the late seventeenth century, when many persecuted French Huguenots fled to South Carolina's coastal Low Country. Then, a couple of zealous killjoys identified the distinctive specialty as a modern dessert with antecedents in the Arkansas and Missouri Ozarks and even learned that a certain Evelyn Florance made an "Ozark Pudding" during the 1940s in Charleston's old Huguenot Tavern. No matter—just as it doesn't matter that the fluffy dessert is really not a torte. Mother first came upon the torte when Charleston's Junior League included it in the first (1950) edition of their now-legendary cooking bible, *Charleston Receipts,* and after years of tampering, she finally developed what she considers to be the ultimate version—fully worthy of her Thanksgiving table.

¼ cup all-purpose flour
2½ teaspoons baking powder
¼ teaspoon salt
2 large eggs
1½ cups granulated sugar
½ teaspoon pure vanilla extract
1 cup finely chopped pecans
1 cup cored, peeled, and finely chopped apples
1 cup heavy cream
1 tablespoon sweet sherry

*P*reheat the oven to 350°F. Grease the bottom and sides of a medium-size baking dish and set aside.

*S*ift the flour, baking powder, and salt together into a large mixing bowl. In a medium-size mixing bowl, whisk the eggs, sugar, and vanilla together till frothy, then add to the dry mixture and stir till well blended. Gently fold the pecans and apples into the batter, scrape the batter into the prepared baking dish, and bake till a cake tester or straw inserted in the center comes out clean, about 35 minutes. Let the torte cool completely.

*I*n a small mixing bowl, beat the cream and sherry together with an electric mixer till stiff peaks form, spread the cream mixture evenly over the top of the torte, and cut the torte into squares to serve.

YIELD 6 servings

CRANBERRY-APPLE COBBLER

One Thanksgiving, Mother tried this altogether different approach to the traditional Southern cobbler by topping the autumn-inspired filling with a loose batter instead of firm, rolled-out pastry, and the results were so successful that she later applied the technique to both a blackberry-raspberry cobbler and one made with pears and apricots. I've even had luck with this recipe using mango and a combination of berries.

3½ cups fresh cranberries, stemmed and rinsed
1 cup cranberry juice
2 small Granny Smith apples
1 tablespoon finely chopped orange rind
1 cup all-purpose flour, plus more if needed
2 teaspoons baking powder
1 cup granulated sugar
2 large eggs, beaten
1 cup milk
1 teaspoon pure vanilla extract
1 teaspoon grated lemon rind
Whipped cream or vanilla ice cream

In a large, heavy, nonreactive saucepan, combine the cranberries and cranberry juice, bring to a boil, reduce the heat to low, and simmer till the cranberries pop, about 10 minutes. Meanwhile, core, peel, and cut the apples into ½-inch-thick slices (about 2 cups). Add them to the cranberries with the chopped orange rind, return the heat to the simmer, and cook about another 10 minutes.

Preheat the oven to 375°F. Grease a 2-quart baking dish and set aside.

Sift the flour and baking powder together into a large mixing bowl, then add the sugar, eggs, milk, vanilla, and lemon rind and stir with a wooden spoon till well blended, adding a little more flour if necessary to produce a loose but not wet batter.

Pour the cranberry-apple mixture into the prepared baking dish, scrape the batter evenly over the top, and bake till the top is golden brown, 35 to 40 minutes. Serve the cobbler hot or at room temperature with dollops of whipped cream or scoops of ice cream on top.

YIELD 6 servings

UNCA' NALLE'S BUTTERSCOTCH PUDDING

Since Nalle Belliveau was orphaned as a baby and raised by my maternal grandmother and great-grandmother, Mother always referred to him as her half-brother, I simply as Unca' Nalle. Utterly passionate about butterscotch in any form and a real jokester, he loved nothing more than to ask waitresses in restaurants if they had his beloved butterscotch pie, knowing full well that nobody except Mother made the dessert. Then, one time he was caught off guard when he was told, "No, sir, but we do have butterscotch pudding." Suffice it to say that nothing would do then but for Mother to concoct a butterscotch pudding and, since Unca' Nalle was always partly in charge of the annual Halloween celebration, to feature the dessert at this jovial affair. One tip: To prevent a "skin" from forming on the tops while chilling, fit small pieces of waxed paper over the ramekins.

1 quart milk
5 large egg yolks
1 cup firmly packed dark brown sugar
⅓ cup cornstarch
3 tablespoons butter, cut into pieces and softened
1 tablespoon pure vanilla extract

In a medium-size mixing bowl, combine 1 cup of the milk, the egg yolks, brown sugar, and cornstarch, whisk till well blended and smooth, and set aside.

In a large saucepan, heat the remaining 3 cups milk almost to a boil, taking care not to scorch it, and remove from the heat. Whisking vigorously and constantly, gradually add a little of the hot milk to the egg yolk mixture, then, over moderate heat, gradually pour the warmed yolk mixture into the hot milk, whisking steadily. Bring to a boil, whisking, and let cook for 2 minutes. Remove from the heat, add the butter and vanilla, and whisk till well blended.

Strain equal amounts of the mixture through a fine sieve into six individual glass or ceramic ramekins, let cool, and then chill for 2 hours before serving.

YIELD 6 servings

FIRST COUSIN BAKED APPLE PUDDING

*F*or years, one of Mother's three to four desserts at our large Thanksgiving dinner was a classic Brown Betty. Then, deciding she wanted to lighten the dessert and give it a different character, she added eggs, vanilla, and a few nuts and served it with a little brandy sauce. I'm not sure how much lighter this first cousin to Brown Betty is, but it is certainly a felicitous apple pudding to serve after a traditional turkey and dressing feast. And if you want something truly unusual and equally delectable, substitute, as I've done on occasion, Bosc pears for the apples and add about a tablespoon of pure maple syrup to the batter.

⅓ cup (about ¾ stick) butter, softened
1 cup granulated sugar
1 large egg, beaten
1 cup all-purpose flour
1 teaspoon baking soda
½ teaspoon salt
¼ teaspoon ground cinnamon
¼ teaspoon ground nutmeg
2 large Granny Smith or Rome apples, unpeeled, cored and grated
½ cup chopped nuts (pecans or walnuts)
1 teaspoon pure vanilla extract
Brandy Sauce (page 259)

*P*reheat the oven to 350°F. Lightly grease an 8-inch square baking pan and set aside.

*I*n a large mixing bowl, cream the butter and sugar together with an electric mixer till light and fluffy. Add the egg and beat till well blended. In a small bowl, combine the flour, baking soda, salt, cinnamon, and nutmeg and mix well, then add to the creamed mixture and stir till well blended. Add the apples, nuts, and vanilla and stir till well blended. Scrape the mixture into the prepared pan and bake till a toothpick inserted in the center comes out clean, about 35 minutes. Serve the pudding warm or cold with the sauce spooned over the top.

YIELD **6 to 8 servings**

MECKLENBURG COUNTY PERSIMMON PUDDING

North Carolina's Mecklenburg County is known for its superior persimmons harvested in late fall, and when I say persimmons, I'm referring to the genuine reddish-orange, fat, succulent, native American persimmon, not the smaller, less flavorful Japanese variety found in many areas of the country. "I hope those persimmons won't pucker your mouth," Mother used to kid Mr. Norwood when he'd deliver the fall fruits and vegetables he'd brought from his farm in Matthews, aware as any Tarheel that unripe persimmons have the most disagreeably acidic, astringent taste of any fruit on earth. Persimmons are generally perfect around Thanksgiving, and while Mother certainly knows how to use them to make cakes, pies, and preserves, our Thanksgiving dinner (which typically involves three to four desserts) just wouldn't be the same without this pudding with rum-spiked sauce that her mother and grandmother also prided themselves in serving.

2 cups boiling water
4 large, ripe persimmons, stemmed and rinsed well
1¼ cups firmly packed light brown sugar
3 large eggs
1¼ cups all-purpose flour
1 teaspoon baking powder
1 teaspoon baking soda
½ teaspoon salt
2 teaspoons ground cinnamon
¾ teaspoon ground nutmeg
¾ teaspoon ground ginger
2½ cups half-and-half
¼ cup (½ stick) butter, melted
Hard Sauce (page 259)

Preheat the oven to 325°F. Grease a large baking dish and set aside.

In a large mixing bowl, pour the boiling water over the persimmons and stir for about 2 minutes, then drain in a colander. Run the persimmons through a food mill to produce 2 cups of pulp, then, in a large mixing bowl, combine the pulp, brown sugar, and eggs and beat with a fork till well blended. In a small mixing bowl, combine the flour, baking powder, baking soda, salt, and spices and stir this mixture alternately with the half-and-half into the persimmon mixture. Add the butter and stir till well blended and smooth. Scrape the mixture into the prepared baking dish and bake till firm, about 1½ hours. Serve the pudding warm topped with hard sauce.

YIELD 10 to 12 servings

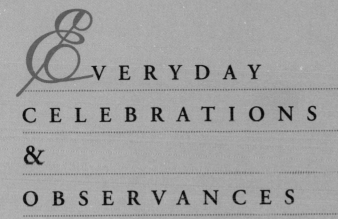

EVERYDAY CELEBRATIONS & OBSERVANCES

Birthdays

&

Christenings

Hummingbird Cake

Snowflake Coconut Cake with
Seven-Minute Frosting

Paw Paw's Birthday Caramel Cake with
Caramel Frosting

Baptism Coconut Pound Cake

Baptism Marble Chocolate Cheesecake

Chocolate-Orange Cupcakes

Chocolate Pecan Pie

Fellowship Coffee Cake Muffins

Essie's Apple Dumplings

Pussycat Syllabub

Peanut Butter Oatmeal Cookies

Little Tots Sugar Frosties

Dixie Saucepan Fudge Brownies

*L*et anybody (man, woman, child, friend, or relative stranger) so much as mention that so-and-so has a birthday coming up, and, without hesitation, Mother will announce that he or she "must have a cake"—meaning, in her parlance, anything sweet. If it's a question of an adult family member and a party is planned, most likely she'll make a big ceremonious cake, plus maybe Apple Dumplings; if the celebrant is a youngster, an assortment of cookies, iced cupcakes, and brownies are more in order; and if it's a friend being feted in someone else's home, she'll offer to bring something like a pecan pie or her beloved Hummingbird Cake. And if it's my own birthday—no question about it: the same lavish, fabulous, inimitable Caramel Cake with Caramel Frosting that she used to fix for her father's birthday. Never is the Southern obsession with rich, dramatic desserts more obvious than when Mother goes to town over a birthday, and never (I'm convinced) does she enjoy baking more than for this most special of occasions.

I don't know whether christenings (or baptisms) in other parts of the country are transformed into major social celebrations, but rest assured that in the South, no such religious occasion is complete without a festive after-service reception attended by the entire family, close friends, and, indeed, the participating minister. Occasionally the event is held in the parish house of the church, but if Mother has any say, nothing will do but for everyone to gather at home for her traditional Marble Chocolate Cheesecake or stunning Snowflake Coconut Cake—usually accompanied by cups of winey Pussycat Syllabub.

HUMMINGBIRD CAKE

I have no idea how many decades this rich, complex cake has been in our family, but it was only recently that Mother finally proffered the following quaint explanation of the name: "You see, the cake is sweet as molasses, and everybody knows how hummingbirds love red sugar water and the sweet nectar in flowers. Of course I've never put a cake outside to see if hummingbirds will eat it, but the reasoning makes sense—don't you think?" I guess it's as good an explanation as any, but whatever the origins of the name, Mother makes Hummingbirds for birthdays (young people especially love it) and at Christmas.

For the cake
3 cups all-purpose flour
2 cups granulated sugar
1 teaspoon baking soda
1 teaspoon ground cinnamon
1 teaspoon salt
3 large eggs, beaten
1½ cups vegetable oil
1½ teaspoons pure vanilla extract
One 8-ounce can crushed pineapple, undrained
1 cup chopped nuts (pecans, walnuts, or hazelnuts)
2 cups chopped bananas

For the frosting
Two 8-ounce packages cream cheese, softened
1 cup (2 sticks) butter, softened
Two 1-pound boxes confectioners' sugar, sifted
2 teaspoons pure vanilla extract

1 cup chopped nuts (pecans, walnuts, or hazelnuts)

*P*reheat the oven to 350°F. Grease and flour three 9-inch cake pans, tapping out any excess flour, and set aside.

*T*o make the cake, combine the flour, granulated sugar, baking soda, cinnamon, and salt in a large mixing bowl. Add the eggs and oil and stir till the dry ingredients are moistened, taking care not to overmix. Stir in the vanilla, pineapple, nuts, and bananas. Divide the batter evenly among the prepared pans. Bake till a cake tester or straw inserted in the center comes out clean, 25 to 30 minutes. Let the cakes cool in their pans for 10 minutes, then turn out onto a wire rack to cool completely.

*T*o make the frosting, combine the cream cheese and butter in a large mixing bowl and cream together with an electric mixer till smooth. Add the confectioners' sugar, beat till light and fluffy, and stir in the vanilla. Spread the frosting between the layers of the cakes, frost the top and sides, and sprinkle the nuts over the top.

YIELD One 3-layer 9-inch cake; about 12 servings

Martha's Sweet Note

Overbeating cake and cookie batters with an electric mixer can have a terrible effect on the way they rise (as with biscuit dough). Even when gradually adding eggs and liquids to a mixture, beat only till the ingredients are well blended—no more.

SNOWFLAKE COCONUT CAKE WITH SEVEN-MINUTE FROSTING

*L*ike her mother and grandmother, Mother still saves any extra milk drained from fresh coconuts just so she can make this wondrous, moist cake that graces the table after babies of relatives and friends have been christened—served ceremoniously, of course, with small glasses of chilled sweet white wine. Just the mention of ordinary coconut cakes made with canned flaked coconut and frosted with a heavy, overly sweet, innocuous white icing makes Mother cringe. "They're dry as a bone, tasteless, just awful," she says with a scowl, "so if you're not willing to deal with fresh coconut and produce a nice, light frosting in a double boiler, you'd be better off making another cake." And that's that!

1 medium-size coconut (see Sweet Note on page 17)
2¼ cups granulated sugar
3 cups cake flour (see Sweet Note on page 27)
2 teaspoons baking powder
1 cup (2 sticks) butter, softened
1 cup milk
1 teaspoon pure vanilla extract
6 large egg whites
Seven-Minute Frosting (page 252)

*P*ierce the eyes of the coconut with an ice pick or small screwdriver, strain the milk into a container, add enough water to measure 1 cup, and pour into a small saucepan. Add ¼ cup of the sugar, bring to a boil over moderate heat, stirring, and set aside to cool. Crack the coconut with a hammer and remove the meat from the shell. Trim off the brown skin with a sharp paring knife and discard, grate the coconut onto a plate, and set aside.

*P*reheat the oven to 350°F. Grease and flour three 8-inch round cake pans, tapping out any excess flour, and set aside.

*I*n a medium-size mixing bowl, combine the flour and baking powder and mix well. In a large mixing bowl, cream the butter and the remaining 2 cups sugar together with an electric mixer till light and fluffy. Beat the dry mixture alternately with the milk and vanilla into the creamed mixture till well blended, ending with the dry mixture.

*W*ash and dry the mixer beaters, then, in another large mixing bowl, beat the egg whites till stiff but not dry peaks form. With a rubber spatula, gently fold them into the creamed mixture. Scrape the batter evenly into the prepared pans and bake till a cake tester or straw inserted in the center comes out clean, about 30 minutes. Cool the cakes in the pans for about 10 minutes, then turn them out onto a wire rack to cool completely.

*P*lace a cake layer on a cake plate, drizzle about one quarter of the coconut milk mixture over the top, spread about ¾ cup of the frosting over the top, and sprinkle about one quarter of the grated coconut over the frosting. Repeat with the second layer, then top with the third and spread the remaining frosting over the top and around the sides of the cake and press the remaining grated coconut into the top and sides. Drizzle the remaining coconut milk over the top, cover the cake with plastic wrap, and chill for at least 24 hours before serving.

YIELD One 3-layer 8-inch cake; 10 to 12 servings

Martha's Sweet Note

If batter scraped into a baking pan seems uneven and I want a perfectly even cake layer, I gently "spank" the bottom for even distribution and to minimize any bubbles that have formed.

PAW PAW'S BIRTHDAY CARAMEL CAKE WITH CARAMEL FROSTING

Mercy, this cake is wonderful, and I can remember, as a child, looking forward to my grandfather Paw Paw's birthday only because I knew Mother would be making a big caramel cake for him and I'd be allowed to lick the frosting bowl and spoon. (She now makes it for my birthday.) The cake has been in our family at least four generations, and Mother has already handed down the recipe to my young niece. For me, this has always been the supreme birthday cake. Paw Paw had to have vanilla ice cream with his caramel cake; I like mine plain—and eaten with my fingers.

2⅔ cups all-purpose flour
2 teaspoons baking powder
1 teaspoon salt
2 cups granulated sugar
1 cup (2 sticks) butter, softened
4 large eggs, separated
1 cup milk
1 teaspoon pure vanilla extract
Caramel Frosting (page 253)

Preheat the oven to 350°F. Grease and flour three 9-inch square baking pans, tapping out any excess flour, and set aside.

Combine the flour, baking powder, and salt in a medium-size mixing bowl and mix well. In a large mixing bowl, cream the granulated sugar and butter together with an electric mixer till light and fluffy, then add the egg yolks one at a time, beating after each till creamy. Alternately add the dry ingredients and milk to the batter, beginning and ending with the dry ingredients. In another large mixing bowl, beat the egg whites till stiff peaks form, then fold them gently into the batter. Stir in the vanilla. Scrape the batter into the prepared baking pans and bake till a cake tester or straw inserted in the centers comes out clean, 20 to 30 minutes.

Stack the layers on top of each other, spreading the frosting over the top of each layer, then all around the sides, with a knife.

YIELD One 3-layer 9-inch square cake; 10 to 12 servings

BAPTISM COCONUT POUND CAKE

*T*he first time I tasted this sumptuous pound cake was over thirty years ago, when Mother served it on a buffet celebrating my nephew Charles's baptism, an event that began a tradition that continues to this day when babies of family and friends are christened. She originally got the recipe from the wife of one of my daddy's partners in the printing business, and when Mother questioned the lady about the *tablespoon* of lemon extract, Dot emphasized how that was the secret to the cake. For optimum flavor and moistness, Mother insists on using only fresh coconut, and the cake is so rich that it doesn't need to be frosted.

1 cup (2 sticks) butter, softened
3 cups granulated sugar
4 large eggs
1 tablespoon pure lemon extract
3 cups all-purpose flour
½ teaspoon baking powder
⅛ teaspoon salt
1 cup milk
1 cup grated fresh coconut (see Sweet Note on page 17)

*P*reheat the oven to 325°F. Grease and flour a 10-inch tube pan, tapping out any excess flour, and set aside.

*I*n a mixing bowl, cream the butter and sugar together with an electric mixer till light and fluffy, then add the eggs one at a time, beating well after each. Add the lemon extract and beat till well blended. In a medium-size mixing bowl, combine the flour, baking powder, and salt and alternately add the dry ingredients and milk to the creamed mixture, beating till well blended and smooth. Add the coconut and stir till well blended. Scrape the batter into the prepared pan and bake till a cake tester or straw inserted in the center comes out clean, about 1 hour and 10 minutes. Turn the cake out onto a wire rack, let cool completely, and then remove the pan.

YIELD One 10-inch tube cake; 12 to 14 servings

BAPTISM MARBLE CHOCOLATE CHEESECAKE

*I*n the South, most baptism ceremonies are traditionally held at twelve noon, followed by a reception at the home of the parents or grandparents, where no more than one substantial sweet dish and coffee (or sweet wine) are served to celebrate the occasion. Mother both hosts and attends lots of baptism receptions, and so popular has this "adult" cheesecake become at these affairs that friends simply refer to it as "Martha Pearl's baptism cake."

Three 8-ounce packages cream cheese, softened
1 cup granulated sugar
Grated rind of 1 small orange
½ teaspoon pure vanilla extract
¼ cup all-purpose flour
5 large eggs
½ cup heavy cream
One unbaked 9-inch Chocolate Wafer Pie Shell (page 248)
2 ounces semisweet chocolate, melted

*P*reheat the oven to 300°F.

*I*n a large mixing bowl, combine the cream cheese, sugar, orange rind, and vanilla and beat with an electric mixer till well blended and smooth. Add the flour and beat till well blended. Add the eggs one at a time, beating well after each addition. Add the cream and beat till well blended, then spoon half of the mixture into the pie shell. Stir the chocolate into the cream cheese mixture left in the bowl, then swirl that mixture over the top of the pie and gently cut it into the plain cream cheese mixture with four evenly spaced slashes of a knife. Bake the cheesecake till a cake tester or straw inserted in the center comes out clean, 50 minutes to 1 hour. Let the cake cool for about 10 minutes, then transfer to a wire rack to cool completely. Transfer the cheesecake to a serving plate, cover with plastic wrap, and chill till very cold and firm, at least 3 hours, before serving.

YIELD **One 9-inch cheesecake; at least 12 servings**

CHOCOLATE-ORANGE CUPCAKES

Mother certainly often makes these small, yummy cupcakes for her morning coffees, guild meetings, and afternoon teas, but at no occasion are they more appreciated than at a child's festive birthday party—each cake stuck with a colorful candle. I don't think I've ever opened Mother's freezer without seeing half a dozen of the cakes stored in plastic bags.

⅓ cup (about ¾ stick) butter, softened
⅔ cup granulated sugar
2 large eggs
1¼ cups cake flour (see Sweet Note on page 27)
2 teaspoons baking powder
⅛ teaspoon salt
½ cup plus 2 tablespoons milk
Grated rind of 1 orange
2 ounces unsweetened baking chocolate, broken into pieces

Preheat the oven to 375°F. Line a 12-cup mini muffin tin with paper cupcake liners and set aside.

In a large mixing bowl, cream the butter with an electric mixer till fluffy, then gradually add the sugar and beat till light and fluffy. Add the eggs and beat till well blended. In a small mixing bowl, combine the flour, baking powder, and salt and mix well. Add the flour mixture alternately with ½ cup of the milk to the creamed mixture, ending with the flour. Beat till well blended. Stir in the orange rind.

In a small bowl, combine the chocolate and the remaining 2 tablespoons milk, place the bowl over a shallow pot of hot water, and stir till the chocolate melts. Add the chocolate to the batter and stir till well blended.

Using a large spoon, fill each muffin cup three quarters full with batter, then bake till lightly browned and a cake tester or straw inserted in the center comes out clean, 25 to 30 minutes. Let the cupcakes cool in the tin for 10 minutes, then transfer to a wire rack to cool completely.

YIELD 1 dozen cupcakes

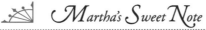 *Martha's Sweet Note*

When making muffins or cupcakes (large or small), I often fit the tins with paper muffin cups instead of greasing the tins. The cups are much easier to handle, and even if the muffins or cupcakes contain ingredients that might seep out, they're much less likely to stick.

CHOCOLATE PECAN PIE

When it was noticed that my nephew, Charles Royal, wouldn't touch Mother's sacred Southern pecan pie when he was a child, she modified the recipe by deleting the corn syrup and adding chocolate, only to realize that she'd created a pie with an altogether different flavor and texture. To this day, Mother still makes this pie for Charles's birthday, and I must grudgingly admit that once you've tasted this creamy chocolate version, the regular classic leaves a little something to be desired. "I've learned that lots of children won't eat plain nut desserts," Mother explains, "but add a little chocolate—to cakes, pies, cookies—and they gobble them up."

⅔ cup evaporated milk
2 tablespoons butter
One 6-ounce bag (1 cup) semisweet chocolate chips
2 large eggs, beaten
1 cup granulated sugar
2 tablespoons all-purpose flour
¼ teaspoon salt
1 teaspoon pure vanilla extract
1 cup chopped pecans
1 unbaked 9-inch Basic Pie Shell (page 243)

Preheat the oven to 375°F.

In a small saucepan, combine the evaporated milk, butter, and chocolate, stir constantly over low heat till the chocolate melts completely, and remove the pan from the heat.

In a large mixing bowl, combine the eggs, sugar, flour, salt, vanilla, and pecans and stir till well blended. Add the chocolate mixture and stir well, then scrape into the pie shell. Bake the pie just till the filling is soft in the center when the pie is gently shaken, 40 to 45 minutes. Cool the pie completely on a wire rack.

YIELD One 9-inch pie; 6 to 8 servings

The Holiday White Fruitcake *(page 6)*

Cinnamon-Walnut
Coffee Cake *(page 13)*
and Christmas Ambrosia
(page 19)

Tidewater Trifle (page 16) and
Santa Claus Hand-Dipped Candy Balls *(page 20)*

Chilled Grasshopper Soufflé *(page 36)*

Sunshine Chiffon Cake with Orange Butter Frosting (page 44) and *Bridal Snowballs with Lemon Filling (page 129)*

The One and Only Authentic Southern Strawberry Shortcake *(page 70)*

Frank's
Lemon Meringue
Pie *(page 74)*

*F*resh Peach Crisp *(page 78)*
and Vade Mecum Dewberry
Cobbler *(page 160)*

Satan Chocolate Pound Cake with
Chocolate-Marshmallow Frosting *(page 86)*

*R*eal McCoy Southern
Pecan Pie *(page 89)* and
Hootie's Eggnog-Walnut Pie
(page 14)

*S*nowflake Coconut Cake with Seven-Minute Frosting *(page 106)*

*B*aptism Marble Chocolate Cheesecake *(page 110)*

*E*ssie's Apple Dumplings *(page 114)* and
Fancy Coffee-Almond Parfaits *(page 203)*

Damson Plum Roll
(page 162)

Pearl's Snow Cream with Raspberry Sauce *(page 186)*

Carolina Peach Ice Cream *(page 211)*, Peanut Butter Blossoms *(page 81)*, Pecan Diamonds *(page 228)*, and Maple Chocolate Meringue Fluffs *(page 231)*

FELLOWSHIP COFFEE CAKE MUFFINS

Mother is forever modifying her basic approach to coffee cake, the latest manifestation being these unusual muffins she contributed to an after-church Sunday brunch held by members of her altar guild. Like any coffee cake, the muffins freeze beautifully, so consider doubling or tripling the recipe. The muffins are best when buttered, and Mother also serves them with homemade jam on the side at her christening receptions.

For the filling
½ cup firmly packed dark brown sugar
½ cup chopped pecans
2 tablespoons all-purpose flour
2 teaspoons ground cinnamon
2 tablespoons butter, melted

For the batter
1½ cups all-purpose flour
½ cup granulated sugar
2 teaspoons baking powder
½ teaspoon salt
¼ cup Crisco shortening
1 large egg, beaten
½ cup milk

Preheat the oven to 375°F. Line a 12-cup muffin tin with paper muffin cups and set aside.

To make the filling, combine the brown sugar, pecans, flour, cinnamon, and butter in a medium-size mixing bowl, stir till well blended, and set aside.

To make the batter, sift together the flour, granulated sugar, baking powder, and salt into a large mixing bowl, then add the shortening and cut it in with a pastry cutter or two knives till the mixture resembles coarse crumbs. In a small bowl, combine the egg and milk, add to the flour mixture, and stir just till moistened.

Fill each prepared muffin cup about one quarter full of batter and cover with a thin layer of the pecan mixture. Spoon the remaining batter evenly over the top, then spoon the remaining pecan mixture over the top, filling each cup about two thirds full. Bake till the muffins are lightly browned, about 20 minutes, remove the paper cups, and serve the muffins warm.

YIELD 1 dozen muffins

ESSIE'S APPLE DUMPLINGS

Mother makes apple dumplings a dozen different ways, and while a version with hard sauce is hard to beat, this technique she learned from her mother's black maid, Essie, produces the most classic and delicious dumplings I know. These are the dumplings that Essie would make for my grandfather, Paw Paw, when he'd come home from work for "dinner" in the middle of the day, and they're the same ones I remember our old family friend Charlie Rougeux begging Mother to bake every time he had a birthday.

For the dumplings

2 cups all-purpose flour
1 teaspoon salt
3 tablespoons confectioners' sugar, sifted
⅔ cup Crisco shortening
¼ cup ice water
6 Granny Smith or Golden Delicious apples
Granulated sugar
1 teaspoon ground cinnamon
1 teaspoon ground nutmeg
Cold butter, cut into small pieces

For the syrup

1 cup granulated sugar
2 cups water
3 tablespoons butter
1 teaspoon ground cinnamon

Heavy cream (optional)

Preheat the oven to 400°F. Grease a large casserole or baking dish and set aside.

To prepare the pastry, combine the flour, salt, and confectioners' sugar in a medium-size mixing bowl and mix well. Cut in the Crisco with a pastry cutter or two knives until the mixture resembles coarse meal, add the ice water, and mix with a fork till the dough can be pressed together. Divide the dough into six portions and, on a floured work surface, roll each portion out into a 7- to 8-inch square.

Peel and core the apples and place one on each pastry square. Fill the opening of each apple with granulated sugar, add pinches of cinnamon and nutmeg to each, push small pieces of butter into the openings, and sprinkle a little more sugar on top. Moisten the edges of the pastry squares with water and bring the opposite corners of the pastry up over the apples to encase them completely, sealing the edges well. Place the apples about 2 inches apart in the prepared casserole or baking dish.

*T*o make the syrup, combine all the ingredients in a small, heavy saucepan, bring to a boil, and cook for 3 minutes, stirring. Pour the syrup around but not over the apples and bake till golden, about 40 minutes. (If the dumplings start to brown too much, reduce the heat to 375°F.) Serve the dumplings plain or with cream spooned over the tops.

YIELD **6 servings**

PUSSYCAT SYLLABUB

All that anybody knows about the origins of syllabub is that part of the name probably derives from the Elizabethan word *bub* (a bubbling drink) and that it was once a pudding-like dessert. It evolved in the American South as a thick but delicate dessert drink spiked with wine, Madeira, or sherry and intended to be served with tea cakes—often at Christmas or New Year's but also during the summer months. My maternal great-grandmother, Sweet Maa, and grandmother, Maw Maw, made syllabub with homemade scuppernong or blackberry wine stored in huge crocks in the cellar, and ever since Maw Maw's cat once lapped up every ounce of a syllabub placed on the back porch to cool, Mother has referred to it by this appropriate name. Syllabub can be drunk directly from the cup or eaten with a spoon, and today Mother most often serves it at afternoon teas and christening receptions.

¼ cup fresh lemon juice, strained
2 cups sweet white wine or Madeira
½ cup superfine sugar
2 teaspoons finely grated lemon rind
3 cups half-and-half

In a large, stainless-steel or glass bowl, combine the lemon juice, wine, and sugar and stir till the sugar is completely dissolved. Add the lemon rind and stir till well blended. Add the half-and-half and beat the mixture with an electric mixer till stiff peaks form. Cover with plastic wrap and chill for 30 minutes. When ready to serve, pour the syllabub into a cut-glass bowl, then ladle into punch cups.

YIELD 6 to 8 servings

PEANUT BUTTER OATMEAL COOKIES

Since these cookies need as much texture as possible to provide their delightful crunch, don't even think of making them if all you have in the house is instant oatmeal and smooth peanut butter. Since I'm such a (crunchy) peanut butter fiend, Mother created the cookies just for me, but since it seems that this is one nut dessert that children love, she now bakes them up for lots of birthday parties. For even more interesting texture, sometimes I also add about a quarter cup of dark raisins when stirring in the peanut butter. They don't affect the crunch at all, and the added flavor makes the cookie truly sumptuous. Do not overmix this cookie dough.

1 cup (2 sticks) butter, softened
1 cup granulated sugar
1 cup firmly packed dark brown sugar
1 teaspoon pure vanilla extract
2 large eggs, beaten
1 cup crunchy peanut butter
2 cups all-purpose flour
1½ cups old-fashioned rolled oats
2 teaspoons baking soda
1 teaspoon salt

Preheat the oven to 350°F. Grease two large baking sheets and set aside.

In a large mixing bowl, cream together the butter, two sugars, and vanilla with an electric mixer, then add the eggs and beat just till well blended. With a wooden spoon, stir in the peanut butter till well blended. In a medium-size mixing bowl, combine the flour, oats, baking soda, and salt, and mix well. Gradually add the dry mixture to the creamed mixture and stir till the dough is smooth. Using your hands, roll the dough into small balls and place about 1 inch apart on the prepared baking sheets. With the back of a floured fork, press a crisscross design onto the balls and bake till lightly browned, around the edges, about 10 minutes.

YIELD About 6 dozen cookies

LITTLE TOTS SUGAR FROSTIES

Obviously, these are a favorite cookie that Mother bakes both for the young children in our family and for neighbors' children. With candied cherry or pecan halves pressed into the centers before baking, they've also become a major staple of her vast Christmas cookie output—either served at various holiday celebrations or included in one of her gift tins. When the frosties are made strictly for a child's birthday (and I think Mother loves cooking for children more than for anyone else), she often sprinkles the tops with red and green colored sugar. She always makes these in large quantities.

1 pound (4 sticks) butter, softened
1½ cups granulated sugar
1 large egg
1 teaspoon pure vanilla extract
1 teaspoon pure almond extract
4 cups all-purpose flour

Preheat the oven to 350°F. Grease two large baking sheets and set aside.

In a large mixing bowl, cream the butter and sugar together with an electric mixer. Add the egg and extracts, beat till well blended, then gradually beat in the flour till well blended and smooth. Drop the batter by the teaspoon about 1 inch apart on the prepared baking sheets and press each down slightly with the bottom of a small floured glass. Bake till the frosties are slightly browned around the edges and just soft in the middle, about 15 minutes. Using a spatula, carefully transfer the frosties to paper towels and let them cool completely.

YIELD About 100 frosties

DIXIE SAUCEPAN FUDGE BROWNIES

Southerners are known for their laziness and short-cuts in cooking, and never was this trait made more apparent than when, for her great-granddaughter's birthday just a couple of years ago, Mother decided not to dirty up lots of bowls and spoons but to simply prepare the batter for her rich fudge brownies in a single saucepan. "Lord, they're easy to make this way," she informs, "and what's funny is that they're actually the best brownies I make." For this type of child's party, she typically serves the brownies with Dixie cups of vanilla ice cream, and she leaves out the nuts, since she's convinced that children don't like them. She now also includes the brownies at her big outdoor Labor Day bash, sometimes using as many as four different varieties of nuts. If you really want something good, eat one of these brownies with a glass of cold milk before going to bed. In any case, don't overcook them—they should be nice and soft, almost gummy.

¾ cup (1½ sticks) butter
4 ounces unsweetened baking chocolate
2 cups granulated sugar
4 large eggs, beaten
1½ cups all-purpose flour
½ teaspoon salt
1½ teaspoons pure vanilla extract
1¾ cups coarsely chopped nuts (pecans, walnuts, hazelnuts, or peanuts)

Preheat the oven to 375°F. Lightly grease a medium-size baking dish and set aside.

In a large, heavy saucepan, stir the butter and chocolate together over low heat till they melt and remove the pan from the heat. Add the sugar, eggs, and flour, beating well with an electric mixer after each addition. Add the salt, vanilla, and nuts and stir till well blended. Scrape the batter into the prepared baking dish and bake till the cake just begins to pull away from the sides, 30 to 35 minutes. Let the cake cool, then cut into square brownies.

YIELD   16 brownies

Weddings

&

Graduations

Emergency Lemon Buttermilk Wedding Cake

Skillet Pineapple Upside-Down Cake

Marty's Fudge Sundae Pie

Icebox Chocolate Pie

Bridal Lemon Tarts

Bridal Snowballs with Lemon Filling

Good-Luck Brownie Pudding

Chocolate-Almond Bavarian

Rum Chocolate Mousse

Coconut-Apricot Cookie Rolls

Butter Walnut Turtle Bars

Grand wedding receptions in the South, as elsewhere, are always catered affairs, which doesn't mean there have not been times (for much more modest celebrations) when Mother has not had her offer accepted to produce a dazzling cake equal to (and certainly tasting better than) the fanciest four-layer commercial extravaganzas. Where she really excels, however, is in the imaginative preparation of various desserts featured at bridal luncheons and buffet suppers attended by everyone involved in the wedding. If these events are not held in homes, the most popular venue is a country club, but, in either case, it's never unusual for women cooks to bring the sweet delicacies that they're particularly proud of and that add even more glamour to the food being served. If Mother is hosting the party at home, her dessert might be a Rum Chocolate Mousse, Brownie Pudding, or her well-known Bridal Snowballs, but if she's asked to contribute something sweet to a more formal buffet, she's likely to arrive with her elegant Lemon Tarts or beautiful Lemon Buttermilk Cake. "And I'll tell you something about those tarts," she boasts modestly. "You better make plenty, because people think nothing of eating two or three and they disappear in no time."

I went through four graduations in my youth, each of which Mother celebrated (both at home and away) by producing desserts with a Ph.D. It was the same for my sister, the same for cousins, the same for my niece and nephew, and I'm sure it'll be the same for Mother's great-grandchildren if they make it to the podium before she retires to the celestial table. When I was once awarded an advanced degree and Mother discovered the day before that no really great dessert had been planned by the generous friends giving the reception, she marched imperiously into their kitchen and proceeded to make her fabulous Icebox Chocolate Pie. "People forget today that graduation is one of the most important moments in youngsters' lives—I know because I never graduated from anyplace—and I believe in doing something special that they'll remember." I remember.

EMERGENCY LEMON BUTTERMILK WEDDING CAKE

"Martha Pearl, we're in a real fix," Mother's friend Sally almost sobbed over the phone just hours before her daughter's small wedding, explaining how the neighbor who'd offered to bake a big frosted angel food cake for the modest reception had had a bad accident . . . and it was too late to call a caterer . . . and where could she find a really good commercial cake? "Nonsense!" Mother reassured. "Honey, don't you worry yourself one minute longer. It won't be the fanciest cake in the world, since we don't have much time to fool around, but Betty Jane will have a homemade cake—that I can promise you." And this is the lemon buttermilk cake that Mother baked in a flash. The ladies decorated the cake with various ornaments the best they could, and the bride indeed had a cake that may not have been very elaborate but at least tasted wonderful. This also makes a nice and unusual birthday cake.

For the cake

4 large eggs
2 cups granulated sugar
1 cup Crisco shortening
1 cup buttermilk (see Sweet Note on page 10)
3 cups all-purpose flour, sifted
2 tablespoons pure lemon extract
½ teaspoon baking powder
½ teaspoon baking soda
½ teaspoon salt

For the glaze

5 tablespoons orange juice
5 tablespoons fresh lemon juice
2½ cups confectioners' sugar, sifted
½ teaspoon salt

Preheat the oven to 325°F. Lightly grease and flour a large tube pan and set aside.

To make the cake, combine the eggs, granulated sugar, shortening, and buttermilk in a large mixing bowl and beat with an electric mixer till frothy. Add the flour 1 cup at a time, beating constantly, then add the lemon extract, baking powder, baking soda, and salt, beating till well blended. Scrape the mixture into the prepared pan and bake till golden and a cake tester or straw inserted in the center comes out clean, about 1 hour.

Meanwhile, combine the ingredients for the glaze in a medium-size mixing bowl and whisk till well blended and smooth.

Loosen the edges of the hot cake with a knife, spread about half of the glaze over the top, and return the cake to the oven for 3 minutes. Transfer the cake to a large serving plate, drizzle the remaining glaze down the sides, and let cool completely.

YIELD 1 large tube cake; 8 to 10 servings

SKILLET PINEAPPLE UPSIDE-DOWN CAKE

I remember having this age-old skillet cake as a child when my maternal grandmother made it, but the occasion at which it made the greatest impression on me was when Mother served it as dessert for my high school graduation dinner—a tradition that has continued as other youngsters in the family have donned their robes. "Teenagers love the cake, and I usually have to do two skillets," she says proudly. Well, so do adults, I hasten to add, and once you've tasted a slightly gummy pineapple upside-down cake made in a cast-iron skillet, the more common classic pales by comparison. I eat it hot, warm, cold, any way, all ways.

¼ cup (½ stick) butter
⅔ cup firmly packed dark brown sugar
9 slices canned pineapple, ¼ cup of the juice reserved
9 maraschino cherries
2 large eggs, separated
¾ cup granulated sugar
¾ cup all-purpose flour
⅛ teaspoon salt
½ teaspoon baking powder
Whipped cream or vanilla ice cream (optional)

*P*reheat the oven to 325°F.

*I*n a 9-inch cast-iron skillet, melt the butter over low heat, then add the brown sugar and spread the mixture evenly over the bottom. Off the heat, arrange the pineapple slices over the top, fit a cherry into the hole of each slice, and set aside.

*I*n a large mixing bowl, beat the egg yolks with an electric mixer till very thick, then gradually beat in the granulated sugar till well blended. In a small saucepan, heat the reserved pineapple juice over low heat, then gradually add it to the egg-and-sugar mixture, beating constantly. Add the flour, salt, and baking powder and mix till well blended and smooth. Wash and dry the mixer beaters, then, in a medium-size mixing bowl, beat the egg whites till stiff but not dry peaks form. Using a rubber spatula, gently fold them into the batter, then scrape the batter over the pineapple slices and bake till a cake tester or straw inserted in the center comes out almost clean, about 1 hour. Loosen the edges of the cake with a knife and invert onto a serving plate. Serve the cake hot or cold with optional whipped cream or ice cream spooned over each portion.

YIELD One 9-inch cake; 8 to 10 servings

MARTY'S FUDGE SUNDAE PIE

Although I'm not crazy about this sort of frozen pie that Southern housewives like my cousin Marty in Fayetteville, North Carolina, find so "refreshing" on hot summer days, Mother serves it at graduation parties and says the youngsters gobble it up as if it were chocolate cake. "You just don't understand the pie," she chides me. "No, it's not very sophisticated to adults, but the graham cracker crust is different and, as anybody in the South knows, nothing goes together better than graham crackers and chocolate." Hummm. I'd forgotten that.

1 cup evaporated milk
One 6-ounce bag (1 cup) semisweet chocolate chips
1 cup small marshmallows
¼ teaspoon salt
1 quart vanilla ice cream
1 prebaked 9-inch Graham Cracker Pie Shell (page 247)
½ cup chopped pecans

In a medium-size, heavy saucepan, combine the evaporated milk, chocolate chips, marshmallows, and salt and cook over moderate heat till thickened, stirring constantly. Remove the pan from the heat and let cool to room temperature.

Spoon half the ice cream into the pie shell and cover with half the chocolate mixture. Repeat with the remaining ice cream and chocolate mixture, sprinkle the pecans on top, and freeze the pie for 4 hours before serving.

YIELD One 9-inch pie; 6 to 8 servings

Martha's Sweet Note

To cut a pie that has frozen hard, hold a sharp knife momentarily under hot running water, dry it quickly, and then, applying pressure, draw the blade slowly through the pie.

ICEBOX CHOCOLATE PIE

*O*f all the desserts that Mother has devised to surprise and satisfy young people at graduation parties, this chilled pie has probably been the most popular—"and they don't even notice the bourbon." Youngsters no doubt relish the pie, but the few times I've served it to friends at serious dinner parties—once flavored with fine Cognac instead of bourbon—not one morsel was ever left over.

3 large egg whites
Pinch of salt
Pinch of cream of tartar
⅔ cup granulated sugar
½ cup finely chopped hazelnuts
½ teaspoon pure vanilla extract
8 ounces milk chocolate, broken into pieces
¼ cup water
2 tablespoons bourbon
1½ cups heavy cream
½ cup chocolate curls (see Sweet Note) for garnish

*P*reheat the oven to 300°F. Lightly butter a 10-inch pie plate.

*I*n a large mixing bowl, combine the egg whites, salt, and cream of tartar and beat with an electric mixer till foamy. Gradually add the sugar, beating constantly after each addition, and continue beating till the whites form stiff peaks. Fold the hazelnuts and vanilla into the whites, then scrape the mixture into the prepared pie plate. Form a nestlike indentation in the mixture by building the sides up with a spoon ½ inch above the edge of the plate, but not over the rim. Bake the shell till golden brown, about 50 minutes, then let cool completely.

*I*n a small, heavy saucepan, combine the chocolate and water over low heat, stir till the chocolate melts completely, and let cool. Add the bourbon and stir till well blended.

*I*n a large mixing bowl, whisk the cream to soft peaks, then fold in the chocolate mixture. Pile the mixture into the meringue nest, chill for 2 hours, and garnish the top with the chocolate curls.

YIELD One 10-inch pie; 8 servings

 *Martha's Sweet Note*

*T*o make chocolate curls to decorate all sorts of desserts, I have a wonderful adjustable chocolate shaver—available in the best kitchen supply shops. If you can't find one, a sturdy vegetable peeler should work.

BRIDAL LEMON TARTS

These are the nifty little tarts that my grandmother always included on bridal buffets and the ones that Mother also serves today in lace doilies on silver trays at afternoon teas and cocktail parties. Personally, I keep the ones I bake in tins for last-minute dessert emergencies—and for snacking. Since these tarts seem to disappear in no time when served on buffets, you might be smart to double the recipe. These *must* be made with fresh lemon juice.

½ cup (1 stick) butter, softened
2¾ cups granulated sugar
6 large eggs
¼ cup all-purpose flour
Juice of 3 lemons (about ⅔ cup)
1 tablespoon grated lemon rind
Ground nutmeg
3 dozen prebaked Basic Small Tart Shells (page 244)

Preheat the oven to 350°F.

In a large mixing bowl, cream the butter with an electric mixer, then gradually add 2 cups of the sugar, beating well. Add the eggs one at a time, beating well after each addition. In a bowl, combine the flour and the remaining ¾ cup sugar, mix well, and add alternately with the lemon juice to the creamed mixture, beginning and ending with the flour mixture. Stir in the lemon rind. Sprinkle nutmeg very lightly over each tart shell, then spoon 2 tablespoons of the lemon filling into each shell. Place the shells on a large ungreased baking sheet and bake till the filling is set and the crusts lightly browned, 15 to 20 minutes. Let the tarts cool before serving.

YIELD 3 dozen tarts

BRIDAL SNOWBALLS WITH LEMON FILLING

*B*ridal parties in the South remain one of the perfect celebrations where a hostess can display any number of new confections along with her colorful congealed salads and hot casseroles, and when Mother first created these creamy coconut snowballs, virtually every guest pleaded for the recipe. Little did they know that her sole inspiration was a small bowl of leftover lemon filling used to make a birthday cake. Here is still another dessert that almost demands fresh coconut.

For the lemon filling

¾ cup granulated sugar
3 tablespoons cornstarch
¼ teaspoon salt
¾ cup water
2 large egg yolks, slightly beaten
2 teaspoons grated lemon rind
¼ cup fresh lemon juice
2 tablespoons butter, cut into pieces

For the snowballs

Buttermilk Cupcakes (page 241)
1 pint heavy cream, whipped to stiff peaks
Grated coconut from 1 small coconut (see Sweet Note on page 17)
    or, if necessary, about 2 cups frozen grated coconut, thawed

*T*o make the filling, combine the sugar, cornstarch, and salt in a medium-size, heavy saucepan and stir till well blended. Gradually add the water, stirring constantly till well blended and smooth. Stir in the egg yolks, lemon rind, and lemon juice and cook over moderate heat, stirring constantly, till the mixture thickens. Bring to a boil and, stirring constantly, cook till very thick, about 1 minute. Remove the pan from the heat, add the butter, and stir till well blended and smooth. Let the filling cool completely.

*T*o assemble the snowballs, carefully split each cupcake across the middle, then, with a small spoon, scoop out about one spoonful of cake from the center of each top and bottom. Fill the bottom cavities with the lemon filling and firmly place the tops over the bottoms. Spread the whipped cream all over each cupcake and gently press grated coconut into the cream. Place the snowballs on a large baking pan or tray, cover with plastic wrap, and chill well till ready to serve.

YIELD 18 snowballs

GOOD-LUCK BROWNIE PUDDING

Thinking this might be an unusual pudding made with chocolate brownies when Mother first told me about the dessert, I asked her to explain the deceiving name, only to be told, "Don't be silly. You can't make a pudding with brownies, for heaven's sake. It's called brownie pudding all over the South simply because the brown sugar and cocoa make it brown." She then hesitated, as if contemplating something important. "You know, on second thought, crumbled-up brownies just might make a pretty good pudding if you did it right." In any case, the dessert as is has always been a big hit at Mother's bridal receptions, in which case she would usually double this recipe and bake the "good-luck" pudding in a large, ungreased baking dish.

1 cup all-purpose flour
¾ cup granulated sugar
¾ cup chopped pecans
½ cup milk
2 tablespoons butter, melted
1 teaspoon pure vanilla extract
2 teaspoons baking powder
¼ teaspoon salt
1¾ cups hot water
¾ cup firmly packed dark brown sugar
2 tablespoons unsweetened cocoa powder
Whipped cream or ice cream

Preheat the oven to 350°F.

In a large mixing bowl, combine the flour, sugar, pecans, milk, butter, vanilla, baking powder, and salt and stir till well blended and smooth. Spread the batter evenly in an ungreased medium-size baking dish.

In a small mixing bowl, combine the hot water, brown sugar, and cocoa, stir till well blended, and pour the mixture over the batter. Bake the pudding till a cake tester or straw inserted in the center comes out clean, about 35 minutes. Serve warm topped with whipped cream or ice cream.

YIELD 6 to 8 servings

CHOCOLATE-ALMOND BAVARIAN

If you don't think young people like molded desserts, try serving this sinfully rich chocolate Bavarian at a high school or graduation party the way Mother does. "Kids generally think that any congealed dessert is . . . well, blah," she comments in frustration, "but this is one Bavarian that I guarantee they'll love—as do chocoholic adults." In truth, if you forgo the chocolate sauce altogether and increase the almond extract to taste, you'll also have a very subtle, light mold to serve at a bridge luncheon or to top off an ample formal dinner.

1½ envelopes unflavored gelatin
2½ cups milk
⅔ cup granulated sugar
¼ teaspoon salt
½ cup slivered almonds, toasted (see Sweet Note on page 65)
1 teaspoon pure almond extract
1 cup heavy cream, whipped to stiff peaks
1½ cups Chocolate Sauce (page 255)

In a small bowl, sprinkle the gelatin over ½ cup of the milk and let soften.

In the top of a double boiler over simmering (not boiling) water, combine the remaining 2 cups milk, the sugar, and salt and stir till the mixture is hot and well blended. Add the almonds, stir, remove from the heat, cover, and let stand for 15 minutes. Add the gelatin mixture to the almond mixture, set over the simmering water again, and stir till the gelatin is completely dissolved. Remove from the heat and let cool for about 10 minutes, then add the almond extract and beat with an electric mixer till fluffy. Fold in the whipped cream, scrape the mixture into a 5-cup ring mold, and chill till firm, at least 4 hours. Unmold the Bavarian onto a deep platter, coat the top with chocolate sauce, and spoon the remaining sauce into the center of the ring.

YIELD 8 servings

 *Martha's Sweet Note*

To keep the intensity of flavorings and extracts added to cakes, puddings, pies, and candies from fading, I usually add them to the mixture at the very end.

RUM CHOCOLATE MOUSSE

*B*ridesmaids' luncheons (whether sit-down or buffet) are still as staunch a tradition in the South as when Mother herself was a bride some sixty years ago. Occasionally, these special celebrations take place in the home, but, more often than not, they're held at a country club with family and friends bringing the various dishes to be served. Mother has a veritable repertory of desserts intended for such luncheons, but the one the ladies seem to love most is this fluffy mousse served just after the bride gives gifts to her bridesmaids. The mousse maintains its form up to about one hour after having been thoroughly chilled.

8 ounces semisweet chocolate, broken into pieces
¼ cup strong black coffee
⅓ cup (about ¾ stick) butter, softened
3 large eggs, separated
2 tablespoons dark rum
¼ teaspoon salt
¼ cup granulated sugar
1 cup heavy cream, whipped to stiff peaks

*I*n a large, heavy saucepan, combine the chocolate and coffee and stir over very low heat till the chocolate melts. Remove the pan from the heat, add the butter, and stir till well blended and smooth. Add the egg yolks and rum, stirring steadily till well blended.

*I*n a medium-size mixing bowl, beat the egg whites with an electric mixer till foamy, then add the salt and continue beating till the whites form soft peaks. Still beating, add the sugar and beat till the whites form stiff peaks. Fold the whites gently into the chocolate mixture, then fold in the whipped cream. Scrape the mousse into a crystal bowl (or individual coupes), cover with plastic wrap, and chill for 2 to 3 hours before serving.

YIELD 6 to 8 servings

Martha's Sweet Note

*S*ee SWEET NOTE *on page 31 regarding the use of uncooked egg whites.*

COCONUT-APRICOT COOKIE ROLLS

*M*other originally created these unusual cookie rolls for one of her bridal showers, and while she still includes them on the buffet at these festive events, she also finds them an ideal dessert to take to a morning charity workshop held at a friend's home. Since so little coconut is needed, there's no need to bother dealing with the fresh, and Mother often substitutes other preserves (peach, strawberry, fig) for the apricot—or she sometimes might combine two preserves.

½ cup frozen grated coconut
½ cup apricot preserves
¼ cup finely chopped walnuts
1 cup (2 sticks) butter, softened
1 cup sour cream
½ teaspoon salt
2 cups all-purpose flour
Confectioners' sugar for sprinkling

*I*n a small mixing bowl, combine the coconut, preserves, and walnuts and set aside.

*I*n a large mixing bowl, cream the butter with an electric mixer till light and fluffy, then add the sour cream and salt and beat with a spoon till well blended. Gradually stir in the flour till well blended and smooth. Divide the dough into quarters, wrap each packet in aluminum foil, and chill at least 4 hours. Unwrap the packets.

*P*reheat the oven to 350°F. Grease two large baking sheets and set aside.

*O*n a well-floured surface, roll one packet ⅛ inch thick, keeping the remaining dough chilled till ready to use. Cut the dough into 2½-inch squares and spread each square with ½ teaspoon of the coconut mixture. Starting with one corner, carefully roll up each square, moistening the opposite corner with water to seal. Repeat with the remaining dough and coconut mixture. Place the rolls on the prepared baking sheets, seam side up, and bake till the tips are lightly browned, 16 to 18 minutes. Sprinkle the rolls lightly with confectioners' sugar and let cool completely.

YIELD About 5 dozen cookie rolls

BUTTER WALNUT TURTLE BARS

Children and teenagers absolutely relish these gooey little bars, which is why Mother makes them for so many birthday parties and graduation celebrations. When my niece and nephew were children, Mother used to let them help her swirl the chocolate for the marbled effect, and she still believes that encouraging youngsters to participate in making simple confections like these turtles leads to more serious involvement in cooking. "I had you making jelly treats and benne cookies when you were knee-high to a jackrabbit," she likes to remind me. If, like Mother, you suspect that very young children won't eat the bars because of the nuts (and I do often think she imagines this problem), just leave them out and add more chocolate chips.

2 cups all-purpose flour
1½ cups firmly packed light brown sugar
1½ cups (3 sticks) butter, cut into pieces and softened
1 cup walnut halves or coarsely chopped walnuts
One 6-ounce bag (1 cup) semisweet chocolate chips

Preheat the oven to 350°F. Butter a large baking dish and set aside.

In a large mixing bowl, combine the flour, 1 cup of the brown sugar, and ½ cup (1 stick) of the butter and beat with an electric mixer till the mixture resembles coarse meal, about 2 minutes. Press the mixture evenly over the bottom of the prepared dish and arrange the walnuts over the top.

In a small, heavy saucepan, combine the remaining ½ cup brown sugar and 1 cup (2 sticks) butter and, stirring constantly, cook over moderate heat till the mixture comes to a boil. Stirring constantly, boil for 1 minute, then pour the mixture over the walnuts. Bake till the top is bubbly, about 20 minutes, and remove from the oven. Sprinkle the chocolate chips evenly over the top, allow to melt slightly, and then swirl with a fork to create a marbled effect. Let cool completely, then cut into small bars.

YIELD About 3 dozen bars

Bereavements

&

Shut-Ins

Butter Pecan Cake with Butter Pecan Frosting

Divine Grace Coconut Custard Pie

Bereavement Chocolate Bread Pudding

Boiled Custard

Sweet Maa's "Get Well" Baked Custard

Funeral Angel Bavarian

Prune Whip

Spicy Molasses Cookies

Shut-In Gingersnaps

*M*ost non-Southerners are disarmed (if not downright shocked) by the highly social and culinary nature of bereavements that take place throughout the South before and after funerals, but people like my mother take these elaborate buffets as seriously as those set up for the most joyous christenings and weddings. When my father died, for example, there must have been twenty dishes spread across the big mahogany dining room table, all brought by relatives and close friends and periodically replenished as the many visitors came to pay respect and left. Naturally, some bereavement dishes are savory, but by far the vast majority are desserts. ("Sugar produces energy," Mother reminds by way of explanation, "and at times like these, people need something to help their stamina.") Mother considers her Divine Grace Coconut Custard Pie to be the quintessential bereavement dessert, but also high on the list are her Chocolate Bread Pudding, Butter Pecan Cake, and Angel Bavarian. "The whole idea," she says soberly, "is that we are not so much mourning the deceased as celebrating a good life, and what better way than sharing the same beautiful food we know that person would have enjoyed?"

Hospital patients, friends in nursing homes, people recuperating from illness at home, or simply souls who are lonely—to Mother all qualify as shut-ins in need of a little joy and deserving of a nice pudding, a fresh fruit tart, a decorative tin of homemade cookies, or any other confection that she thinks will "up the spirits." When a close friend of ours recently underwent leg surgery three thousand miles away and called to report on the success, Mother was so thrilled that she packed a big box with various cookies and candies, a coffee cake, and shortbread and put it in the mail. She certainly finds nothing noble about such gestures; it's just another of her very personal ways of bringing about a cause for happiness and celebration.

BUTTER PECAN CAKE WITH BUTTER PECAN FROSTING

This is one of Mother's favorite bereavement cakes, a rich but fairly delicate gâteau that she began taking to bereavements after a close friend's mother died and the cakes on the buffet were all the same. "I mean, there were five—mind you, five!—pound cakes on that table," Mother exclaimed, "so I decided then and there to come up with something different that would add a little variety at the next observance." As I've said, bereavements in the South are not exactly celebratory, but they are serious culinary affairs.

For the cake

1 cup (2 sticks) butter, softened
1¼ cups chopped pecans
1⅓ cups granulated sugar
2 large eggs
2 cups all-purpose flour
1½ teaspoons baking powder
¼ teaspoon salt
⅔ cup milk
1½ teaspoons pure vanilla extract

For the frosting

¼ cup (½ stick) butter, softened
One 1-pound box confectioners' sugar, sifted
5 to 7 tablespoons heavy cream
1 teaspoon pure vanilla extract

Preheat the oven to 350°F. Grease and flour two 9-inch round cake pans, tapping out any excess flour, and set aside.

In a small baking pan, melt 3 tablespoons of the butter in the oven, then stir in the pecans and toast till fragrant and lightly browned, about 10 minutes. Remove from the oven and let cool.

To make the cake, cream the remaining butter in a large mixing bowl with an electric mixer and gradually add the granulated sugar, beating till smooth. Scrape the mixture into a large, heavy saucepan and beat over low heat till light and fluffy. Remove from the heat and add the eggs one at a time, beating constantly after each addition. In a small mixing bowl, combine the flour, baking powder, and salt and mix well. Add this to the creamed mixture alternately with the milk and stir well with a wooden spoon till smooth, beginning and ending with the dry mixture. Stir in the vanilla and 1 cup of the toasted pecans, reserving the remaining pecans for the frosting.

$\mathcal{S}$crape the batter into the prepared cake pans and bake till a cake tester or straw inserted in the center comes out clean, about 30 minutes. Cool the layers in their pans for 10 minutes, then remove and let cool completely on a wire rack.

$\mathcal{T}$o make the frosting, cream the butter in a large mixing bowl with the electric mixer, then gradually beat in the confectioners' sugar, cream, and vanilla and beat till light and fluffy. Stir in the reserved pecans. Place one of the cake layers on a cake plate and spread about one third of the frosting smoothly over the top. Place the other layer on top of it and spread the remaining frosting over the top and sides.

YIELD One 2-layer 9-inch cake; 10 to 12 servings

 Martha's Sweet Note

I'm adamant about cooling cakes on wire racks, which allow them to cool evenly on the top, bottom, and sides, preventing "soggy" spots.

DIVINE GRACE COCONUT CUSTARD PIE

*M*other always has a couple of prepared pie shells and grated coconut in the freezer for emergencies, so when a mourner calls at the last minute to ask if she could contribute a dish to a bereavement buffet, nothing is simpler and easier to prepare than this custard pie that requires minimum chilling. "A close friend baked the pie for my daddy's funeral," she remembers, "and I've noticed over the years that even the children at bereavements like it. Of course, I'd prefer to use freshly grated coconut, but sometimes that's just not practical." Without the coconut, the pie is also ideal for friends and relatives on the mend in the hospital.

¼ cup (½ stick) butter, softened
1¼ cups granulated sugar
5 large eggs
½ teaspoon pure vanilla extract
¼ teaspoon salt
2 cups half-and-half
1 cup fresh (see Sweet Note on page 17) or thawed frozen
    grated coconut
1 unbaked 10-inch Basic Pie Shell (page 243)

*P*reheat the oven to 375°F.

*I*n a large mixing bowl, cream the butter and sugar together with an electric mixer till light and fluffy, then beat in the eggs one at a time. Add the vanilla and salt, then gradually beat in the half-and-half till well blended. Stir in the coconut till well blended. Scrape the mixture into the pie shell and bake till a cake tester or straw inserted in the center comes out clean, about 30 minutes. Let the pie cool completely, then chill till ready to serve.

YIELD One 10-inch pie; 8 servings

BEREAVEMENT CHOCOLATE BREAD PUDDING

*M*other always considered bread pudding to be the ideal way to use up stale bread, as well as the perfect bereavement dish, since it's already cooked, needs only to be reheated, and is easy to eat. When a dear friend died a few years ago, however, Mother realized that she was bored with plain old bread pudding and decided to try one with chocolate. Guests (if that's the right word) raved over the dish, so today when one of these doleful observances is staged, nothing will do but for Martha Pearl to bake her chocolate bread pudding and bring along a big tub of whipped cream. Mother says the dish is also great for church suppers, since it can be made in large quantities.

2 cups finely grated stale white bread
2 cups milk, scalded (see Sweet Note on page 18)
⅔ cup granulated sugar
2 ounces unsweetened baking chocolate, melted
1 teaspoon pure vanilla extract
½ cup chopped pecans or walnuts
1 cup heavy cream, whipped to stiff peaks

*I*n a large mixing bowl, combine the grated bread and scalded milk and let stand for 15 minutes.

*P*reheat the oven to 350°F. Grease a 1-quart baking dish.

*A*dd the sugar, chocolate, vanilla, and nuts to the bread mixture and stir till well blended. Scrape the mixture into the prepared baking dish and bake till a cake tester or straw inserted in the center comes out clean, about 1 hour. Serve the pudding hot in dessert bowls with the whipped cream on top.

YIELD *6 servings*

BOILED CUSTARD

*T*his classic custard (which is texturally different from Custard Sauce, page 261) is not only the perfect comfort dish for shut-ins unable to digest most foods easily but also the base of many of Mother's Bavarians, trifles, and puddings. The custard may seem ridiculously simple, but if you're not extremely careful adding the hot milk to the egg mixture, stirring constantly, you can end up with a curdled mess.

1 quart milk
4 large eggs
1 cup granulated sugar
1 teaspoon pure vanilla extract

*I*n the top of a double boiler set over simmering (not boiling) water, heat the milk till hot. In a medium-size mixing bowl, beat the eggs and sugar together till frothy, then, stirring constantly, add about ¼ cup of the hot milk to the egg mixture. Stirring constantly, pour the egg mixture into the milk and cook till it thickens slightly and coats the back of a spoon, about 5 minutes. Remove the custard from the heat, scrape into a bowl, stir in the vanilla, and let cool before serving, whisking gently from time to time.

YIELD **6 servings**

SWEET MAA'S "GET WELL" BAKED CUSTARD

*M*other remembers that years ago when anybody in the family got the least bit sick, her Georgia grandmother, Sweet Maa, would head straight for the kitchen to bake this custard, insisting that it was "strengthening" and "easy to keep on the stomach." Martha Pearl's mother, Maw Maw, did exactly the same; Mother continued the practice with my sister and me; and today the minute she hears that a relative or friend is ill or in the hospital, nothing will do but to bake up a few cups of this quintessential comfort food. As a more substantial dessert, the custard is also very good with fresh macerated fruit spooned over the top, and I've even made it with a little chopped fruit incorporated in the custard itself.

3 large eggs, slightly beaten
¼ cup granulated sugar
¼ teaspoon salt
2 cups milk, scalded (see Sweet Note on page 18)
1 teaspoon pure vanilla extract
Ground nutmeg to taste

*P*reheat the oven to 325°F. Butter a 1-quart casserole or four individual custard cups and set aside.

*I*n a large mixing bowl, combine the eggs, sugar, and salt and mix till well blended. Slowly add the milk, stirring constantly, then add the vanilla, stirring to blend well. Pour the mixture into the prepared casserole or cups and sprinkle nutmeg lightly over the top. Place the casserole or cups in a larger baking pan filled with enough boiling water to come halfway up the sides of the casserole or cups and bake till a knife inserted halfway between the center and the edges comes out clean, about 35 minutes. Remove from the water and let the custard cool completely. Serve at room temperature or chilled.

YIELD 4 servings

 Martha's Sweet Note

When baking custards and custard desserts, never overcook, as that will make them watery. Likewise, while boiled custards are cooling, whisk them occasionally to allow steam to evaporate and keep them from becoming watery.

FUNERAL ANGEL BAVARIAN

*M*other can be as critical of other people's cooking as any proud Southern cook, but she's the first to compliment up and down the dishes of both friends and strangers whose skills she respects. One such lady was Ruth Fisher, a member of Mother's book club and "one of Charlotte's finest cooks," with whom Mother exchanged recipes for decades. "Ruth once said that, of all her desserts, this angel Bavarian was the one she'd like to have served at her bereavement." When I said I found this all rather morbid, Mother snapped, "That's because you still don't understand that what we're doing is celebrating the lives of dear friends who've passed on by preparing something special they would have enjoyed." Yes, I was humbled.

2 envelopes unflavored gelatin
½ cup cold water
2 cups milk
4 large eggs, separated
1 cup granulated sugar
2 tablespoons all-purpose flour
¼ teaspoon salt
Grated rind of 1 large orange
¼ cup fresh orange juice
1 pint heavy cream
One 10-inch Angel Food Cake (page 240)
Grated coconut from 1 small coconut (see Sweet Note on
    page 17)

*I*n a small bowl, sprinkle the gelatin over the water to soften, and set aside.

*I*n a large, heavy saucepan, combine the milk, egg yolks, sugar, flour, and salt, whisk till well blended, and cook over moderate heat, stirring constantly, till the mixture thickens. Remove from the heat, whisk in the gelatin mixture, and let cool completely, stirring several times. Add the orange rind and orange juice and stir till well blended.

*I*n a medium-size bowl, beat half of the cream with an electric mixer till stiff peaks form and fold into the cooled custard. Wash and dry the beaters, then, in a large mixing bowl, beat the egg whites till stiff but not dry peaks form and gently fold them into the custard.

*B*reak the angel food cake up into small pieces and line the bottom of a large tube pan with half of the pieces. Cover with half of the custard, then repeat the procedure with the remaining cake and custard, ending with custard. Cover with plastic wrap and let stand overnight in the refrigerator.

*T*urn the cake out onto a cake plate. In a medium-size mixing bowl, beat the remaining cup of cream with an electric mixer till stiff peaks form and spread over top of the cake. Sprinkle the coconut all over the top.

YIELD 12 to 14 servings

◺ *Martha's Sweet Note*

See SWEET NOTE on page 31 regarding the use of uncooked egg whites.

PRUNE WHIP

I didn't like prunes as a child (I'm still not crazy about them), so, since Mother was convinced of their nutritional value, she concocted this enticing dessert to fool me. She says I ate it and loved it, and gradually the dessert evolved as a favorite with friends in the hospital and with shut-ins. I should add that when I was food poisoned in a restaurant a few years ago and left weak as a dishrag, this prune whip proved to be a wonderful restorative.

1½ cups pitted dried prunes
1½ cups water
3 large egg whites
¼ teaspoon salt
6 tablespoons granulated sugar
2 tablespoons fresh lemon juice
¼ cup chopped filbert nuts

In a medium-size, heavy saucepan, combine the prunes and water and bring to a boil, then reduce the heat to low, cover, and simmer for 10 minutes. Drain the prunes, cut them into small pieces, place in a small bowl, and set aside.

In a large mixing bowl, beat the egg whites with an electric mixer till soft peaks form. Add the salt, gradually add the sugar, and beat till stiff peaks form. Pour the lemon juice over the prunes, mix well, and fold the prunes into the egg whites. Add the nuts and stir gently. Spoon the whip into sherbet dishes and chill well before serving.

YIELD 6 to 8 servings

◺ *Martha's Sweet Note*

See SWEET NOTE on page 31 regarding the use of uncooked egg whites.

SPICY MOLASSES COOKIES

Let Mother notice that milk in the refrigerator has gone sour (which infuriates her) and, unlike others who would just pour it down the sink, she'll most likely grab a jar of molasses and bottles of spices and bake up a batch of these wondrously light cookies to serve at her next charity social or take to a shut-in. You have to be careful with this dough. If it's not thoroughly chilled (preferably overnight), the cookies won't cut out neatly and evenly, and if it's rolled too thin, they'll crumble. Also, watch them carefully while baking to make sure they don't overcook—they should be just barely browned.

½ cup (1 stick) butter, softened
½ cup Crisco shortening
1 cup firmly packed light brown sugar
1 cup molasses
2 large eggs
2 teaspoons ground ginger
1 teaspoon ground cinnamon
½ teaspoon ground nutmeg
½ teaspoon ground cloves
4 cups all-purpose flour
2 teaspoons salt
2 teaspoons baking soda
½ cup soured milk

In a large mixing bowl, cream the butter, Crisco, and brown sugar together with an electric mixer till light and fluffy. Add the molasses and eggs and beat till well blended. Add the spices and beat till well blended.

Into another large mixing bowl, sift together the flour, salt, and baking soda, then add to the molasses mixture and stir till well blended. Add the soured milk and stir till the mixture is smooth. Cover the dough with plastic wrap and chill for at least 6 hours (preferably overnight).

Preheat the oven to 400°F. Grease two baking sheets and set aside.

On a floured surface, roll out the dough about ¼ inch thick, cut out 3-inch cookies, and place about 1½ inches apart on the prepared baking sheets. Gather up the excess dough, reroll, and cut out more cookies. Bake till slightly browned, 8 to 10 minutes. Let the cookies cool completely.

YIELD **About 40 cookies**

SHUT-IN GINGERSNAPS

*M*other openly confesses to having gotten this basic recipe from a local TV cooking show, though, typically, she tampered with the ingredients till she finally produced "the only gingersnaps I know that don't get hard." Unlike most gingersnaps, Mother's contain no vinegar or ground cloves, both of which she feels kill the taste of the ginger. She makes the cookies for any number of occasions but loves nothing more than baking up a batch, packing the snaps carefully in one of her colorful gift boxes, and taking them to sick friends in the hospital or at home. I'm utterly addicted to these.

¼ cup Crisco shortening
1 cup granulated sugar
1 large egg
¼ cup dark molasses
2 cups all-purpose flour
2 teaspoons baking soda
½ teaspoon salt
1 tablespoon confectioners' sugar, sifted
1 teaspoon ground cinnamon
1 teaspoon ground ginger
Granulated sugar for coating

*P*reheat the oven to 350°F. Grease two large baking sheets and set aside.

*I*n a large mixing bowl, cream together the Crisco and sugar with an electric mixer till light and fluffy, then add the egg and molasses and beat till well blended. In a medium mixing bowl, combine the flour, baking soda, salt, confectioners' sugar, cinnamon, and ginger, then gradually fold the dry ingredients into the molasses mixture. Pinch off small pieces of the dough and, using your hands, roll each into a ball about the size of a large marble. Roll the balls lightly in sugar, place about 1 inch apart on the prepared baking sheets, and bake till golden, 10 to 12 minutes, being careful not to overbake. Transfer the gingersnaps to a wire rack and let cool slightly, then roll again lightly on both sides in sugar and let cool completely. Store the snaps in an airtight container to maintain their softness.

YIELD 55 to 60 gingersnaps

 *Martha's Sweet Note*

If cookies, brownies, meringues, and other such confections stored in tins begin to harden too much, adding a piece of soft white bread will resoften them in just a couple of hours.

Picnics

&

Cookouts

Charity League Fudge Cake

"Two Mamas" Banana Cake

Stone Fence Applesauce Cake

Glazed Banana Caramel Pound Cake

Banana Split Pie

Pawley's Island Pie

Fig, Apricot, and Strawberry Tart

Secession Brown Betty

Vade Mecum Dewberry Cobbler

Molded Maple Delight

Damson Plum Roll

World's Greatest Cookie

other's desserts for picnics and cookouts are virtually interchangeable, meaning that she's just as likely to prepare a hefty Dewberry Cobbler or Glazed Banana Caramel Pound Cake for one of her church suppers or picnics as for the annual pork barbecue at my place to which we invite up to twenty-five guests every July. Outdoor (and certain indoor) eating in the South almost always implies not only lots of people but a staggering array of food, a reality Mother has to address when deciding which desserts to make and how much. "The thing you have to remember when cooking for a big crowd," she advises, "is that, because there are so many other dishes, people will not necessarily eat as many sweets as they would at a more modest event. At home, for instance, guests might eat two, even three squares of Fudge Cake at a simple hamburger cookout, but at a big political or fund-raising church barbecue where there are tons of meat and Brunswick stew and beans and coleslaw and hush puppies, only a glutton could eat that much cake."

As you can see from the relatively large yields for most of the recipes, these sturdy, rich confections are designed to serve a minimum of eight persons (some up to fifteen). Remember, however, that if you're baking the Secession Brown Betty, Pawley's Island Pie, or "Two Mamas" Banana Cake for the type of truly large crowd Mother is talking about, this does not necessarily mean that you've got to triple the recipes to be on the safe side.

Note also that, with the exceptions of the Banana Split Pie and Molded Maple Delight (both ideal for a small gathering), none of the desserts requires chilling, making them easy to transport when necessary and assuring that their integrity remains intact over a long period of time.

CHARITY LEAGUE FUDGE CAKE

For years, Mother's friend Grace Reid, president of Charlotte's Charity League, would bring her famous fudge cake to afternoon workshops and absolutely refuse to divulge the recipe to other members. Utterly frustrated, Mother eventually had "serious words" with Grace about the sumptuous cake and was finally told, "Okay, Martha Pearl, if you call me on the phone in private, I'll tell you— and only you!—how to make it." Of course there's nothing really that special about the recipe, but when Mother takes the cake to a picnic ("Ideal, since it's served out of the dish it's baked in"), the squares "disappear like lightning."

For the cake
½ cup (1 stick) butter
2 ounces unsweetened baking chocolate
1 cup granulated sugar
½ cup all-purpose flour
¼ teaspoon salt
2 large eggs, beaten
1 teaspoon pure vanilla extract
1 cup pecan pieces

For the frosting
¼ cup (½ stick) butter
1 ounce unsweetened baking chocolate
2¼ cups confectioners' sugar, sifted
¼ teaspoon salt
1 teaspoon pure vanilla extract

Preheat the oven to 350°F. Grease and flour a medium-size baking dish, tapping out any excess flour, and set aside.

To make the cake, melt the butter and chocolate together in the top of a double boiler set over simmering water, then remove from the heat. Stirring constantly, add the granulated sugar, flour, salt, eggs, and vanilla, then stir in the pecans till well blended. Scrape the batter into the prepared pan and bake till a cake tester or straw inserted in the center comes out clean, 20 to 25 minutes. Let the cake cool in the pan.

To make the frosting, melt the butter and chocolate together in the top of a double boiler set over simmering water. Remove from the heat and, with a spoon, gradually beat in the confectioners' sugar, salt, and vanilla. (If necessary, add a little cream or milk to make the frosting spreadable.) Frost the top of the cake, let cool completely, cover with plastic wrap, and, if desired, chill briefly before cutting into small squares.

YIELD 1 medium-size cake; about 24 squares

"TWO MAMAS" BANANA CAKE

*W*hat could be more Southern than two Mississippi grandmothers, the first called One Mama, the other Two Mama? A bit eccentric, to be sure, but such was the case when one of Mother's dearest friends and next-door neighbor, Ann Scarborough, was growing up in the Delta and being weaned on wholesome country food. Ann doesn't talk much about One Mama's dishes, but apparently Two Mama was a phenomenal cook whose banana cake was known far and wide. Ann brought the recipe with her when she moved to North Carolina, Mother had a fit when she first tasted it, and almost overnight it became one of her favorite desserts to take to cookouts—"since it's not only the best banana cake on earth but big enough to serve a crowd." Just recently, the recipe for the spicy cake was passed down to me, and I now include it on large buffets to be eaten with ice cream.

¼ cup (½ stick) butter, softened
½ cup vegetable oil
2 cups granulated sugar
4 large eggs
3 cups all-purpose flour
½ teaspoon salt
1½ teaspoons baking soda
1 teaspoon baking powder
2 teaspoons ground cinnamon
1½ teaspoons ground cloves
6 ripe bananas, peeled and mashed
1 teaspoon pure vanilla extract
1½ cups seedless golden raisins
1½ cups chopped pecans

*P*reheat the oven to 325°F. Grease and flour a 10-inch tube pan, tapping out any excess flour, and set aside.

*I*n a large mixing bowl, cream the butter, oil, and sugar together with an electric mixer till well blended and smooth, then add the eggs one at a time, beating well after each addition. In a medium-size mixing bowl, combine the flour, salt, baking soda, baking powder, and spices and gradually add to the creamed mixture, stirring well. Add the bananas and vanilla and stir well, then fold in the raisins and pecans. Scrape the batter into the prepared pan and bake till a cake tester or straw inserted in the center comes out clean, about 1¼ hours. Let the cake cool in the pan for about 10 minutes, then turn it out onto a wire rack to cool completely before serving.

YIELD One 10-inch tube cake; 10 to 12 servings

STONE FENCE APPLESAUCE CAKE

*T*his is one of Mother's favorite picnic cakes, so reminiscent of weekends spent at our cabin on the Catawba River outside Charlotte when I was a child and at Sunday outings with neighbors in Freedom Park. Since the spicy cake holds up beautifully, it's perfect for picnics even in the hottest weather. As for the name, the explanation is simple: At the river, there was a stone fence behind the cabin where Mother would place her cakes to cool quickly—despite hungry gnats!

¾ cup (1½ sticks) butter, softened
1 cup granulated sugar
1½ cups firmly packed dark brown sugar
2 large eggs
3 cups all-purpose flour
1½ cups whole wheat flour
1 tablespoon baking soda
1½ teaspoons ground cinnamon
1½ teaspoons ground nutmeg
1½ teaspoons ground allspice
2¼ cups unsweetened applesauce
¾ cup shredded raw carrots
1½ cups chopped nuts (pecans or walnuts)
1½ cups seedless golden raisins
Confectioners' sugar for sprinkling

*P*reheat the oven to 350°F. Grease and flour a 10-inch Bundt or tube pan, tapping out any excess flour, and set aside.

*I*n a large mixing bowl, cream the butter with an electric mixer till fluffy, then gradually beat in the two sugars. Add the eggs and beat till well blended. In a medium-size mixing bowl, combine the two flours, baking soda, and spices and mix till well blended. Add the dry ingredients, applesauce, and carrots alternately to the butter mixture, then fold in the nuts and raisins until thoroughly blended. Scrape the batter into the prepared pan and bake till the cake is browned and firm to the touch, about 1 hour and 20 minutes. Cool the cake completely and transfer to a cake plate before cutting into thin slices sprinkled with confectioners' sugar.

YIELD One 10-inch tube or Bundt cake; 12 to 15 servings

GLAZED BANANA CARAMEL POUND CAKE

*E*very May, Mother's church sponsors a huge informal picnic attended by at least one hundred members, many of whom bring fried chicken, sandwiches, pastas, salads, bread, and the like. Mother's contribution is always two or three glazed pound cakes, "which feed lots of people and which the children just love." Note that this cake is not actually frosted; you simply pour the glaze over the top and let it drip down the sides. Personally, however, I like to double the quantity of glaze.

For the cake

1 cup (2 sticks) butter, softened
½ cup Crisco shortening
2 cups firmly packed light brown sugar
1 cup granulated sugar
5 large eggs
3 cups all-purpose flour
½ teaspoon salt
½ teaspoon baking powder
½ teaspoon baking soda
½ cup milk
2 teaspoons pure vanilla extract
1 large ripe banana, peeled and well mashed
1 cup coarsely chopped pecans

For the glaze

¼ cup (½ stick) butter, melted
¼ cup firmly packed light brown sugar
¼ cup granulated sugar
¼ cup heavy cream
1 teaspoon pure vanilla extract

*P*reheat the oven to 325°F. Grease a 10-inch tube pan and set aside.

*T*o make the cake, place the butter, Crisco, and two sugars in a large mixing bowl and cream together with an electric mixer till light and fluffy, then add the eggs one at a time, beating well after each addition. In a medium-size mixing bowl, combine the flour, salt, baking powder, and baking soda. Add the dry mixture alternately with the milk to the creamed mixture, beating till well blended. Add the vanilla and mashed banana and stir well, then stir in the pecans. Scrape the batter into the prepared pan and bake till a cake tester or straw inserted in the center comes out clean, about 1 hour and 20 minutes. Let the cake cool for about 10 minutes, then turn out onto a cake plate to cool completely.

continued

To make the glaze, combine all the ingredients in a small bowl and stir till well blended. Pour the glaze slowly over the top of the cake, letting it drip down the sides.

YIELD One 10-inch tube cake; 10 to 12 servings

BANANA SPLIT PIE

This crazy pie that Mother fixes for various informal cookouts is unapologetically exotic, rich, sinful, and so reminiscent of lazy youthful days spent at soda fountains eating banana splits. If you plan to serve the pie outside in hot weather (it's great for backyard barbecues when kids are present), be sure to chill it for at least two hours so that it holds its shape when cut.

One 12-ounce box vanilla wafers, crushed
¾ cup (1½ sticks) butter, melted, plus 1 cup (2 sticks) butter, softened
2 cups confectioners' sugar, sifted
2 large eggs
5 to 6 ripe bananas, peeled and sliced
One 20-ounce can crushed pineapple, drained
1 pint heavy cream, whipped to stiff peaks
1 cup chopped nuts (pecans, walnuts, or peanuts)
Maraschino cherry halves for garnish

In a large mixing bowl, combine the vanilla wafers and melted butter and mix well, then press the mixture onto the bottom and sides of a large baking dish. Set aside.

In another large mixing bowl, combine the sugar, softened butter, and eggs and beat steadily for 15 minutes with an electric mixer (do not underbeat). Spread the sugar mixture over the vanilla wafer crust and arrange the sliced bananas evenly over the top. Cover the bananas with the crushed pineapple, spread the whipped cream over the pineapple, and sprinkle the nuts over the top. Garnish the edges of the pie with cherries and chill for at least 2 hours, then cut into squares.

YIELD At least 15 servings

PAWLEY'S ISLAND PIE

*T*oday, Louis Osteen is the celebrated chef at Louis' restaurant in Charleston, South Carolina, but when my family first met him years ago, he was just beginning his career up the coast at Pawley's Island Inn and Restaurant. We raved about his succulent crab cakes and hearty Southern stews, but the dish that Mother really had a fit over (and wasted no time getting the recipe for) was Louis' chocolate-walnut pie—really a variation on old-fashioned shoofly pie. Today, Mother sometimes makes the pie for her Kentucky Derby party as well as for any number of picnics and cookouts.

1 cup granulated sugar
½ cup all-purpose flour
2 large eggs
1 teaspoon pure vanilla extract
½ cup (1 stick) butter, melted and cooled
1 cup chopped walnuts
One 6-ounce bag (1 cup) semisweet chocolate chips
1 unbaked 10-inch Basic Pie Shell (page 243)

*P*reheat the oven to 350°F.

*I*n a large mixing bowl, combine the sugar, flour, eggs, and vanilla and stir till well blended. Add the butter and stir till completely incorporated and smooth. Add the walnuts and chocolate chips and stir till well distributed.

*S*crape the batter into the pie shell and bake till golden brown, about 30 minutes. Let the pie cool completely before serving.

YIELD One 10-inch pie; at least 8 servings

FIG, APRICOT, AND STRAWBERRY TART

*F*igs are ready!" our next-door neighbor would call out to Mother in mid-summer, referring to the ripe, green wonders that filled two fig trees near his house and garage. Mother would then go over, fill a large bag full, and the making of pudding, ice cream, preserves, and tarts would begin—after, of course, we'd picked out the most luscious beauties to eat plain, wrap in thin slices of country ham, or cut up over ice cream.

Since figs are so fragile, Mother rarely cooks them except to make preserves, the explanation of why the only item baked in this recipe is the tart shell. The tart contains no cream, so it's ideal for summer picnics and cookouts, and, depending on the exact season, you can substitute fresh raspberries, blueberries, or peaches for the strawberries and apricots and design the tart accordingly. Just make sure the figs are not too mushy.

½ cup apricot preserves
¼ cup Amaretto liqueur
6 large or 8 medium-size ripe figs, stemmed, washed, and patted dry
1 baked 10-inch Almond Tart Shell (page 246)
1 pint fresh strawberries, washed, hulled, and patted dry

*I*n a small mixing bowl, combine the preserves and Amaretto, mix well, and set aside. Cut the figs lengthwise in half.

*U*sing a pastry brush, spread 3 tablespoons of the preserve mixture over the bottom of the tart shell and arrange a ring of the figs cut side up around the edges. Arrange the remaining figs in the center of the tart. Arrange about 4 strawberries in the center of the figs and fill the spaces between the figs in the center and those around the edges with the remaining strawberries. Brush the tops of the figs and strawberries with the remaining preserve mixture, place the tart on a serving plate, and chill for about 1 hour before serving.

YIELD One 10-inch tart; 8 servings

SECESSION BROWN BETTY

The apocryphal story goes that when the Confederacy seceded from the Union in 1861, Southerners celebrated by eating what was considered a symbolic rebel dessert: Brown Betty—or, as some referred to it, "Secession Cobbler." I don't suppose it matters that this basic crumble was a staple in rural England centuries before our War for Southern Independence, or that the origins of the name "Betty" are totally unknown, or that the dish was not even mentioned in print in the United States till after the war. What *is* true is that the dessert was a good way to use stale bread and remains (at least for Mother) the ideal dish to take to picnics and cookouts. Mother got the idea of adding citrus rinds from an old regional cookbook with a recipe by Nancy, Lady Astor of Devon, England, who indicated that the Betty should be served with Devonshire cream "made as soon as possible after milking." We settle for ordinary heavy cream or a zesty lemon sauce.

6 large Granny Smith or Rome apples
2 tablespoons fresh lemon juice, plus extra for sprinkling on the apples
2 cups stale bread crumbs
½ cup (1 stick) butter, melted
1 cup granulated sugar
1 teaspoon ground cinnamon
Grated rind of ½ lemon
Grated rind of ½ orange
½ cup boiling water
Heavy cream or Lemon Sauce (page 256)

*P*reheat the oven to 350°F. Grease a large baking dish and set aside.

*P*eel and core the apples, thinly slice them, sprinkle with a little lemon juice to prevent discoloration, and set aside.

*P*lace the bread crumbs in a medium-size mixing bowl. In a small bowl, combine the butter and the 2 tablespoons lemon juice and stir till well blended, then pour over the bread crumbs and mix well. In another small bowl, combine the sugar, cinnamon, and citrus rinds and mix well.

*A*rrange a layer of apples in the bottom of the prepared baking dish, spoon about one third of the bread-crumb mixture over the apples, and sprinkle part of the sugar mixture over the crumbs. Repeat the procedure till all the ingredients are used up, but before you add the final layer of crumbs, pour the boiling water over the top, then add the remaining crumbs and sugar mixture. Cover the dish with aluminum foil and bake till the apples are soft, about 30 minutes. Uncover and bake till the top is browned, about another 10 minutes. Serve warm in bowls with spoonfuls of heavy cream or lemon sauce.

YIELD At least 8 servings

VADE MECUM DEWBERRY COBBLER

Dewberry and blackberry cobblers are almost a religious experience for Mother. Sweet dewberries, which are little more than large blackberries, are not common in most states, but are plentiful throughout most of the South and are used interchangeably with their smaller cousins to make delicious cobblers and pies.

Mother got this prized recipe years ago when she and other ladies of the Women's Auxiliary of the Episcopal Church went to the retreat of Vade Mecum in the Blue Ridge Mountains. One day, they and the presiding minister decided to go blackberry picking, an outing that produced chigger bites but also bucket after bucket of fat blackberries and dewberries that the cook at the camp turned into huge "sheets" of cobbler.

A major secret to this cobbler (or any cobbler) is to cook the bottom pastry till it's dry, before adding any berries.

Dough for 1 double 10-inch Basic Pie Shell (page 243)
5 cups ripe dewberries and/or blackberries, rinsed
1¼ cups granulated sugar
¼ cup water
2 tablespoons all-purpose flour
3 tablespoons butter, cut into small pieces
Hard Sauce (page 259) or vanilla ice cream

Preheat the oven to 375°F.

Roll out half the dough on a floured work surface to generously fit a 2-inch-deep 10-inch pie plate. Line the greased pie plate with the dough, trim off any excess, and crimp the edges. Place the crust in the oven till the pastry is dry, about 5 minutes. Roll out the remaining dough ⅛ inch thick and cut into ½-inch-wide strips. Place half of the strips on a lightly greased baking sheet and bake till lightly browned, about 10 minutes. Remove from the oven and let cool.

Increase the oven temperature to 425°F.

In a large, heavy saucepan, combine the berries, 1 cup of the sugar, and the water and stir gently over low heat till the berries are softened. In a small bowl, combine the flour and the remaining ¼ cup sugar, stir, and add to the berries. Increase the heat to moderate and, stirring constantly, cook till the mixture has thickened slightly. Spoon the berries into the prepared pie shell, distributing the cooked pastry strips throughout the filling as you add the berries. Dot with the butter. Making a lattice pattern, cover the top of the cobbler with the uncooked pastry strips and bake till the pastry is browned, about 25 minutes.

Serve the cobbler warm with hard sauce or vanilla ice cream on top.

YIELD   One 10-inch cobbler; 12 servings

MOLDED MAPLE DELIGHT

This congealed dessert, so suggestive of brisk but balmy air and falling leaves, has considerably more body than most, making it perfect for any number of early fall celebrations. If Mother decides to present dishes on a backyard buffet, this mold is always included, and if she's asked to prepare an easy-to-serve dessert for a fall church supper or barbecue, she might make at least two and have them kept chilled till ready to serve.

1 envelope unflavored gelatin
¼ cup milk
6 tablespoons granulated sugar
3 tablespoons cornstarch
2 large eggs, beaten
1 quart milk, heated
2 tablespoons pure maple extract
3 tablespoons firmly packed light brown sugar
1 pint heavy cream, whipped to stiff peaks
¼ cup chopped hazelnuts, toasted (see Sweet Note on page 65)

In a small bowl, sprinkle the gelatin over the ¼ cup milk and let soften.

In the top of a double boiler, combine the granulated sugar, cornstarch, and eggs and beat with a whisk over simmering (not boiling) water till thickened and smooth. Gradually add the heated milk, whisking till thick and smooth. Whisk in the gelatin mixture, remove from the heat, and stir till the gelatin is completely dissolved, then let the mixture cool completely.

In a medium-size mixing bowl, combine the extract, brown sugar, and half of the whipped cream and stir till well blended, then add the mixture to the cooled gelatin mixture, stirring. Scrape the mixture into a medium-size baking dish and chill till firm, 4 to 6 hours. Unmold, cut into squares, top with the remaining whipped cream, and sprinkle the hazelnuts over the tops.

YIELD At least 8 servings

 *Martha's Sweet Note*

To facilitate the unmolding of congealed desserts, wrap a warm, damp towel around the mold before loosening the sides with a knife.

DAMSON PLUM ROLL

*M*emory is faint, but I can still recall Mother's egg man, old Henry, calling out from his truck, "Damsons, Miss Martha, I got some mighty nice damsons I just picked off the tree this morning." And I also recall Mother assigning me the difficult and loathsome task of cutting the flesh off those tart damson plums and scraping the seeds clean so she'd have plenty to make pies, fools, puddings, and the preserves used in this wonderful roll that was so perfect for picnics and cookouts. Today, damson plums are scarce as hens' teeth, but when Mother spots them during summer at Southern farmers' markets, she's been known to buy the whole lot. Just recently at a roadside stand on Long Island, we came across jars of very good homemade damson preserves produced in Arkansas, so, no matter where you live, keep your eyes open.

4 large eggs
¾ cup granulated sugar
¾ cup all-purpose flour
½ teaspoon baking powder
¼ teaspoon salt
1 teaspoon pure vanilla extract
Confectioners' sugar for sprinkling
1½ cups damson plum preserves

*P*reheat the oven to 400°F. Line a 15 × 10 × 1-inch jelly roll pan with waxed paper, grease it well, even to the corners, and set aside.

*I*n a large mixing bowl, beat the eggs with an electric mixer till frothy, then gradually add the granulated sugar, beating till light and thick, about 8 minutes. In a small mixing bowl, stir together the flour, baking powder, and salt, add to the egg mixture, and stir till well blended. Add the vanilla and stir till well blended. Scrape the batter onto the prepared pan, spreading it evenly toward the corners, and bake till firm, about 13 minutes. Trim off any crisp edges of the cake and turn the cake out onto a clean kitchen cloth or tea towel sprinkled with confectioners' sugar. Remove the waxed paper and carefully and firmly roll up the cake evenly in the cloth, making sure the cake is completely covered with cloth. Place the roll on a wire rack to cool completely.

*C*arefully unroll the cake, spread the preserves evenly over the top, roll again, and sprinkle with confectioners' sugar. To serve, cut the roll into 1-inch-thick slices.

YIELD 1 large jelly roll; 8 to 10 servings

WORLD'S GREATEST COOKIE

My sister was the first lady in the family to carry on Mother's proud baking tradition, and today my niece and Mother's namesake, Martha Crawford, follows in the footsteps of both her grandmother and mother. When young Martha showed up at the house with a bag of what she had confidently determined was "the world's greatest cookie," Mother, Hootie, and I glanced at one another suspiciously. Once we'd taken a first bite of the light, buttery, crisp marvels, we all three agreed that if the cookie was not necessarily the world's best, it was certainly one of the most exceptional we'd ever tasted. "Sweetheart," Mother confessed lovingly to Martha, reaching in the bag for another cookie, "I must say I couldn't have done better myself." Martha makes huge batches of the cookies when she and her family vacation with friends at Wrightsville Beach, North Carolina, and Mother finds them perfect for both cookouts and ice cream socials.

1 cup rolled oats
1 cup cornflakes
1 cup frozen grated coconut, thawed
½ cup crumbled pecans
3½ cups all-purpose flour
1 teaspoon baking soda
1 teaspoon salt
1 cup (2 sticks) butter, softened
1 cup firmly packed light brown sugar
1 cup granulated sugar
1 large egg
1 cup vegetable oil
1 teaspoon pure vanilla extract

In a blender or food processor, combine the oats, cornflakes, coconut, and pecans, reduce to a fine texture, and set aside. In a large mixing bowl, combine the flour, baking soda, and salt, mix till well blended, and set aside.

Preheat the oven to 325°F.

In a large mixing bowl, cream together with an electric mixer the butter and two sugars till light and fluffy, then add the egg and mix till well blended. Add the oil and vanilla and mix till well blended. Add the oat mixture and stir till well blended, then add the flour mixture and stir till the batter is very smooth.

Drop the batter by teaspoons about 1½ inches apart on large ungreased baking sheets and make a crisscross design on the tops with a fork, dipping the fork periodically into water. Bake till the cookies are slightly browned around the edges, 12 to 15 minutes, and let them cool completely. Store the cookies in airtight containers.

YIELD About 100 cookies

Bridge Luncheons, Book Clubs & Charity Socials

Jes' Pie

Plain Ole Dixie Chocolate Pie

Lady Baltimore Tarts

Margo's Banana Pudding

Miss Patsy's Tipsy Pudding

Bridge Cranberry Mousse

No-Trump Toffee Bars

Raisin and Pecan Oaties

Sugared Pecans

Sugared Baked Peanuts

Of all the culinary events in Mother's active social life, none are more important than those that revolve around playing bridge and holding various meetings and workshops at home. Typically for bridge, eight friends gather at around 10:30 in the morning, play cards till hunger strikes, stop for a glass of wine and lunch, and continue playing till midafternoon, when it's time for more liquid and solid sustenance. At Mother's monthly book club, composed of eight members and always held on Tuesday morning, everyone reports on new books read, but certainly not before slices of pie or cookies have been served with plenty of strong chicory coffee. Church guild meetings, which usually involve fifteen or twenty guests, a devotional, and a program on various fund-raising projects, are more serious affairs where most hostesses take the opportunity to display an ample array of cakes, pies, puddings, and cookies on a handsome dessert buffet. The major purpose of the monthly five-hour charity workshops is to make by hand dozens of exquisite Christmas items (ornaments, tree skirts, napkins, stockings, etc.) that are sold at an annual Charity League bazaar with profits used to support a local child care center, but noble and beneficial as these workshops certainly are, they are also the ideal occasion for the ladies to boast endlessly about new cake variations, exchange recipes (sometimes), and, indeed, show off their latest dessert creations.

Only rarely have I been privy to these traditional, age-old socials as Mother interprets them in her home, but, believe me, if you don't believe that Southerners are as obsessed with desserts as with well-aged bourbon and pit-cooked pork barbecue, you really should hear the continuous banter (and arguments) about pound cakes, syllabubs, congealed Bavarians, parfaits and fools, and, of course, fruitcakes. Like most of the other ladies, Mother has certain desserts virtually designed, in her mind, for these socials, and, like the others, she's convinced that her confections are unique. Needless to say, jealousies abound and some recipes are guarded scrupulously, but all these ladies love to eat as much as Mother, and they're all part of a proud Southern tradition that Mother is determined to pass on to anyone with an exceptional sweet tooth.

JES' PIE

The story goes that a man, wildly impressed with the delicious pie once served him in an Alabama diner, asked the waitress, "What *is* this pie?" only to be told, "Why, that's jes' pie." Another anecdote traces Southern chess pie back to an eighteenth-century English "cheese pie," while still another links the pie with a Southern piece of kitchen furniture called a pie chest, where confections were stored (Mother says her family had one years ago). Whatever the origins of this simple pie and its name, I was raised seeing Jes' Pie written on "receipt" cards, and that's the way we still pronounce it today. Mother often makes it with lemon or coconut for her book club meetings, or she might substitute light brown sugar for the white, but no matter the modification, the little secret to her pies is the teaspoon of cider vinegar.

4 large eggs, beaten
1½ cups granulated sugar
2 teaspoons yellow cornmeal
¼ teaspoon salt
¼ cup (½ stick) butter, melted
¼ cup heavy cream
1 teaspoon pure vanilla extract
1 teaspoon cider vinegar
1 unbaked 9-inch Basic Pie Shell (page 243)

Preheat the oven to 350°F.

In a large mixing bowl, combine the eggs, sugar, cornmeal, salt, butter, cream, vanilla, and vinegar and beat with an electric mixer till well blended and smooth. Scrape the mixture into the pie shell and bake till a cake tester or straw inserted in the center comes out clean, about 30 minutes. Let the pie cool and serve at room temperature.

YIELD One 9-inch pie; 6 to 8 servings

LEMON CHESS PIE *Add ¼ cup fresh lemon juice and 2 teaspoons grated lemon rind to the other ingredients.*
COCONUT CHESS PIE *Increase the heavy cream to ½ cup and add ½ cup fresh (see Sweet Note on page 17) or frozen grated coconut to the other ingredients.*

PLAIN OLE DIXIE CHOCOLATE PIE

*P*eople ask me more for my basic chocolate pie recipe than for any other chocolate dessert," Mother informs. "It's not a black bottom pie, or a mud pie, or a chocolate chess pie. It's just plain old Dixie chocolate pie like I ate as a child, and my mother and grandmother ate, and you ate." Mother loves to serve this pie at her bridge luncheons, and when she wants to make it fancy, she beats the leftover 4 egg whites with 6 tablespoons of sugar till stiff peaks form, spreads the meringue over the top of the pie, bakes it at about 350°F just till the top browns, and chills it briefly.

½ cup unsweetened cocoa powder
¼ cup cornstarch
4 large egg yolks
⅛ teaspoon salt
1½ cups granulated sugar
2 cups milk
2 teaspoons pure vanilla extract
1 prebaked 9-inch Chocolate Wafer Pie Shell (page 248)
1 cup heavy cream, whipped to stiff peaks

*I*n a large, heavy saucepan, combine the cocoa, cornstarch, egg yolks, salt, and sugar and beat well with a whisk till blended. Over low heat, gradually add the milk, whisk till smooth, and cook slowly till thickened, stirring constantly. Remove the pan from the heat, add the vanilla, stir, and let cool. Pour the mixture into the pie shell, chill till slightly firm but not hard, and serve topped with the whipped cream.

YIELD One 9-inch pie; 6 servings

LADY BALTIMORE TARTS

I thought you folks might like to taste my new tarts," drawled Mother's neighbor and close friend, Mac Mahone, holding a large tray full of colorful, freshly baked confections covered with plastic wrap. And when Mac brings a dessert over to the house to be sampled, she never brings only a single portion but enough to feed a party. Mother and Mac have been exchanging recipes for years, but this modification of the famous cake once served at the Lady Baltimore Tea Room in Charleston, South Carolina, is one that Mother truly prizes and loves to serve at both bridge luncheons and afternoon teas. Mac does not disapprove of using 3-inch unbaked commercial tart shells for the recipe, in which case the yield is 16 to 18 tarts; Mother always makes her own 2-inch shells.

3 large eggs, well beaten
1½ cups firmly packed light brown sugar
½ cup light corn syrup
1½ cups chopped pecans or walnuts
1 cup frozen grated coconut, thawed
½ cup chopped crystallized cherries
1 teaspoon pure vanilla extract
½ teaspoon pure almond extract
24 (double recipe) 2-inch unbaked Basic Small Tart Shells (page 244)

*P*reheat the oven to 300°F.

*I*n a large mixing bowl, combine the eggs, brown sugar, and corn syrup and mix till well blended and smooth. Stir in the nuts, coconut, cherries, and two extracts and mix till the filling is well blended.

*A*rrange the 24 unbaked tart shells on a large, heavy, ungreased baking sheet, spoon about ¼ cup of the filling into each shell, and bake till the filling is set and the pastry golden, about 40 minutes. Allow the tarts to cool completely before serving.

YIELD **24 tarts**

MARGO'S BANANA PUDDING

*W*hen Margo Cummings, one of Mother's fellow volunteers in the Charity League workshop, arrived one day with her banana pudding, Mother knew the second she saw and tasted it that the pudding was like no other— "mainly because folding the whipped cream into the custard made it so light and fluffy." Like so many Southern desserts, the pudding no doubt evolved from the classic English trifle, and the very day that one of my friends recently gave Mother a crystal trifle bowl as a thank-you gift, she wasted no time testing the dish with this recipe. Of course, this is not really Margo's recipe, since, typically, Mother decided that vanilla wafers work much better than the original chocolate chip cookies. Both yield a delicious pudding, so make your choice.

½ cup granulated sugar
⅓ cup all-purpose flour
¼ teaspoon salt
2 cups milk, scalded (see Sweet Note on page 18)
3 large egg yolks, beaten
1 teaspoon pure vanilla extract
1 cup heavy cream, whipped to stiff peaks
One 12-ounce box vanilla wafers
5 medium-size ripe bananas, peeled and thinly sliced

*I*n a large, heavy saucepan, combine the sugar, flour, and salt and mix well, then gradually stir in the scalded milk. Cook the mixture over moderate heat, stirring constantly, till slightly thickened. Very gradually, stir about ¼ cup of the hot mixture into the egg yolks, then add the yolks to the hot mixture and cook, stirring constantly, till the mixture is fully thickened and coats a spoon. Remove from the heat and stir in the vanilla. Let cool completely, then fold in half of the whipped cream.

*I*n a trifle or large crystal bowl, alternately layer the vanilla wafers and banana slices, pouring custard over each layer and ending with vanilla wafers. Spread the remaining whipped cream over the top and chill briefly. (If any vanilla wafers are left over, crumble and sprinkle them over the whipped cream.)

YIELD **6 to 8 servings**

MISS PATSY'S TIPSY PUDDING

Miss Patsy Goodwin was a true Southern eccentric, a "Miss Daisy"–type lady who lived in a large Colonial house, drove an old Cadillac, wore feather boas, and belonged to every civic club and social organization in Charlotte. She was a dear friend of Mother's, and, like Martha Pearl herself, a liberal tippler, and she liked to serve this infamous rich, highly spiked pudding at the various meetings she'd hold at home. When she gave Mother the recipe, she specified that the pudding had to be served in an *old* cut-glass bowl and that "little extra glasses of sipping sherry just add to the pleasure." Miss Patsy loved to cook and dropped dead in her kitchen at the age of ninety. I met her a number of times when I was young and wish I'd gotten to know her better.

One 13 × 9-inch Sponge Cake (page 239)
2 cups sweet sherry
1½ cups granulated sugar
1 tablespoon all-purpose flour
4 large eggs, beaten
1 quart milk
1 teaspoon pure vanilla extract
1 quart heavy cream
½ cup slivered almonds, toasted (see Sweet Note on page 65)
12 crystallized cherries (available in specialty food shops and some supermarkets)

In a large crystal bowl, break up the sponge cake into bite-size pieces. Pour the sherry over the cake and let stand for 30 minutes.

In a large, heavy saucepan, combine 1 cup of the sugar and the flour and mix well. Add the eggs and mix till well blended, then gradually stir in the milk. Stirring constantly, cook the mixture over moderate heat till thick enough to coat the back of a spoon, never letting it boil. Remove the custard from the heat, stir in the vanilla, and let cool completely.

In a large mixing bowl, combine the cream and the remaining ½ cup sugar and beat with an electric mixer till stiff peaks form.

Pour the cooled custard sauce over the soaked cake, cover with the sweetened whipped cream, and decorate the pudding with the almonds and cherries. Serve the pudding at room temperature or slightly chilled.

YIELD 6 to 8 servings

BRIDGE CRANBERRY MOUSSE

*W*ith all the eating breaks they take while playing bridge, I often wonder how Mother and the other members in her club ever finish a rubber. Typically, the ladies stop for lunch a little after noon, but when Mother has prepared a really special dessert, like this fall cranberry mousse (to celebrate a birthday, for example), she'll hold off serving it till midafternoon, when it's time for sherry. This is a beautiful mousse that can also be served at a formal dinner—and, best of all, straight from the refrigerator. Fresh cranberries are impossible to find except during the winter months, so if you have any idea of making this mousse or any other cranberry dessert in spring or summer, be sure to stock up on packages when you can and freeze them.

Two 12-ounce packages fresh cranberries, stemmed and rinsed
2 cups water
Grated rind of 2 oranges
3 cups granulated sugar
12 large eggs
1 pint heavy cream

*I*n a large heavy saucepan, combine the cranberries, water, orange rind, and sugar and bring to a boil over high heat. Reduce the heat to moderate and cook till the cranberries burst, about 5 minutes. Remove from the heat.

*I*n a large mixing bowl, beat the eggs with an electric mixer till frothy. Stirring constantly, add about 1 cup of the hot cranberry mixture to the eggs, then, still stirring constantly, return the eggs and cranberries to the saucepan of cranberries. Cook the mixture over low heat, stirring constantly, till the cranberries thicken slightly, about 10 minutes, then remove from the heat and let cool completely, stirring occasionally. (The mixture will be thick.)

*W*ash and dry the mixer beaters, then, in a medium-size mixing bowl, beat the cream till stiff peaks form. Fold the cream into the cranberry custard, scrape the mousse into twelve stemmed crystal glasses, and chill for at least 4 hours before serving.

YIELD 12 servings

NO-TRUMP TOFFEE BARS

*T*he routine remains the same: Mother and her bridge partners play a few hands, break for a long, stylish lunch with wine, deal a few more cards, and then end the afternoon with coffee and more sweets. Of course, each lady prides herself in her particular confection, and none more so than Martha Pearl with these sinfully rich toffee wonders. "It's embarrassing to admit," confesses Mother, "but we really do lots more talking and eating than playing bridge."

1 cup (2 sticks) butter, softened
1 cup firmly packed dark brown sugar
1 large egg yolk
1 cup all-purpose flour
Six 1½-ounce milk chocolate bars
⅔ cup crushed hazelnuts or almonds, toasted (see Sweet Note on page 65)

*P*reheat the oven to 350°F. Lightly grease a large jelly roll pan and set aside.

*I*n a mixing bowl, cream the butter and brown sugar together with an electric mixer until light and fluffy, then add the egg yolk and beat till well blended. Gradually add the flour, beating till well blended and smooth. Spread the dough in the prepared jelly roll pan and bake till medium brown, 15 to 20 minutes. Remove the pan from the oven, immediately arrange the chocolate bars over the top, and allow them to melt. With a knife, spread the chocolate evenly over the cookie base. Sprinkle the nuts on top, let cool, and cut into small bars or diamonds. Store in airtight containers.

YIELD **About 75 bars**

RAISIN AND PECAN OATIES

*M*other got the recipe for these oaties from my dear friend Pat Brown and immediately began serving them with coffee at her book club meetings. Unlike Pat, however, who prefers her cookies crisp and thus lets them "drain" on a brown paper bag, we let ours cool on the pans so they'll remain chewy. By no means should you use instant oatmeal for this recipe. To make the oaties even more gooey, I sometimes add about half a cup of chocolate chips to the batter, leading both Pat and Mother to accuse me of destroying their integrity. I disagree.

1 cup (2 sticks) butter, softened
¾ cup granulated sugar
¾ cup firmly packed dark brown sugar
1 teaspoon pure vanilla extract
1 large egg
1½ cups all-purpose flour
1 teaspoon baking soda
1 teaspoon ground cinnamon
½ teaspoon salt
½ cup old-fashioned rolled oats
1 cup chopped pecans
1 cup seedless dark raisins

*P*reheat the oven to 375°F. Butter two baking sheets and set aside.

*I*n a large mixing bowl, cream together the butter and two sugars with an electric mixer until light and fluffy, then add the vanilla and egg and beat till well blended. In a medium-size mixing bowl, combine the flour, baking soda, cinnamon, salt, and oats and stir till well blended, then add to the creamed mixture and stir till well blended. Add the pecans and raisins and fold them into the batter till evenly distributed. (The batter will be very sticky.) Drop the batter by the teaspoon about 1½ inches apart onto the prepared baking sheets, flatten slightly with a knife, and bake till golden, about 10 minutes. Let cool completely on the sheets.

YIELD **About 50 oaties**

SUGARED PECANS

$\mathcal{P}$ecans are almost a symbol of Southern cooking, and nowhere do nuts figure more prominently than in our numerous desserts. Culinarily, Mother would literally be lost without her pecans, which is why, when a man calls every September to announce, "We're shelling," she orders an entire case (twenty-four one-pound packages) from her favorite Atwell Pecan Company in Wrens, Georgia. Nothing, of course, is simpler or better than toasted, salted fresh pecan halves at cocktail parties, but when Mother wants to put out bowls of treats for nibbling at bridge games and book club meetings, these sugared pecans are always at the top of the list. Remember not to make these pecans on a damp, humid day, as they will not firm up properly, and be sure to store them in tightly closed tins. Also, stored in sealed freezer bags, fresh pecans prepared in any manner maintain their integrity for up to a year in the freezer.

½ cup granulated sugar
½ cup heavy cream
1 tablespoon white corn syrup
Grated rind of 1 medium-size orange
1 tablespoon butter
2 cups pecan halves

$\mathcal{I}$n a small, heavy saucepan, combine the sugar, cream, corn syrup, orange rind, and butter and bring to a low boil over moderate heat, stirring constantly, till the syrup registers 240°F on a candy thermometer or forms a soft ball when a small glob is dropped into ½ cup of cold water. Remove the pan from the heat, scrape the syrup into a medium-size mixing bowl, and beat with a whisk till cool. Add the pecans and mix till well coated, then scatter them over a baking sheet and let them cool completely before storing.

YIELD 2 cups pecans

 Martha's Sweet Note

$\mathcal{F}$orget about making sugared nuts on a wet or cloudy day. If you do, they won't be hard and crisp.

SUGARED BAKED PEANUTS

*P*eanuts play almost as important a role in Southern cooking as pecans, and when friends send Mother a big sack of shelled raw Virginia goobers (and, despite what Georgians might declare, the large, unctuous runner peanuts of Virginia and northeastern North Carolina have no equal), she wastes no time baking up a sugared batch for snacking at the bridge table.

1 cup granulated sugar
½ cup water
2 cups shelled raw peanuts

*P*reheat the oven to 300°F.

*I*n a large, heavy saucepan, combine the sugar and water over low heat and stir till the sugar is dissolved. Add the peanuts and stir steadily till all the syrup adheres to the peanuts. Pour the nuts into a shallow baking pan and bake for exactly 30 minutes, stirring several times. Let the nuts cool completely and keep stored in a tightly covered container.

YIELD 2 cups peanuts

Cocktail Parties

&

Formal Dinners

Carrot Cake with Almond—Cream Cheese Frosting

Old English Blackberry Fool

Peaches Supreme

Fresh Lemon Charlotte Rousse with Strawberries

Pearl's Snow Cream with Raspberry Sauce

Miss Lucy's Wine Jelly

Baby Pecan Tassies

Cocktail Brandy-Rum Balls

othing baffles visitors to the South more than the way Southerners always serve and truly relish sweet confections at their many cocktail parties. (And, by the way, only in the South today does the term "cocktail party" still imply bourbon and branch and stiff martinis and not just wimpy wine and mineral water.) I must admit that I too find it difficult nibbling sugared nuts and crackers spread with cream cheese and hot pepper jelly with my Manhattans, but I do know that if Mother were to throw a party (especially at Christmas) that didn't include her Brandy-Rum Balls, Baby Pecan Tassies, and who knows what other such delicacies, her friends would think seriously of having her committed. The phenomenon only goes to prove that there is indeed no occasion in life where Southerners (like the English) don't manifest their absolute passion for sweets.

If there is a tendency in some parts these days to reduce desserts at formal home dinners to flourless cakes, herb sorbets, and anemic berry "soups," rest assured that no such trend will ever find its way to the table of Martha Pearl Villas. Although Mother is basically as down-to-earth a cook as you'll find, she also routinely hosts exquisite formal dinner parties (for up to ten or twelve persons) where the very finest china, heavy silver, cut-glassware, and linen napery are brought out and where the art of refined Southern cooking reaches its apogee. The occasion might be to celebrate a couple getting married, or a friend promoted to a high position in business, or simply some festive holiday, but whatever the reason, guests can always expect something like a majestic roasted wild duck stuffed with bourbon dressing or jellied daube glacé, glorious squash soufflé or sweet potato and pecan pudding, and, above all, a memorable dessert like Lemon Charlotte Rousse with Strawberries, Snow Cream with Raspberry Sauce, or moist Carrot Cake with Almond–Cream Cheese Frosting. If the main meal is particularly extravagant, Mother might wisely serve only a little Blackberry Fool or Wine Jelly, but, more often than not, this sort of dinner calls for a dessert that really makes a statement—with a Southern accent.

CARROT CAKE WITH ALMOND–CREAM CHEESE FROSTING

*W*hen carrot cake was first a rage in the South about thirty years ago, few people realized that the reason it can be so good when properly prepared is the moistness from the carrots. Like everybody else, Mother initially made the cake with pecans, but then, striving for a more delicate flavor, she substituted toasted almonds—still the ingredient that makes the frosting on her cake distinctive. Overcooked, dry carrot cake is wretched, so be sure to start testing the texture of the layers with a straw or cake tester after about twenty-five minutes of baking (the straw should be slightly moist, not fully clean, when pulled out).

For the cake

2 cups all-purpose flour
2 cups granulated sugar
2 teaspoons baking soda
2 teaspoons ground cinnamon
1 teaspoon salt
4 large eggs
1½ cups vegetable oil
3 cups grated carrots

For the frosting

½ cup (1 stick) butter, softened
One 8-ounce package cream cheese
One 1-pound box confectioners' sugar, sifted
1 teaspoon pure vanilla extract
1 cup chopped almonds, toasted (see Sweet Note on page 65)

*P*reheat the oven to 350°F. Grease and flour three 9-inch round cake pans, tapping out any excess flour, and set aside.

*T*o make the cake, combine the flour, granulated sugar, baking soda, cinnamon, and salt in a large mixing bowl and mix well. Add the eggs and oil and beat with an electric mixer for 2 minutes. Add the carrots and stir till well blended. Scrape the batter into the prepared cake pans and bake just till a cake tester or straw inserted in the center comes out barely clean, 25 to 30 minutes. Cool the cakes in their pans for 10 minutes, then turn out onto wire racks to cool completely.

*T*o make the frosting, cream the butter and cream cheese together in a large mixing bowl with an electric mixer till light and fluffy. Gradually beat in the confectioners' sugar, then add the vanilla and beat till well blended. Add the almonds and stir till well blended. When the cake layers have cooled completely, frost between the layers, along the sides, and on top.

YIELD One 3-layer 9-inch cake; 10 to 12 servings

OLD ENGLISH BLACKBERRY FOOL

*S*ince Mother's maternal great-grandmother (a Johnston) came from England to settle in Virginia before marrying (an Irish Malone) and moving to Georgia (got that straight?), this berry fool recipe can be traced back at least to the eighteenth century. Whether the word derives from the French *fouler* ("to crush") is debatable, but for centuries a fool has been any puree of stewed fruit folded into or combined with whipped rich cream to produce an elegant dessert. Mother remembers her Georgia grandmother, Sweet Maa, serving blackberry fool at sit-down yard picnics, but today she finds the froth more appropriate for stylish brunches, afternoon socials, and even formal dinners. The fool is also very good made with other berries, as well as with plums, peaches, or mangoes.

1 quart (4 cups) fresh blackberries, rinsed
½ cup seedless blackberry jam
½ cup granulated sugar
2 strips of orange rind
1 pint heavy cream
½ teaspoon pure vanilla extract
1 cup sliced almonds, toasted (see Sweet Note on page 65)

*I*n a large, heavy, nonreactive saucepan, combine the blackberries, jam, sugar, and orange strips, slowly bring the mixture to a boil over moderately low heat, and stir constantly till the berries are soft, about 10 minutes. Remove the pan from the heat and cool completely. Remove and discard the orange strips, puree the berries through a food mill or a sieve into a bowl (do not use a food processor or blender), cover with plastic wrap, and chill for about 1 hour.

*I*n a large bowl, whip the cream and vanilla together with an electric mixer till thick but not stiff. In crystal goblets, layer the berry mixture alternately with the cream, ending with cream, then chill till ready to serve. Sprinkle the almonds over the tops before serving.

YIELD 6 to 8 servings

PEACHES SUPREME

This simple but rather elegant dessert was created by Polly Mickle, one of Mother's oldest friends and one of the ladies with whom Mother exchanges recipes at one of those bridge games where there's more talking about food than playing bridge. Since the dish is not too sweet, it's ideal after an elaborate formal dinner. Note that drained canned peach halves—if necessary—can be substituted successfully for the fresh fruit.

Juice of 2 large or 3 medium-size oranges
2 tablespoons peach brandy
12 macaroons, crushed
¼ cup (½ stick) butter, melted
¼ cup sliced almonds
3 large fresh, ripe peaches, peeled (see Sweet Note on page 76), pitted, and halved
Vanilla or peach ice cream

Preheat the oven to 300°F. Butter a 9-inch pie plate and set aside.

In a small bowl, combine the orange juice and brandy, mix well, and set aside. In a medium-size bowl, combine the macaroons, butter, and almonds, mix well, and set aside.

Arrange the peach halves cut side up in the buttered pie plate, spoon equal amounts of macaroon mixture into each indention, and pour the orange juice and brandy over the top. Bake till the tops are browned and the peaches soft, about 20 minutes, basting twice. To serve, top each portion with ice cream.

YIELD 6 servings

FRESH LEMON CHARLOTTE ROUSSE WITH STRAWBERRIES

This is an elegant dish that my sister, Hootie, often served at formal dinner parties at her home in Wilmington, North Carolina, and that Mother was quick to adopt. Although light, it is a quintessential Southern dessert, one that any lady takes great pride in preparing. The trick is to make sure that the gelatin is dissolved completely to avoid lumpiness, and to help the ladyfingers to stand evenly and gracefully, Mother always trims the rounded ends. A classic Charlotte Rousse is made with strawberries, but sometimes Mother and I will substitute fresh blackberries, raspberries, or blueberries when they're in season.

1 package unflavored gelatin
½ cup fresh lemon juice
4 large eggs, separated
1½ cups granulated sugar
¼ teaspoon salt
3 tablespoons butter
2 teaspoons grated lemon rind
1 teaspoon pure lemon extract
16 plain ladyfingers, split
1 pint heavy cream
1 pint fresh strawberries, rinsed, patted dry, hulled, and sprinkled with ½ cup granulated sugar

In the top of a double boiler set over simmering water, soften the gelatin in the lemon juice, stirring till completely dissolved. In a medium-size mixing bowl, combine the egg yolks and sugar and beat with an electric mixer till thickened. Add the salt and beat well. Add the egg mixture to the gelatin and cook over simmering water, stirring constantly, till thick and smooth, about 8 minutes. Add the butter and stir till well blended. When the mixture is again thickened, add the lemon rind and extract and stir well. Remove the pan from the hot water and let cool.

Line the bottom and sides of a 9-inch springform pan with the split ladyfingers. In a medium-size mixing bowl, beat 1 cup of the cream with an electric mixer till stiff peaks form. In a large mixing bowl, beat the egg whites till stiff peaks form. Scrape the cooled lemon mixture into another large mixing bowl and gently fold in the whipped cream and egg whites with a rubber spatula. Scrape the mixture into the prepared pan, cover with plastic wrap, and chill overnight.

When ready to serve, remove the sides of the pan and transfer the Rousse to a crystal serving plate. Whip the remaining cup of cream with the mixer till stiff peaks form, spread evenly over the top, and decorate with the strawberries.

YIELD 6 to 8 servings

PEARL'S SNOW CREAM WITH RASPBERRY SAUCE

Although Pearl Byrd Foster hailed proudly from a distinguished family in Virginia, she spent much of her long life as the dynamic, demanding proprietor and chef of a famous little restaurant in Manhattan called Mr. & Mrs. Foster's Place. She was an important mentor to me back in the 1970s, when she was creating some of the most innovative American dishes ever conceived, the recipes for which she guarded scrupulously, almost defiantly. Pearl and Mother hit it off from the start as Southern ladies seriously involved in cooking, which no doubt is why Pearl eventually agreed to send her sacred and much sought-after snow cream recipe (handwritten on personalized Tiffany stationery) with the understanding that "it remain a secret till I'm gone." Today the dessert is still one of the most unusual and elegant in Mother's repertory, served only at formal dinners, as Pearl would have suggested.

For the snow cream

2 teaspoons unflavored gelatin
⅓ cup water
1 pint heavy cream
1⅓ cups superfine sugar
1⅓ cups sour cream
One 8-ounce package cream cheese, softened
2 teaspoons pure vanilla extract

For the sauce

One 10-ounce package frozen raspberries, thawed
1¼ teaspoons cornstarch, dissolved in ¾ cup water
⅔ cup granulated sugar
3 tablespoons orange liqueur

1⅓ cups heavy cream, whipped to stiff peaks

To make the snow cream, sprinkle the gelatin over the water in a small bowl and let soften for 3 minutes.

In a large, heavy saucepan, bring the heavy cream to a boil, then remove from the heat, add the gelatin mixture, and stir till it is completely dissolved. Add the superfine sugar, stir till well blended, and let the mixture cool. Add the sour cream, cream cheese, and vanilla and whisk the mixture till very smooth. Scrape the mixture into a crystal serving bowl or individual crystal serving dishes, cover with plastic wrap, and chill till firm, about 2 hours.

To make the sauce, combine the raspberries, dissolved cornstarch, and granulated sugar in a blender, blend till very smooth, and push through a sieve, to remove the seeds, into a saucepan. Heat the mixture over low heat, stirring constantly, till it thickens. Remove from the heat. Add the liqueur, stir till well blended, and chill the sauce till ready to serve.

Serve the snow cream with one or two tablespoons of sauce spooned over each portion and topped with dollops of whipped cream.

YIELD **8 servings**

MISS LUCY'S WINE JELLY

*W*ine jelly is unique to the South, a zesty, elegant, very light congealed dessert often served with butter cookies at formal dinners. This particular version goes back some sixty years to when Mother, a young bride, was being trained to teach Sunday school and attended a dinner for upcoming teachers in the old Colonial home of the head of Charlotte's primary school department. "Miss Lucy, a real grande dame and fierce taskmaster, also happened to be a very good cook, and when she served this jelly, I stayed head over heels till I finally got up the nerve to ask her for the recipe. And in all these years, I've never once modified an ingredient or procedure."

2 envelopes unflavored gelatin
1½ cups water
2 lemons
1 orange
1¼ cups granulated sugar
1 cup sweet sherry
½ cup red port
1 cup heavy cream, whipped to stiff peaks, or Custard Sauce (page 261)

*I*n a small bowl, sprinkle the gelatin over ½ cup of the water and let soften. Cut thin strips of rind from the lemons and orange and set aside. Squeeze enough juice from the lemons and orange into a bowl to measure ½ cup and set aside.

*I*n a medium-size heavy saucepan, combine the remaining cup of water, the lemon and orange strips, and sugar, bring to a boil over moderate heat, and stir for 5 minutes. Remove the pan from the heat, strain the contents into a medium-size mixing bowl, and stir in the gelatin mixture. Let cool, then stir in the lemon and orange juice, sherry, and port. Pour into eight stemmed crystal glasses and chill till firm, at least 4 hours. To serve, spoon a dollop of whipped cream or custard sauce over each portion.

YIELD **8 servings**

BABY PECAN TASSIES

A sure hit at Mother's cocktail parties, these tiny tassies are unusual, mainly because of the sapid cream cheese crust. This is one dessert recipe that Mother is constantly modifying: a splash of sour cream added to the creamed cheese mixture, more or less vanilla and pecans, extra butter in the filling. "It's not that the basic recipe doesn't produce good tassies," she tries to explain, "but, for some reason, I always think I can make them taste even better." So feel free to experiment—within reason.

One 3-ounce package cream cheese, softened
½ cup (1 stick) plus 1 tablespoon butter, softened
1 cup all-purpose flour
1 large egg
1 cup firmly packed light brown sugar
1 teaspoon pure vanilla extract
⅛ teaspoon salt
¾ cup coarsely chopped pecans

In a medium-size mixing bowl, cream the cream cheese and ½ cup of the butter together with an electric mixer, then gradually add the flour and mix well to form a firm, smooth dough. Cover with plastic wrap and chill for 1 hour.

Preheat the oven to 325°F.

Remove the chilled dough from the refrigerator and, with your hands, roll into twenty-four 1-inch balls. Place the balls in twenty-four ungreased 1¾-inch mini muffin tins and press the dough against the sides and bottoms of each tin.

Wash and dry the mixer beaters. In a medium-size mixing bowl, combine the egg, brown sugar, the remaining tablespoon of butter, the vanilla, and salt and beat with the mixer till smooth. Sprinkle about half of the pecans into the bottoms of the prepared tins, fill each with an equal amount of the egg mixture, and sprinkle the remaining nuts over the tops. Bake till the filling is just set, about 25 minutes. Let them cool completely before removing from the tins.

YIELD 2 dozen small tassies

Martha's Sweet Note

I always keep my hands lightly floured while rolling dough into balls to make certain cookies. Likewise, if the balls have to be pressed out slightly or indented (as with Jimbo Treats, page 227) before baking, I make sure my fingers are floured to combat the stickiness and prevent possible unsightly cracks and splits in the dough.

COCKTAIL BRANDY-RUM BALLS

Quite frankly, I've never understood the way Southerners absolutely relish these sorts of sweet confections with cocktails, a character fault on my part, no doubt, that has led Mother more than once to scowl, "You've just become too much of a Yankee!" The irony is that I love these sweets with Mother's subtle blend of honey, rum, and brandy, but I much prefer to serve them with cookies as a simple dessert. In any case, when Mother makes these balls for her cocktail parties (and, believe me, they're gone in no time), she always makes enough extra ones to add to her fancy gift jars with decorative ribbons intended for special friends.

Two 7½-ounce packages vanilla wafers, crushed into fine crumbs
½ cup honey
½ cup light or dark rum
⅓ cup brandy
1 pound walnut pieces, finely ground
Vegetable oil
Granulated sugar for rolling

In a large mixing bowl, combine the wafer crumbs, honey, rum, brandy, and walnuts and mix till well blended. Rub a little vegetable oil on your hands and roll small pieces of the mixture between your palms to form balls about the size of large marbles. Roll each ball in granulated sugar and store in an airtight container up to 2 weeks.

YIELD About 55 balls

Morning Coffees, Afternoon Teas

&

Weekend Brunches

Mama's Solarium Lemon Cheese Cake

Sour Cream Coffee Cake

Banana-Chocolate Coffee Cake

Orange-Cranberry Tea Bread

Strawberry Preserve Breakfast Tart

Jelly-Filled Brunch Muffins

Lemon Drop Cookies

Lace Cookies

Fancy Coffee-Almond Parfaits

Polished Poached Oranges

Spiced Dried Fruit Compote

As if breakfast, bridge and charity lunches, cocktail parties, and various dinners were not enough food events to fill Mother's day, she also sponsors any number of informal morning coffees and afternoon teas to celebrate one happening or another, to work with friends on diverse projects, or simply to be with someone she hasn't seen in a long time. Typically, her coffees take place at about ten A.M. and last as long as it takes to catch up on gossip and finish a small coffee cake, or fruit preserve tart, or elegant parfaits. Afternoon tea is usually at four o'clock sharp and involves such delicacies as her Orange-Cranberry Tea Bread, Lemon Cheese Cake, and/or cookies. And don't forget that in the South it is not only traditional but socially acceptable for friends to just drop in "to visit" at any time of day, in which case Mother is forever ready to put on a pot of coffee or tea and open a few tins of homemade goodies.

When my daddy was alive, weekend brunches at the house were almost a bimonthly ritual, entailing lots of guests, big crystal bowls of his potent punch, and Mother's buffet groaning with fancy egg dishes, two or three types of meat, casseroles, salads and fresh fruits, breads and coffee cakes, and even rich pies and tarts. Today, Mother can still serve a pretty prodigious Sunday brunch when there's reason for celebration (a wedding or graduation, family or friends in from out of town, a successful church pledge drive), but generally she now prefers a more subdued affair on Saturdays featuring a nice egg dish, poached or dried fruit preparations, perhaps her warm Jelly-Filled Muffins, and certainly a beautiful coffee cake (with homemade preserves on the side).

MAMA'S SOLARIUM LEMON CHEESE CAKE

*N*obody loved the ceremony of afternoon tea like my Georgia grandmother, and none of her "sweets" was so popular with the ladies as the lemon cheese cake she taught Mother how to bake. When Maw Maw finally had to go into a nursing home in her nineties, what she asked Mother for most was this tart cake, which she would take into the solarium and serve her friends and nurses at "tea parties" just like those she had held at home. Mother once asked Maw Maw why she called the dessert a "cheese cake" when it didn't contain a trace of cheese, only to have her mother give the very sensible response, "Because it's the color of cheese." Nobody ever argued with Maw Maw, no matter how absurd her culinary wisdom, and the name has stuck to this day.

For the cake

6 large egg whites (yolks reserved)
1 cup (2 sticks) butter, softened
2 cups granulated sugar
3 cups all-purpose flour
2 teaspoons baking powder
¼ teaspoon salt
1 cup milk
1½ teaspoons pure lemon extract

For the frosting

1½ cups granulated sugar
3 rounded tablespoons all-purpose flour
6 large egg yolks, slightly beaten
1 cup milk
2 tablespoons butter
Grated rind of 2 lemons
½ cup fresh lemon juice

*P*reheat the oven to 350°F. Grease and flour four shallow 8-inch baking pans, tapping out any excess flour, and set aside.

*T*o make the cake, beat the egg whites with an electric mixer in a large mixing bowl till stiff peaks form and set aside.

*I*n another large mixing bowl, cream the butter and sugar together with the mixer till light and fluffy. Into a medium-size bowl, sift together the flour, baking powder, and salt. In a small bowl, combine the milk and lemon extract and mix well. Add the dry ingredients and milk mixture alternately to the creamed mixture and stir with a wooden spoon till well blended. With a rubber spatula, gently fold in the egg whites, then divide the batter among the prepared baking pans. Bake till a cake tester or straw inserted in the center comes out clean, about 20 minutes, remove the pans from the oven, and let cool.

*T*o make the frosting, combine all the ingredients in a large, heavy saucepan and stir slowly over low heat till thickened enough to spread. Remove the cake layers from the pans and spread the frosting evenly between the layers, on top, and around the sides of the cake.

YIELD One 4-layer 8-inch cake; 10 to 12 servings

SOUR CREAM COFFEE CAKE

This, in Mother's opinion, is the queen of all coffee cakes and the one that usually joins company with the Champagne punch, egg, sausage, and grits casserole, country ham biscuits, fried green tomatoes, fresh fruit compote, and strawberry preserves at one of her more elaborate Sunday brunches. It's not the easiest coffee cake to make, but if you love fresh coffee cake, you'll remember this one for a long time. Best of all, it freezes beautifully and can be reheated in a matter of ten to fifteen minutes.

3 cups all-purpose flour
1½ teaspoons baking powder
1½ teaspoons baking soda
¼ teaspoon salt
1½ cups (3 sticks) butter, softened
1½ cups granulated sugar
2½ teaspoons pure vanilla extract, plus 2 tablespoons pure vanilla extract combined with 2 tablespoons water
3 large eggs
1½ cups sour cream
¾ cup chopped walnuts
¾ cup firmly packed dark brown sugar
1½ teaspoons ground cinnamon
Confectioners' sugar for dusting

*P*reheat the oven to 350°F. Generously grease a 10-inch Bundt or tube pan and set aside.

*I*n a medium-size mixing bowl, combine the flour, baking powder, baking soda, and salt, mix till well blended, and set aside. In a large mixing bowl, cream the butter and granulated sugar together with an electric mixer till light and fluffy, then add the 2½ teaspoons vanilla and the eggs, beating well after each addition. Gradually beat in the sour cream, then add the flour mixture and beat till the mixture is well blended. In a small bowl, combine the walnuts, brown sugar, and cinnamon and mix well.

*S*poon one third of the batter into the prepared pan and sprinkle half of the nut mixture over the surface, taking care not to sprinkle all the way to the edges of the pan (which could cause the cake to break when turned out). Repeat with the second third of the batter and the remaining nut mixture, and top with the remaining batter. Spoon the vanilla-water mixture evenly over the top and bake the cake in the center of the oven for 30 minutes. Reduce the heat to 325°F and continue baking till the cake feels quite firm and a cake tester or straw inserted in the center comes out clean, about 45 minutes. Cool the coffee cake on a wire rack for 10 minutes before loosening the edges with a knife and turning it out onto a serving plate. Let cool completely and dust with confectioners' sugar just before serving in wedges.

YIELD One 10-inch Bundt or tube cake; 10 to 12 servings

BANANA-CHOCOLATE COFFEE CAKE

*M*other no longer serves many Sunday brunches, but when she does, it can be a production. Typically, she and friends will go to early church, after which she returns home to cook and await their arrival for Bloody Marys or mimosas on the sun porch at about eleven A.M. Then, shortly after noon, everybody partakes of a buffet that might include cheese and eggs or vegetable omelettes, creamed chipped beef, grits soufflé, fresh fruit, chicory coffee, and, perched on a crystal cake pedestal, Mother's popular banana-chocolate coffee cake, prepared the day before. So delicious is this coffee cake that I've been known to serve it for dessert at casual dinner parties.

Unsweetened cocoa powder for dusting plus ½ cup
1¼ cups all-purpose flour
1 teaspoon baking powder
½ teaspoon baking soda
¼ teaspoon salt
½ cup (1 stick) butter, softened, or ½ cup Crisco shortening
1 cup firmly packed dark brown sugar
1 teaspoon instant coffee granules
2 large eggs, well beaten
1 cup peeled and mashed bananas
One 6-ounce bag (1 cup) semisweet chocolate chips

*P*reheat the oven to 325°F. Grease and dust with cocoa powder a 10-inch Bundt pan, tapping out any excess cocoa, and set aside.

*I*n a medium-size mixing bowl, combine the flour, ½ cup cocoa powder, baking powder, baking soda, and salt, mix well, and set aside.

*I*n a large mixing bowl, cream together with an electric mixer the butter, brown sugar, and instant coffee till smooth. Add the eggs and mashed bananas and mix well with a wooden spoon. Add the dry ingredients and mix well with the spoon, then fold in the chocolate chips. Scrape the batter into the prepared pan. Bake till a cake tester or straw inserted in the center comes out clean, about 45 minutes, let cool in the pan, and invert onto a large plate.

YIELD One 10-inch Bundt cake; 10 to 12 servings

ORANGE-CRANBERRY TEA BREAD

*M*other makes this delectable sweet bread year-round to serve at afternoon tea socials for her lady friends, but the time of year she really produces the bread in quantity is at Thanksgiving and Christmas, when fresh cranberries are plentiful and she makes the bread in small aluminum tins to give away as holiday gifts. She actually developed this recipe as a modified fruit-cake made tart with the cranberries, and she almost insists that it should be heated slightly to bring out the blend of flavors. I personally love to toast the bread for breakfast.

1 cup granulated sugar
¼ cup (½ stick) butter, melted
4 large eggs
Grated rind of 2 medium-size oranges
3 cups all-purpose flour
2 teaspoons baking powder
2 teaspoons baking soda
2 teaspoons ground cinnamon
1 teaspoon salt
1 cup fresh orange juice
1 cup fresh cranberries, stemmed, rinsed, and patted dry
1 cup chopped walnuts
1 cup seedless golden raisins

*P*reheat the oven to 350°F. Butter and flour two medium-size loaf pans, tapping out any excess flour, and set aside.

*I*n a large mixing bowl, combine the sugar, butter, eggs, and orange rind and beat with an electric mixer till well blended and smooth. In a medium-size mixing bowl, combine the flour, baking powder, baking soda, cinnamon, and salt, then add the dry ingredients alternately with the orange juice to the egg mixture, beating till well blended. Stir in the cranberries, walnuts, and raisins, then scrape the batter evenly into the prepared pans and bake till a cake tester or straw inserted in the center comes out clean, about 1¼ hours. Cool the loaves in the pans for about 10 minutes, then turn them out onto a wire rack to cool completely. Serve the bread at room temperature or reheated, with a little butter spread over the top.

YIELD **2 medium-size loaves**

STRAWBERRY PRESERVE BREAKFAST TART

*B*reakfast in Mother's (and my) home has always been a royal production, an affair often just as elaborate as brunch (especially when guests are invited), involving platters of fresh fruit, eggs, meats, grits, biscuits, and homemade preserves—every morning, any morning. Mother originally came up with this tasty tart to appeal to children not interested in omelettes, country ham, and the like, but today I notice that adults are the first to sneak a wedge. You can use any preserves (damson, peach, apricot, raspberry), and if Mother knows that certain children are particularly picky, she will even make the tart with grape jelly. She often serves this tart at one of her morning coffee socials.

¼ cup all-purpose flour
1¼ cups granulated sugar
2 tablespoons butter, melted
¾ cup strawberry preserves
1 tablespoon grated orange rind
1 cup tepid water
3 large eggs, beaten
One 9-inch Basic Pie Shell (page 243), prebaked for 5 minutes

*P*reheat the oven to 350°F.

*I*n a medium-size mixing bowl, combine the flour and sugar and mix till well blended. Add the butter and stir till the mixture is crumbly. In a small mixing bowl, combine the preserves, orange rind, and water and stir till syrupy, then add to the flour mixture and stir till well blended. Add the eggs and stir till well blended and smooth. Scrape the batter into the pie shell and bake till the crust is nicely browned and the middle of the tart is firm, about 25 minutes. Serve the tart warm.

YIELD One 9-inch tart; 6 servings

JELLY-FILLED BRUNCH MUFFINS

Years ago, Mother came up with these unusual muffins as a means to use up the syrupy remains in the jars of her homemade fruit preserves, and almost immediately they became a staple on her weekend brunch buffets (elegantly presented in a silver wire basket with a linen roll cover). The muffins can be made with any fruit jelly, jam, or preserves. Since the jam/jelly/preserves could ooze out of the muffins while baking, it's both easier and neater to use paper muffin cups. The muffins can be served at room temperature, but they're much better eaten warm.

4 cups all-purpose flour
½ cup granulated sugar
2 tablespoons baking powder
1 teaspoon salt
2 large eggs, slightly beaten
2 cups milk
½ cup (1 stick) butter, melted
Fruit jelly, jam, or preserves

Preheat the oven to 400°F. Line three 6-cup muffin tins with paper muffin cups and set aside.

In a large mixing bowl, combine the flour, sugar, baking powder, and salt, mix well, and set aside. In a medium-size bowl, combine the eggs, milk, and butter and mix well. Make a well in the center of the dry ingredients, pour in the liquid ingredients, and gradually stir just till the dry ingredients are moistened. Fill each prepared muffin cup one-quarter full with the batter. Spoon about 1 teaspoon of jelly into the center of each muffin cup and spoon the remaining batter over the jelly, filling each cup about half full. Bake till a cake tester or straw inserted in the center comes out clean, 20 to 25 minutes. Immediately remove the muffins from the tins.

YIELD **18 muffins**

LEMON DROP COOKIES

*M*other loves lemon in any form, and though at first I snickered when she said she'd come up with these unusual cookies to serve at her afternoon teas ("Basically, I wanted to add a little crunch to plain old lemon snaps"), the second I tasted a chewy one, I proclaimed it delicious—and intriguing. Do make the effort to find pure (not artificial) lemon drop candy, and since the drops do not melt while baking, be sure to crush them very fine—"unless you want to risk breaking a tooth," Mother advises casually. (To crush the candy, wrap in a clean towel and beat with a hammer.) I like these cookies with any chocolate, coffee, or nut ice cream.

½ cup (1 stick) butter, softened
¾ cup granulated sugar
1 large egg
1 teaspoon grated lemon rind
1 tablespoon heavy cream
1½ cups all-purpose flour
1 teaspoon baking powder
½ teaspoon salt
½ cup (one 6½-ounce package) pure lemon drop candy, very finely crushed

*P*reheat the oven to 350°F. Grease a large baking sheet and set aside.

*I*n a large mixing bowl, cream the butter and sugar together with an electric mixer till light and fluffy, then add the egg and beat till well blended. Add the lemon rind and cream and stir till well blended. In a small mixing bowl, combine the flour, baking powder, and salt and mix well, then add to the creamed mixture and stir till well blended. Add the crushed candy and stir till well blended. Drop the batter by the teaspoon about 1 inch apart onto the prepared baking sheet and bake till lightly browned around the edges, about 10 minutes. Let the cookies cool completely before removing from the sheet.

YIELD About 3 dozen cookies

LACE COOKIES

*T*hese delicate cookies hail from friends in Mississippi and are perfect with afternoon tea or at ice cream socials. Mother can't emphasize enough how careful you need to be when peeling the cookies off the foil (if you rush, they'll come apart in pieces), and since they harden very quickly and don't resoften well in tins even when a piece of fresh bread is added, the cookies should be served as soon after baking as possible. I also like them made with maple instead of vanilla extract.

2 cups old-fashioned rolled oats
2 cups firmly packed light brown sugar
2 tablespoons all-purpose flour
½ teaspoon salt
1 cup (2 sticks) butter
1 large egg, beaten
1 teaspoon pure vanilla extract

*P*reheat the oven to 375°F. Line a large baking sheet with greased aluminum foil and set aside.

*I*n a large mixing bowl, combine the oats, brown sugar, flour, and salt, mix well, and set aside. In a medium-size, heavy saucepan set over moderate heat, melt the butter till very hot but not bubbly, pour over the oat mixture, and stir till the sugar is dissolved. Add the egg and vanilla and stir till well blended. Drop the batter by a slightly rounded ¼ teaspoon at least 2 inches apart onto the baking sheet and bake the cookies till slightly browned, about 7 minutes. When the cookies are cool enough to handle, carefully peel them off the foil and let them completely cool on a wire rack before serving.

YIELD About 2 dozen cookies

FANCY COFFEE-ALMOND PARFAITS

*L*et a friend report a new grandchild, or have a neighbor return from a long trip, or hear that a church fund-raising canvas has surpassed its goal, and Mother will have reason to celebrate the occasion by hostessing a late-morning coffee. Generally, she serves shortbread, muffins, coffee cake, or gingerbread at her coffee socials, but when the celebration is really special, something like these fancy little parfaits are more in order. "People just rave about them," she boasts, "but the truth is, they're so simple a child could make them."

1 pint heavy cream
½ cup confectioners' sugar, sifted
½ cup coffee liqueur
½ gallon coffee ice cream
1 cup toasted (see Sweet Note on page 65) and chopped almonds

*I*n a large mixing bowl, combine the heavy cream, confectioners' sugar, and ¼ cup of the liqueur and whisk vigorously till well blended.

*F*ill eight parfait glasses half full with the ice cream and spoon equal amounts of the cream mixture into each glass. Sprinkle the chopped nuts over the cream, then spoon equal amounts of the remaining ¼ cup liqueur over the top of each parfait. Serve the parfaits well chilled.

YIELD 8 individual parfaits

POLISHED POACHED ORANGES

*T*his is not only one of the simplest and cleverest brunch dishes you can serve but one that Mother is constantly modifying by using different liqueurs and extracts and adding other compatible flavoring agents, such as chopped toasted nuts sprinkled over the tops. You really can't baste these oranges enough—the more "polished," the better.

8 medium-size navel oranges
2 cups granulated sugar
1 cup water
3 tablespoons orange liqueur
2 teaspoons pure maple extract

*P*eel the oranges without pulling them into sections, remove and discard all traces of white pith, and then cut enough of the rind into thin slivers to measure about ¼ cup.

*I*n a large, heavy nonreactive saucepan, combine the rind slivers, sugar, and water, bring to a low boil, and cook, without stirring, till the syrup thickens slightly, about 8 minutes. Arrange half of the oranges in the syrup, reduce the heat to low, and cook for 5 minutes, basting the oranges constantly with the hot syrup. Transfer the oranges to a large serving dish and repeat the procedure with the remaining oranges. Remove the pan from the heat, add the liqueur and extract to the remaining syrup, stir till well blended, and pour over the oranges.

*C*over the oranges with plastic wrap and chill for 2 hours, basting them occasionally with the syrup, before serving.

YIELD **8 servings**

MANGO ICE CREAM

Although Mother has always loved to eat mangoes while traveling in tropical and subtropical climes, they never figured in her cooking for the simple reason that they weren't widely available in Charlotte till a few years ago. Once she could lay hands on the luscious fruit, however, the first thing she did was turn it into this refreshing ice cream—and to great acclaim at a neighborhood social. Do notice that there is no cooked custard in the ice cream— the eggs are raw. So isn't Mother afraid of the possibility of salmonella and who knows what else in these vigilant times? "Oh, sure I'm aware," she allows, "but I've been cooking with raw eggs for over sixty years, my eggs are always fresh and well refrigerated, and I'm still around to tell about it."

4 large, ripe mangoes, peeled, pitted, and cut into chunks
Juice of 2 limes
Grated rind of 1 lime
2 cups granulated sugar
3 large egg yolks, beaten
5 cups half-and-half
½ teaspoon pure vanilla extract

In a blender or food processor, combine the mangoes, lime juice, and rind and process till very smooth. Transfer the puree to a large mixing bowl, add the sugar, egg yolks, half-and-half, and vanilla, and stir till well blended and smooth. Scrape the mixture into the container of an electric ice cream freezer and freeze according to the manufacturer's directions. (Or scrape the mixture into a large bowl, whisk briskly till very smooth, cover, and freeze in the refrigerator freezer.) Serve as soon as the ice cream is frozen.

YIELD About ½ gallon ice cream; at least 8 servings

SPICED DRIED FRUIT COMPOTE

Since today dried fruits are high as a cat's back in price, Mother rarely buys them, but when more reckless and loving friends give her a big Christmas basket of dried figs, apricots, and the like, you can rest assured that the luscious fruits will show up in this spicy compote on her next weekend brunch buffet. And what's also nice is that any leftover fruits keep, covered, in the refrigerator for weeks. Do be sure to serve this compote at room temperature so that the fruits exhibit their full flavors.

½ pound *each* dried apricots, figs, pears, and peaches
3 cups water
1 cup dry white wine
4 thin lemon slices, seeded
One 3-inch cinnamon stick
½ cup honey
¼ cup dark rum
¼ teaspoon ground allspice

In a large, nonreactive saucepan, combine the fruits, add the water, wine, lemon slices, and cinnamon stick, and stir well. Bring to a boil, then reduce the heat to low and simmer till the fruits begin to swell, about 20 minutes. With a slotted spoon, transfer the fruits to a plate.

Add the honey, rum, and allspice to the saucepan, increase the heat to high, and cook, stirring, till the liquid is reduced by half. Return the fruits to the saucepan, stir well, remove from the heat, and let cool completely. Transfer the fruits and liquid to a deep serving dish, cover with plastic wrap, and chill overnight. Bring the fruits back to room temperature before serving with a slotted spoon.

YIELD At least 8 servings

Ice Cream Socials

of Benne Cookies (page 230), Peanut Butter Oatmeal Cookies (page 117), Jimbo Treats (page 227), and Gingersnaps (page 147).

Finally, Mother wouldn't dream of hosting an ice cream social without the appropriate clear glass or cut-crystal dishes, small silver spoons, and large cloth napkins for catching inevitable spills and drips. And the best way to serve the ice cream itself? Directly from the ice-cold metal canister in the churn.

Martha's Sweet Note

To avoid having to repack ice cream made in an electric freezer with ice and salt, simply place the ice cream container in the refrigerator freezer (if there is sufficient space) or transfer the ice cream to a plastic carton and store in the freezer (for up to 2 weeks).

CAROLINA PEACH ICE CREAM

If my mother is an author-
ity on anything, the subject
she could almost write a
book about is peaches. And
never is she touchier about
peaches than when she
makes this celestial ice
cream from July through
September, refusing to use
June cling peaches ("too
small and not juicy
enough") and traveling
down to South Carolina to
buy freestone Elbertas by
the peck the day the picking starts. Remember to
look for peaches that have
fuzz and no blemishes and
are ripe (but not too soft)
and juicy. We usually serve
this ice cream with plain
Pound Cake (page 238).

6 large fresh, ripe peaches
1½ cups granulated sugar
3 large eggs
2 cups half-and-half
2 tablespoons cornstarch
Dash of salt
1 pint heavy cream
2 tablespoons pure vanilla extract

*P*eel (see Sweet Note on page 76) and pit the peaches, cut them
into small pieces, and place half the pieces in a medium-size mixing
bowl. Add 1 cup of the sugar and stir till the sugar is dissolved.
Cover the peaches tightly with plastic wrap and let stand in the
refrigerator for at least 2 hours. In another bowl, mash the remaining peaches with a heavy fork and refrigerate with the peach pieces.

*I*n a large, heavy saucepan, whisk the eggs till frothy, add the half-
and-half, and whisk till well blended. In a small bowl, combine the
cornstarch, the remaining ½ cup sugar, and the salt, mix till well
blended, and gradually whisk this into the egg mixture. Cook the
mixture over low heat, stirring constantly, till the custard thickens
slightly. Remove the pan from the heat, let cool, cover, and chill for
2 hours.

*I*n a bowl, combine the mashed peaches, heavy cream, and vanilla,
add this to the cold custard, and stir till well blended. Pour the mixture into the container of an electric ice cream freezer and freeze
according to the manufacturer's directions. When the ice cream is
frozen (it will still be slightly soft), remove the dasher and stir the
peach pieces and any juice into the ice cream. Cover the container,
pack more ice and ice cream salt around the container, and allow the
ice cream to mellow for 2 to 3 hours before serving.

YIELD About ¾ gallon ice cream; 12 to 15 servings

GINGERED PEACH ICE CREAM

*M*other got the idea for this tangy peach ice cream when she once grated fresh ginger into the filling for a peach pie. The ice cream is not quite as rich and full-bodied as her traditional Carolina classic, but when she serves it at one of her backyard socials—with various cookies—people rave over it. Follow the advice about peaches provided in the headnote to Carolina Peach Ice Cream (page 211).

10 medium-size fresh, ripe peaches, peeled (see Sweet Note on page 76), pitted, sliced, and mashed (about 6 cups)
2½ cups granulated sugar
3 large eggs
2 tablespoons all-purpose flour
½ teaspoon salt
1 quart milk
1 cup heavy cream
½ cup peeled and finely chopped fresh ginger

*I*n a large mixing bowl, combine the peaches and 1 cup of the sugar, stir till well blended, and set aside.

*I*n a large, heavy saucepan, beat the eggs with an electric mixer till frothy. In a small mixing bowl, combine the remaining 1½ cups sugar, the flour, and salt, mix well, and gradually add to the eggs, beating till thickened. Add the milk and stir well. Cook the mixture over low heat, stirring constantly till the custard thickens enough to coat a spoon, about 12 minutes. Remove the pan from the heat, place it in a large bowl of ice water, and stir till completely cooled. Add the peaches, cream, and ginger, stir till well blended, pour into the container of an ice cream freezer, and freeze according to the manufacturer's directions. When frozen, remove the dasher, cover the container, pack more ice and ice cream salt around the container, and allow the ice cream to mellow for 2 to 3 hours before serving.

YIELD About 1 gallon ice cream; at least 15 servings

STRAWBERRY ICE CREAM

Notice that Mother does not use an egg custard to make strawberry ice cream, which she feels would detract from the brilliant taste of the berries. Likewise, she has learned that nothing balances the ultra-sweetness of fully ripe, fresh strawberries like lemon juice. When picking or shopping for strawberries, forget the (false) notion that smaller berries are necessarily sweeter, and concentrate on large, plump berries that are bloodred and firm—with not a trace of green or white. After rinsing strawberries to be used to make ice cream, drain them thoroughly on paper towels to prevent "icy" ice cream and guarantee creaminess. Mother and I agree that nothing goes better with homemade strawberry ice cream than her Coconut Pound Cake (page 109) or Snowflake Coconut Cake (page 106).

5 pints fresh, ripe strawberries, rinsed, hulled, and patted dry
1¾ cups granulated sugar
1 pint half-and-half
1 pint heavy cream
½ cup fresh lemon juice

*I*n a large mixing bowl, mash the berries well with a fork, add the sugar, and stir till well blended. Add the half-and-half, cream, and lemon juice and stir till thoroughly blended. Cover the bowl with plastic wrap and chill for at least 2 hours.

*S*crape the mixture into the container of an ice cream freezer and freeze according to the manufacturer's directions. When the ice cream is frozen, remove the dasher, cover the container, pack more ice and ice cream salt around the container, and allow the ice cream to mellow for 2 to 3 hours before serving.

YIELD About 1 gallon ice cream; about 15 servings

CLASSIC VANILLA ICE CREAM

All I can say is that once you've tasted home-made vanilla ice cream, eating the commercial stuff is a monumental bore. Mother often tops cobblers, pies, and puddings with this ice cream, and at socials she usually serves a chocolate, butterscotch, or mocha sauce (see pages 255 or 257) to be spooned over the creamy scoops.

1 quart milk
4 large eggs
2 cups granulated sugar
2 tablespoons all-purpose flour
½ teaspoon salt
1 quart half-and-half
1 quart heavy cream
4 teaspoons pure vanilla extract

In a large, heavy saucepan, scald the milk over moderate heat (see Sweet Note on page 18). In a medium-size bowl, combine the eggs, sugar, flour, and salt and whisk till well blended. Whisking constantly, gradually add the scalded milk to the egg mixture, then return the mixture to the saucepan and cook over low heat till slightly thickened, about 10 minutes. Remove the pan from the heat and let cool completely. Pour the custard into a large mixing bowl, cover, and chill for at least 3 hours.

Remove the bowl from the refrigerator, add the half-and-half, cream, and vanilla, and stir till well blended. Scrape the custard into the container of an electric ice cream freezer and freeze according to the manufacturer's directions. When the ice cream is frozen, remove the dasher, cover the container, pack more ice and ice cream salt around the container, and allow the ice cream to mellow for 2 to 3 hours before serving.

YIELD About 1 gallon ice cream; at least 15 servings

Martha's Sweet Note

To make plain ice cream very special, I often spoon a sauce (see pages 255–262) over it and add toasted nuts.

CRUNCHY PEANUT BUTTER ICE CREAM

*T*his ice cream is so rich it'll take the top off your head," Mother quips without apology. Of course children love it, but since Mother's convinced that they don't appreciate the peanut crunch the way adults do, she will use smooth peanut butter when she knows there'll be lots of kids at a social. Any chocolate cookie goes perfectly with this ice cream.

1½ cups crunchy peanut butter
Two 15-ounce cans sweetened condensed milk
Two 13-ounce cans evaporated milk
2 tablespoons pure vanilla extract

*I*n the top of a double boiler, melt the peanut butter over briskly simmering (not boiling) water and remove from the heat.

*I*n a large mixing bowl, combine the condensed milk, evaporated milk, and vanilla and stir till well blended. Add the melted peanut butter and stir till well blended and smooth. Scrape the mixture into the container of an electric ice cream freezer and freeze according to the manufacturer's directions. When the ice cream is frozen, remove the dasher, cover the container, pack more ice and ice cream salt around the container, and let the ice cream mellow for 2 to 3 hours before serving.

YIELD About 1 gallon ice cream; at least 15 servings

COCONUT-PINEAPPLE ICE CREAM

Although it's best to use fresh coconut in this ice cream, Mother says that frozen or sweetened flaked coconut is "acceptable" so long as you reduce the sugar in the recipe by a half cup. On the other hand, since fresh pineapple is much too coarse and difficult to crush properly, always use the canned product. This is a truly remarkable ice cream.

1½ cups grated fresh coconut (see Sweet Note on page 17)
6 cups milk
2 cups granulated sugar
5 large egg yolks
1½ cups canned crushed pineapple, drained
1 pint heavy cream
2 teaspoons pure almond extract

In a large bowl, combine the coconut and milk, stir well, and chill for 1 hour.

In a large, heavy, nonreactive saucepan, beat the sugar and egg yolks together with an electric mixer till frothy, then add the coconut mixture and cook over low heat, stirring constantly, till the custard thickens slightly, about 10 minutes. Remove the pan from the heat, place in a larger pan or bowl of ice water, and stir till completely cooled. Add the pineapple, cream, and extract and stir till well blended, then scrape the mixture into the container of an electric ice cream freezer and freeze according to the manufacturer's directions. When the ice cream is frozen, remove the dasher, cover the container, pack more ice and ice cream salt around the container, and allow the ice cream to mellow for 2 to 3 hours before serving.

YIELD About 1 gallon ice cream; at least 15 servings

BIG PUDDIN'S FRUIT ICE CREAM

*T*his recipe comes from one of Mother's neighbors and dearest friends, Ann Scarborough, who, in turn, got it from the Mississippi grandmother she called Big Puddin. Apparently, Big Puddin was sick and tired of the same old ice creams served at Sunday socials, so one hot summer afternoon when she had invited friends over to the big house for "something cool and refreshing," she created this unusual ice cream on the spot with ingredients she found in the kitchen.

3 medium-size oranges, well rinsed
3 lemons, well rinsed
One 15-ounce can crushed pineapple, drained
2 cups granulated sugar
One 5-ounce can condensed milk
1 pint heavy cream
1 quart half-and-half

*G*rate the rinds of the oranges and lemons onto a plate, then squeeze the juice from them all into a bowl.

*I*n a large mixing bowl, combine the rinds and juices, add the pineapple and sugar, and stir till well blended. Add the condensed milk, cream, and half-and-half and stir till well blended. Scrape the mixture into the container of an electric ice cream freezer and freeze according to the manufacturer's directions. When the ice cream is frozen, remove the dasher, cover the container, pack more ice and ice cream salt around the container, and allow to mellow for 2 to 3 hours before serving.

YIELD About 1 gallon ice cream; at least 15 servings

MOUNT PLEASANT BUTTERMILK ICE CREAM

*W*hen, some years ago, a few charming South Carolina ladies of Charleston's Junior League invited Mother, Daddy, and me to eat roasted dolphin, shrimp pie, and Huguenot torte at a beach house over in Mount Pleasant, Mother was beside herself to find out the major ingredient in the homemade ice cream served with the torte. "Why, it's just buttermilk," one young lady informed us almost timidly, "plain old buttermilk." Slightly embarrassed, Mother hastily jotted down the simple recipe and has never since stopped telling the story of that stupendous meal when she failed to recognize the flavor of the buttermilk she drinks regularly. This is one ice cream that's best just frozen in the freezer.

1 quart buttermilk (see Sweet Note on page 10)
1 pint heavy cream
1½ cups granulated sugar
1 teaspoon pure vanilla extract
¼ cup sweet white wine

*I*n a large mixing bowl, combine the buttermilk, cream, sugar, vanilla, and wine and stir till blended thoroughly. Pour the mixture into a 2-quart plastic container and place in the refrigerator freezer. When the mixture begins to freeze (after about 2 hours), remove and stir well again. Return to the freezer and freeze till almost hard, about 2 hours.

YIELD About ½ gallon ice cream; at least 8 servings

BANANA-RUM ICE CREAM

*I*t almost killed Mother to admit it, but the second she tasted my food-obsessed friend Lowell Judson's banana ice cream, she was forced to proclaim it better than the one she'd been making for decades. One secret, of course, is the rum, but after lengthy discussion with Lowell and further experimentation, she decided that what makes the ice cream's texture truly exceptional is pureeing the bananas not in a food processor or blender (which makes the pulp "too foamy"), but simply with a fork.

2 cups milk
1 pint half-and-half
1½ cups granulated sugar
6 large egg yolks, beaten
8 ripe bananas, peeled
1 tablespoon light rum

*I*n a large, heavy saucepan, combine the milk, half-and-half, sugar, and egg yolks and, stirring constantly, cook over moderately low heat till the mixture begins to thicken, 6 to 8 minutes. *(Do not let the mixture boil.)* Cool the mixture completely.

*M*eanwhile, in a large mixing bowl, mash the bananas well with a heavy fork to produce about 4 cups of puree. When the milk mixture has cooled, gradually add it to the puree. Whisk briskly and steadily to produce a smooth mixture, scrape into an electric ice cream freezer, and freeze according to the manufacturer's directions till almost frozen. Add the rum, stir well, and continue freezing till almost hard. Pack more ice and ice cream salt around the container and allow the ice cream to mellow for 2 to 3 hours before serving.

YIELD About 1 gallon ice cream; at least 15 servings

Friendship Gifts

Lunch Box Brownies

....

Aunt Ella's Buttermilk Gingerbread

....

Sassy Shortbread

....

Jimbo Treats

....

Pecan Diamonds

....

Benne Cookies

....

Maple Chocolate Meringue Fluffs

....

Fig Preserves

....

Friendship Brandied Fruit

A young friend gives birth to an eight-pound baby girl, and Mother makes sure that a large congratulatory jar of Brandied Fruit or Fig Preserves is at the house the day Mary returns from the hospital. When an elderly couple finally decides to sell their home and move into a cheery new condo, Mother wastes no time assembling a colorful tin of brownies, Benne Cookies, and Pecan Diamonds as a welcome gift when she goes to visit. And after I tell her how wonderful and caring a certain veterinarian has been when my beloved beagle has to be put down, her immediate reaction to this virtual stranger is, "I'm going to mail him a Buttermilk Gingerbread this very afternoon."

Edible sweet friendship gifts play as important a role in Mother's cooking routine as cakes and puddings do for birthdays and Charity League luncheons, her lifelong way of celebrating any special happening, expressing thanks, or simply letting someone know she's thinking about them. As a result, there's no time when her canister of Brandied Fruit resting on the counter is not three-quarters full, or when she doesn't have shortbread or gingerbread or small fruitcakes tightly sealed in one of her Tupperware containers, or when there are not at least three varieties of homemade cookies stored in tins. To see the vast array of jars and boxes and cartons and tins that cram the shelves in a closet is almost embarrassing, all just waiting to be filled with goodies, decorated with cloths and ribbons and personalized stickers, and given as gifts at the shake of a hat. To be sure, Mother is a very generous and thoughtful Southern lady, except, on occasion, when it comes to her precious jars used for preserves and other fruit preparations. "Here, honey, I thought you might enjoy this," I've heard her frankly tell very close friends a hundred times, "but remember, I'll skin you alive if you don't give me back that jar."

LUNCH BOX BROWNIES

*L*ong before Mother began making her chewy Saucepan Fudge Brownies (page 119), these were the classic ones that I could often count on being in my school lunch box when I was a child (and I was one child who relished nuts in brownies). These brownies are considerably drier and firmer than the fudge variety, making them perfect not only for lunch boxes but also as a friendship gift.

1 cup granulated sugar
½ cup (1 stick) butter, cut into pieces
3 tablespoons water
One 12-ounce bag semisweet chocolate chips
1 teaspoon pure vanilla extract
2 large eggs, beaten
1 cup all-purpose flour
½ teaspoon baking soda
½ cup chopped pecans

*I*n a medium-size, heavy saucepan, combine the sugar, butter, and water, bring slowly to a boil, and remove from the heat. Add about 1½ cups of the chocolate chips plus the vanilla and stir till the chocolate is melted and the mixture smooth. Scrape the mixture into a large mixing bowl and let cool completely.

*P*reheat the oven to 325°F. Grease a 9-inch square baking pan and set aside.

*A*dd the eggs to the cooled chocolate mixture and stir till well blended. Gradually add the flour and baking soda, stirring till the batter is smooth. Add the remaining chocolate chips and the pecans, stir till well distributed, and scrape the batter into the prepared baking pan. Bake till a cake tester or straw inserted in the center comes out clean, about 30 minutes. Cool the pan on a wire rack, then cut out square brownies.

YIELD **About 18 brownies**

AUNT ELLA'S BUTTERMILK GINGERBREAD

I've never been able to keep track of the score of Georgia aunts and uncles whom Mother and her sister used to visit regularly on their large farms near Macon and Monticello, but apparently the master cook of this brood was a certain Aunt Ella who prided herself on this spicy buttermilk gingerbread that so impressed her nieces. "I truly inherited this recipe from Aunt Ella," Mother informs, and for years she's made it a staple at christenings, graduations, wedding receptions, and any other celebratory event involving lots of guests. When she doubles the recipe for a crowd, the gingerbread is served plain, but when she includes it as part of an afternoon tea spread or small formal dinner, she spoons a little Lemon Sauce (page 256) or Hard Sauce (page 259) on top. And a nine-inch-size unsauced gingerbread also makes a nice friendship gift.

½ cup Crisco shortening
½ cup firmly packed light brown sugar
1 large egg
½ cup molasses
¾ cup buttermilk (see Sweet Note on page 10)
2 cups all-purpose flour
2 teaspoons baking powder
¼ teaspoon baking soda
½ teaspoon salt
2 teaspoons ground ginger
1 teaspoon ground cinnamon
¼ teaspoon ground allspice

*P*reheat the oven to 350°F. Grease and flour a medium baking pan and set aside.

*I*n a large mixing bowl, cream the Crisco and brown sugar together with an electric mixer till smooth and fluffy, then add the egg and beat till well blended. In a small mixing bowl, combine the molasses and buttermilk, stir till well blended, add to the creamed mixture, and beat till well blended. In another small mixing bowl, combine the flour, baking powder, baking soda, salt, ginger, cinnamon, and allspice and mix well, then add to the batter and stir till well blended. Scrape the batter into the prepared pan and bake till a cake tester or straw inserted in the center comes out clean, 40 to 45 minutes. Serve warm or at room temperature.

YIELD 8 servings

SASSY SHORTBREAD

*T*he crispy shortbread that Mother serves at morning coffees and includes in her friendship tins is called "sassy" because it's not made like traditional Scottish shortbread (which contains no eggs or vanilla and is baked in small rounds on baking sheets till just golden and cut into wedges). Given the large amount of butter, however, the confection is definitely a shortbread and shows how so many such British desserts evolved with distinct Southern accents. To prevent overmixing (which would toughen the dough), do not use an electric mixer, and to keep the squares crisp, be sure to store them in layers separated by waxed paper in airtight containers. Sometimes, Mother makes the shortbread more exotic by reducing the sugar to about three cups and adding about three quarters of a cup of sweetened flaked coconut. Now, that *is* taking liberties, but her coconut shortbread is unique.

1 pound (4 sticks) butter (no substitutes), softened
1⅓ cups granulated sugar
1 large egg
5 cups all-purpose flour
⅛ teaspoon salt
1 teaspoon pure vanilla extract

*P*reheat the oven to 300°F. Butter a large baking dish and set aside.

*I*n a large mixing bowl, combine the butter and sugar and mix with a wooden spoon till well blended. Add the egg and mix well, then gradually add the flour, stirring with the spoon or mixing with your hands till well blended and smooth. Add the salt and vanilla and continue mixing till well blended. Spread the batter evenly in the prepared dish, score the top lightly with a fork, and bake for 15 minutes. Reduce the heat to 250°F and continue baking till the shortbread is lightly browned, about 45 minutes. Let the shortbread cool in the dish, then cut into small squares.

YIELD About 5 dozen small squares

JIMBO TREATS

Since Mother had been making these buttery jelly cookies and mailing them to me ever since I left home for college, other members of the family eventually named the treats after me. And why didn't I just bake my own? For the simple (and embarrassing) reason that, till a few years ago with Mother literally standing over me and guiding every motion, any batch I tried to make came out pathetic. So here are the rules: 1) The butter and eggs must be at room temperature; 2) The batter should be beaten as little as possible—just till the ingredients are well blended; 3) Your hands must be repeatedly floured while rolling the balls to attain ultimate smoothness; and 4) The cookies must be baked only on the top rack of the oven and *not* overcooked (the texture should be cakelike). Good luck!

1½ cups (3 sticks) butter, softened
1 cup granulated sugar
4 large egg yolks
4 cups all-purpose flour
Various jellies, preserves, and marmalades

Preheat the oven to 325°F.

In a large mixing bowl, cream the butter and sugar together with an electric mixer till light and fluffy, then add the egg yolks and beat just till well blended. Gradually add the flour and beat till the dough is well blended and firm. Roll pieces of the dough into small balls about the size of a large marble between the palms of your hands and place them on ungreased large baking sheets about 1½ inches apart. Press a fingertip into the center of each and bake till dull in color, about 10 minutes. Remove the cookies from the oven, place a dollop of jelly, preserves, and marmalade in the depressions, and continue baking till the cookies are just slightly browned, about another 10 minutes. Let cool till the jelly is set.

YIELD **About 100 treats**

 *Martha's Sweet Note*

When I store most cookies and all gooey confections (especially those intended for gifts) in tins, I always separate the layers with one or two cutout pieces of waxed paper, not only to keep them from sticking to each other but to minimize unsightly crumbling. Use only waxed paper for this, not plastic wrap or even aluminum foil.

PECAN DIAMONDS

I gave Mother this recipe years ago, and, after baking up a batch of the rather elegant little diamonds, she immediately began including them in her friendship gift tins of cookies. Making the diamonds can be slightly tricky, so be sure to follow the directions to the letter. And I dare anybody to eat just one!

For the dough

⅓ cup (about ¾ stick) butter, softened
4½ tablespoons granulated sugar
3½ tablespoons Crisco shortening
1 large egg
¼ teaspoon pure vanilla extract
1½ cups all-purpose flour
½ teaspoon baking powder
¼ teaspoon salt

For the filling

1 cup (2 sticks) butter
½ cup honey
1¼ cups firmly packed light brown sugar
¼ cup granulated sugar
4 cups chopped pecans
¼ cup heavy cream

*T*o make the dough, combine the butter, granulated sugar, Crisco, egg, and vanilla in a large mixing bowl and cream with an electric mixer until light and fluffy. Sift the flour, baking powder, and salt together into a small mixing bowl and add to the creamed mixture. Stir well with a wooden spoon till the dough is smooth, cover with plastic wrap, and refrigerate overnight.

*P*reheat the oven to 350°F. Lightly grease a large baking sheet and set aside.

*D*ivide the cold dough into three equal parts, place each part between two sheets of plastic wrap, and roll into a 5 × 12-inch rectangle ⅛ inch thick. Remove the top sheet of plastic from one piece of dough, invert the dough onto the prepared baking sheet, and remove the other sheet of plastic. Repeat the procedure with the other two pieces of rolled-out dough, stacking them on the first piece of dough, then prick the top layer with a fork. Bake for 10 minutes, then let cool while you prepare the filling.

*T*o make the filling, combine the butter, honey, and both sugars in a large saucepan over moderate heat, bring the mixture to a boil, and boil for exactly 3 minutes. Remove from the heat and let cool completely. Fold in the pecans and heavy cream, then spread the mixture over the baked crust. Continue to bake till golden on top, about 35 minutes, then let cool completely and cut the confection into small diamonds.

YIELD About 100 diamonds

BENNE COOKIES

One of the many reasons we'd drive down the coast to Charleston and Savannah when I was young was so Mother could stock up on fresh benne (sesame) seeds to make these delectable cookies indigenous to the Low Country. Tinned benne cookies are available all over Charleston and Savannah, but never have I tasted a commercial one even in those gracious old towns that can compare with the fresh, delicate wonders that Mother (like home cooks we know in Charleston) makes on a regular basis. These cookies are a bit tricky to make, so follow the directions carefully.

1 cup benne (sesame) seeds
¾ cup (1½ sticks) butter, melted
1½ cups firmly packed light brown sugar
1¼ cups all-purpose flour
¼ teaspoon baking powder
¼ teaspoon salt
1 teaspoon pure vanilla extract
1 large egg

Preheat the oven to 300°F. Line a baking sheet with aluminum foil, grease the foil, and set aside.

Place the benne seeds on another baking sheet and bake till golden, 10 to 15 minutes, stirring. (Please watch them carefully, because they go from being browned to being burned in a few moments.) Remove from the oven and let cool; increase the oven temperature to 325°F.

In a large mixing bowl, combine all the remaining ingredients and stir with a wooden spoon till thoroughly blended. Drop the batter by the ½ teaspoon onto the prepared baking sheet about 1½ inches apart and bake till evenly browned (if still pale in the center and puffed, the cookies are not ready), 15 to 20 minutes, watching constantly to avoid burning. Remove from the oven, allow the cookies to cool for a few minutes, carefully peel them from the foil, and cool completely on a wire rack. When completely cooled, immediately transfer the cookies to airtight containers.

YIELD About 85 cookies

MAPLE CHOCOLATE MERINGUE FLUFFS

If ever Mother learned a good way to use up left-over egg whites to delectable advantage, it was when we had dinner at the house of a food-obsessed friend, Lowell Judson, and noticed how he'd transformed a bowl of whites into these chewy meringues to be placed in small plastic bags and given guests to take home. Mother now makes the confections not only for friendship gifts but also, of course, for her cocktail parties. I love the fluffs so much that I freeze extra egg whites till I have enough to make a big batch. They do harden very quickly, so be sure to store them in airtight containers.

1 cup granulated sugar
3 large egg whites
½ teaspoon cream of tartar
1 tablespoon pure maple extract
½ cup semisweet chocolate chips

*P*reheat the oven to 200°F. Cover a large baking sheet with parchment paper or foil and set aside.

*I*n a large mixing bowl, combine the sugar, egg whites, and cream of tartar and beat with an electric mixer till stiff peaks form. Add the extract and beat till well blended. Fold in the chocolate chips, then drop the meringue by the teaspoon about 1 inch apart onto the prepared baking sheet and bake till just soft and slightly golden, about 45 minutes. Let the fluffs cool, then transfer them with a spatula to a serving plate.

YIELD **About 15 fluffs**

 *Martha's Sweet Note*

I never make any type of meringue on a rainy or cloudy day, since they won't firm up properly in the humidity.

FIG PRESERVES

As many relatives, friends, and even part-strangers from coast to coast know, Mother is a master at preserving fruits, and to some the most precious of all her gifts is a rare jar of the delectable fig preserves she puts up only in small quantities once a year. One reason is that, unlike most other fruit preserves, these are more a dessert than a condiment, ideal spooned discreetly over vanilla ice cream or used to transform a simple slice of pound or sponge cake into an altogether different concept. Cooking the figs can be a bit tricky, so, after adding the sliced lemons, watch very carefully to make sure that the syrup doesn't overthicken before the figs clear (that is, soften to an almost translucent sheen).

7 cups granulated sugar
¼ cup fresh lemon juice
1½ cups hot water
2 quarts (about 4½ pounds) fresh figs, stemmed
2 lemons, thinly sliced

In a large kettle, combine the sugar, lemon juice, and hot water, bring to a boil, reduce the heat to moderate, and cook, stirring, till the sugar has completely dissolved, about 5 minutes. Add the figs, increase the heat to moderately high, and cook rapidly, stirring occasionally, for 10 minutes. Add the sliced lemons and continue to cook rapidly till the figs clear, 10 to 15 minutes. (If the syrup thickens too much before the figs clear, add about ¼ cup boiling water.)

Pack the figs into ten ½-pint hot, sterilized jars, add syrup to come to ¼ inch from the top of each jar, seal, and allow to cool completely. Store in a cool area.

YIELD Ten ½-pint jars of figs

FRIENDSHIP BRANDIED FRUIT

*R*esting on the counter in Mother's kitchen is a huge, very attractive, glass apothecary canister always full of this delectable brandied fruit, used either to spoon over ice cream and cake or to fill gift jars intended for close friends. "When people are invited to others' homes, they always take the same old wine or flowers or candy," she comments candidly, "so at some point I decided to fill pint jars with my brandied fruit, decorate them with checkered pieces of cloth and pretty ribbons, include a tag with instructions on how to start and 'feed' a batch, and encourage others to make their own mixture." Suffice it that nothing is in more demand today than a jar of Mother's brandied fruit.

1 cup canned pineapple chunks, drained
1 cup canned peach slices, drained
1 cup canned apricot slices, drained
1 cup canned cherries, drained and halved
1 cup granulated sugar, plus more as needed
Good-quality brandy

*I*n a large apothecary canister or decorative glass container with a lid, combine the fruits with the sugar and stir till well blended. Just barely cover the fruit mixture with brandy and stir well. Keep tightly covered at room temperature for at least one week, stirring twice each week. Every 3 weeks, add 1 cup granulated sugar plus 1 cup of any of the above drained fruits, stirring after each addition, and always keep a minimum of 1 cup of mixture as a starter.

*W*hen ready to use as gifts, ladle the fruit into ½- or 1-pint jars with lids and decorate the jars with colorful pieces of cloth or ribbons.

Dessert Basics: Cakes, Pastry Shells, Frostings & Sauces

1-2-3-4 CAKE

Despite the fact that the name quaintly but incorrectly refers to the numerical progression of the first four ingredients, Mother calls this the "workhorse" of all basic cakes, one that lends itself to virtually any frosting (my favorites are Caramel—page 253—and Chocolate-Marshmallow—page 251). Since you do want a perfectly even cake here, be sure to "spank" the batter after it's scraped into the pans.

1 cup (2 sticks) butter, softened
2 cups granulated sugar
4 large eggs
3 cups all-purpose flour
1 tablespoon baking powder
¼ teaspoon salt
1 cup milk
1 teaspoon pure vanilla extract

Preheat the oven to 350°F. Grease and flour three 9-inch round cake pans, tapping out any excess flour, and set aside.

In a large mixing bowl, cream the butter and sugar together with an electric mixer till light and fluffy, then add the eggs one at a time, beating well after each addition. In a medium-size mixing bowl, combine the flour, baking powder, and salt, mix well, and add alternately with the milk to the creamed mixture, beating till smooth. Add the vanilla and beat till well blended.

Divide the batter evenly among the three prepared pans, "spank" the bottoms of the pans to distribute the batter evenly, and bake till a cake tester or straw inserted in the center comes out clean, about 30 minutes. Let the cakes cool in the pans for 10 minutes, then transfer to a wire rack to cool completely.

YIELD One 3-layer 9-inch cake; 10 to 12 servings

 Martha's Sweet Note

When adding dry ingredients alternately with liquids to a creamed mixture for cakes, always end with the dry for best textural results.

POUND CAKE

There are all sorts of so-called pound cakes, but this is the genuine one, made (as the name implies) with a pound of each main ingredient (eggs included). Mother not only uses the cake as the base for any number of fruit shortcakes but loves to serve slices with fresh fruit compotes, ice cream, and puddings or spread with fruit preserves. Unlike Mother, I like my pound cake with a "sad streak" (an undercooked, sweet, moist "streak" running down the middle), in which case the cake should be baked only for about one hour.

1 pound (4 sticks) butter, softened
1 pound (2 cups) granulated sugar
9 large eggs
1 pound (4 cups) all-purpose flour
Dash of salt
2 teaspoons pure vanilla extract
Juice of 1 lemon

Preheat the oven to 325°F. Grease and flour a 10-inch tube pan, tapping out any excess flour, and set aside.

In a large mixing bowl, cream the butter with an electric mixer till smooth, then gradually add the sugar, beating till light and fluffy. Add the eggs one at a time, beating well after each addition. Gradually add the flour and salt, beating constantly. Add the vanilla and lemon juice and continue beating till the batter is well blended and smooth. Scrape the batter into the prepared pan and bake till a cake tester or straw inserted in the center comes out almost clean, about 1¼ hours, taking care not to overcook the cake. Turn the cake out onto a wire rack and let cool completely.

YIELD One 10-inch tube cake; 12 servings

SPONGE CAKE

This very light textured classic is ideal for making such delicate desserts as Tidewater Trifle (page 16) and Tipsy Pudding (page 172), and if you don't care for fruit shortcakes made with biscuit dough as Mother and I do, this sponge cake (cut into rounds or squares) is the alternative.

1 cup cake flour (see Sweet Note on page 27)
1 teaspoon baking powder
¼ teaspoon salt
½ cup milk
¼ cup (½ stick) butter
6 large egg yolks
1 cup granulated sugar
½ teaspoon pure vanilla extract

Preheat the oven to 350°F. Line a 13 × 9 × 2-inch baking pan with waxed paper and set aside.

Into a small mixing bowl, sift together the flour, baking powder, and salt and set aside. In a small saucepan, heat the milk and butter together over moderate heat till the butter melts; keep hot over low heat.

In a large mixing bowl, beat the egg yolks with an electric mixer till thick, then gradually add the sugar, beating constantly. Add the vanilla and beat till well blended. Add the flour mixture and stir just till mixed, then gently stir in the hot milk mixture till well blended. Scrape the batter into the prepared pan and bake till a cake tester or straw inserted in the center comes out clean, 30 to 35 minutes. Let the cake cool in the pan for 5 minutes, then invert onto a wire rack, peel off the waxed paper, and let cool completely.

YIELD One 13 × 9-inch cake

ANGEL FOOD CAKE

*L*ike sponge cake, angel food cake (made with no shortening) can be used as the base of numerous Bavarians, composed puddings, and sweet fruit shortcakes. Also, if you're watching calories (at least partly), this is the perfect cake to frost lightly with Seven-Minute Frosting (page 252) or Orange Butter Frosting (page 254).

1 cup cake flour (see Sweet Note on page 27)
1½ cups granulated sugar
12 large egg whites, at room temperature
1½ teaspoons cream of tartar
¼ teaspoon salt
1½ teaspoons pure vanilla extract

*P*reheat the oven to 375°F.

*I*nto a small mixing bowl, twice sift together the flour and ¾ cup of the sugar and set aside. In a large mixing bowl, combine the egg whites, cream of tartar, and salt and beat with an electric mixer till soft, still slightly moist peaks form. Gradually, add the remaining ¾ cup sugar beating steadily till the whites form stiff peaks. Gradually fold the sifted flour mixture and vanilla into the whites till well blended. Scrape the batter into an ungreased 10-inch tube pan and bake till the cake springs back when touched with a finger, 35 to 40 minutes. Let the cake cool in the pan for 10 minutes, then invert onto a wire rack to cool completely.

YIELD One 10-inch tube cake; 10 to 12 servings

Martha's Sweet Note

*W*hen cooling a sponge or angel food cake, if the tube pan doesn't have little "feet" around the upper rim to hold it up when turned over, you can fit the center tube over an upright bottle to facilitate cooling.

BUTTERMILK CUPCAKES

Although Mother created these tangy cupcakes as a base for her Bridal Snowballs (page 129), they arc also delicious cloaked with virtually any frosting and served at birthday parties, afternoon teas, and ice cream socials.

½ cup (1 stick) butter, softened
1 cup granulated sugar
2 large eggs
2 cups all-purpose flour
½ teaspoon salt
1 teaspoon baking soda
⅔ cup buttermilk (see Sweet Note on page 10)

Preheat the oven to 350°F. Line the cups of three 6-cup muffin tins with paper cupcake liners and set aside.

In a medium-size mixing bowl, cream the butter and sugar together with an electric mixer till light and fluffy, then add the eggs one at a time, beating after each addition till well blended. In a small mixing bowl, combine the flour, salt, and baking soda and mix well. Add alternately with the buttermilk to the creamed mixture, ending with the flour mixture and beating till well blended. Fill the cups of each prepared tin half full with batter and bake till a cake tester or straw inserted in the center comes out clean, 20 to 25 minutes. Let the cupcakes cool in the tins for 10 minutes, then transfer to a wire rack to cool completely.

YIELD 18 cupcakes

PASTRY SHELLS

MARTHA PEARL'S SWEET NOTES ON PASTRY SHELLS

Mother has her own (wise) ideas about dealing with pastry shells, so do take note of these general hints:

1. When vegetable shortening is used to make pastry dough, it should be cold to ensure the flakiest and tenderest crust. Likewise, be sure to measure the shortening carefully, since too much will produce a crust that's too crumbly and dry.

2. When a pastry recipe calls for water to be added to a flour-and-shortening mixture, always use ice water and, for the ideal texture, mix slowly with a fork just till the dough is moist enough to be formed into a ball.

3. Pastry dough (like biscuit dough) does not like to be handled too much, and if you overmix, you'll end up with a heavy, tough crust.

4. Using too much liquid in a dough will result in a heavy, soggy crust; using too little will produce a crumbly one.

5. Always roll out pastry dough on a lightly floured surface and, for even and smooth results, always roll from the center to the edges (not to and fro), rotating the dough as you roll.

6. For a single-bottom pie shell, roll the dough about ⅛ inch thick and 2 to 3 inches wider than the pie plate. For a top crust, roll the dough very thin and just slightly wider than the plate.

7. To fit rolled-out dough into a pie plate, carefully fold the dough in half, position it over the center of the plate, and unfold it to fit loosely in the plate. Gently press the dough into the bottom and sides of the plate, pat gently with your fingers to remove any air pockets, trim the edges, and patch any tears or splits with the excess pieces of dough. If desired, crimp the edges of the dough with your thumb.

BASIC PIE OR TART SHELL

1½ cups all-purpose flour
½ teaspoon salt
½ cup Crisco shortening
4 to 5 tablespoons ice water

*I*n a large mixing bowl, combine the flour and salt, then cut in the shortening with a pastry cutter or two knives till the mixture resembles coarse meal. Stirring with a wooden spoon, gradually add the water till a ball of dough is formed. Wrap the dough in plastic wrap and chill till ready to use.

*T*o bake the pie or tart shell, preheat the oven to 425°F, grease a 9- or 10-inch pie plate or tart pan, and set aside.

*P*lace the chilled dough on a lightly floured surface and roll it out from the center (not to and fro) with a lightly floured rolling pin to a ⅛-inch thickness. Carefully fold the pastry in half, lay the fold across the center of the prepared plate or pan, unfold it, and press it loosely into the bottom and sides of the plate or pan. Prick the bottom and sides with a fork, trim and crimp the edges, place on a heavy baking sheet, and bake till the shell browns evenly, 12 to 15 minutes. Allow the shell to cool completely on a wire rack.

(Note: For pies calling for either a double or lattice crust, use 2 cups all-purpose flour, 1 teaspoon salt, ⅔ cup Crisco shortening, and 5 to 7 tablespoons ice water.)

YIELD One 9- or 10-inch pie or tart shell

SPICY PIE SHELL *Decrease the salt to ¼ teaspoon and add ½ teaspoon each ground cinnamon and nutmeg. Mother uses this shell to add flair to fillings that tend to be a bit bland. Try it for pumpkin pies, sweet potato pies, apple pies, or any pear tart, like her Horse Pear Tart (page 87).*

Martha's Sweet Notes

When I bake pie shells, I never prick the ones I'm only partially cooking (drying out). For a fully baked shell, however, I initially prick the surface of the dough with a fork, then, during the baking, prick any areas that puff up too much. You must watch carefully.

If you want a pie to have a really nice brown crust, give it an initial high blast of heat (at least 400°F), then reduce the heat to the normal baking temperature.

BASIC SMALL TART SHELLS

1 cup all-purpose flour
½ teaspoon salt
⅓ cup Crisco shortening
3 to 4 tablespoons ice water

*P*reheat the oven to 350°F. Grease twelve 2-inch tart shells and set aside.

*I*n a medium-size mixing bowl, combine the flour and salt, then cut in the Crisco with a pastry cutter or two knives till the mixture resembles coarse meal. Using a fork, gradually add the water and mix till the dough is moistened and just holds together. On a lightly floured surface, roll out the dough ⅛ inch thick and cut out 3½-inch circles with a biscuit cutter or small juice glass. Press the circles into the prepared tart shells, rerolling the scraps of dough into more circles. Trim the edges of excess dough with a knife, prick the shells with a fork, place on a large, heavy baking sheet, and bake till slightly browned, 12 to 15 minutes. Let the shells cool completely on a wire rack.

YIELD Twelve 2-inch tart shells

CREAM CHEESE PIE SHELL OR SMALL TART SHELLS

This unusual pastry is ideal for any chocolate or lemon pie, and Mother sometimes uses the tart shells to make miniature pecan or other nut tarts.

½ cup (1 stick) butter, softened
One 3-ounce package cream cheese, softened
1 cup all-purpose flour

In a medium-size mixing bowl, combine the butter and cream cheese, stirring with a wooden spoon till well blended, then gradually add the flour, stirring till well blended and smooth. Using your hands, knead the dough lightly till very smooth, taking care not to overknead, and form into a ball. Wrap the dough in waxed paper and chill for at least 1 hour.

To bake the pie shell or tart shells, preheat the oven to 350°F, grease a 9-inch pie plate or two 6-cup muffin tins, and set aside.

For a pie shell, roll out the chilled dough on a lightly floured surface about ⅛ inch thick, press the dough into the bottom and sides of the pie plate, and prick with a fork. *For small tart shells,* pinch off twelve equal balls of dough, press each into a prepared tin, trim the edges of excess dough with a knife, and prick with a fork. Bake the pie shell or tart shells till slightly browned, 12 to 15 minutes, and allow to cool completely.

YIELD One 9-inch pie shell or twelve 2-inch tart shells

ALMOND PIE OR TART SHELL

*O*ne of the secrets to Mother's delectable Fig, Apricot, and Strawberry Tart (page 158) is this nutty crust, but it's also delicious with any chocolate filling and she sometimes uses it to add new dimension to her Horse Pear Tart (page 87) and Nesselrode Pie (page 30). I find it to be the perfect crust for any fruit tart.

2 cups all-purpose flour
2 tablespoons granulated sugar
½ cup finely ground almonds
⅛ teaspoon salt
½ cup Crisco shortening, chilled
1 teaspoon pure almond extract
¼ cup ice water

*I*n a large mixing bowl, combine the flour, sugar, almonds, and salt, stir till well blended, and cut in the shortening with a pastry cutter or two knives till the mixture resembles coarse meal. In a small bowl, mix together the extract and water and slowly add to the flour mixture, mixing with a fork till the dough just holds together. Wrap the dough in plastic wrap and chill for at least 30 minutes before using.

*T*o bake the shell, preheat the oven to 425°F, grease a 9- or 10-inch pie plate or tart pan, and set aside.

*P*lace the chilled dough on a lightly floured surface and roll it out from the center (not to and fro) with a lightly floured rolling pin to a ⅛-inch thickness. Carefully fold the pastry in half, lay the fold across the center of the prepared pie plate or tart pan, unfold it, and press it loosely into the bottom and sides of the plate or pan. Prick the bottom and sides with a fork, place on a heavy baking sheet, and bake till the shell browns evenly, 12 to 15 minutes. Allow the shell to cool completely on a wire rack.

YIELD One 9- or 10-inch pie or tart shell

 *Martha's Sweet Note*

*T*o make piecrust (as well as biscuit dough) really flaky, you must combine the cold fat (shortening, butter, or lard) with the flour very quickly when mixing with your hands. If you linger, the heat from your hands will melt the fat too soon and leave holes in the crust as it bakes.

COOKIE CRUMB PIE SHELL

*F*or variation, Mother might substitute this crunchy pie shell for a basic one in her Divine Grace Coconut Custard Pie (page 140) and even her Lattice Apple Pie (page 57), and she also suggests using it with virtually any chocolate filling.

1½ cups crushed cookie crumbs (chocolate chip, vanilla wafers, etc.)
½ cup confectioners' sugar, sifted
¾ cup (1½ sticks) butter, melted

*P*reheat the oven to 350°F. Grease a 9-inch pie plate and set aside.

*I*n a medium-size mixing bowl, combine the crumbs, sugar, and butter and stir till the crumbs are well moistened. Press the mixture firmly into the bottom and sides of the prepared pie plate and bake till firm, about 10 minutes. Allow the shell to cool completely on a wire rack.

YIELD One 9-inch pie shell

GRAHAM CRACKER PIE SHELL

*T*his versatile crust is the basis for such creamy concoctions as Marty's Fudge Sundae Pie (page 126), makes a nice substitution in Nalle's Cherry Buttermilk Pie (page 58) and other fruit pies, and enhances any pie with lemon filling. Also try this shell with your favorite nut or peanut butter pie recipe.

1½ cups finely rolled graham cracker crumbs
⅓ cup granulated sugar
⅓ cup (about ¾ stick) butter, softened

*P*reheat the oven to 350°F. Grease a 9-inch pie plate and set aside.

*I*n a medium-size mixing bowl, combine the crumbs, sugar, and butter and stir with a wooden spoon till the mixture is well blended and the crumbs are evenly moistened. Press the mixture into the bottom and sides of the prepared pie plate and bake the shell till firm, about 10 minutes. Allow the shell to cool completely.

YIELD One 9-inch pie shell

CHOCOLATE WAFER PIE SHELL

*M*other's St. Pat's Crème de Menthe Pie (page 33) simply wouldn't be right without this sumptuous chocolate wafer crust, nor would her basic Chocolate Pie (page 169) or rich-as-sin Black Bottom Pie (page 88). The shell is also a nice option for Jes' Pie (page 168), as well as for any nut pie.

1½ cups finely crushed chocolate wafer crumbs
½ cup (1 stick) butter, softened
¼ cup granulated sugar

*P*reheat the oven to 350°F. Grease a 9-inch pie plate and set aside.

*I*n a medium-size mixing bowl, combine the wafer crumbs, butter, and sugar and stir till the mixture is well blended and the crumbs are evenly moistened. Press the mixture into the bottom and sides of the prepared pie plate and bake till firm, about 10 minutes. Allow the shell to cool completely.

YIELD One 9-inch pie shell

*F*ROSTINGS

MARTHA PEARL'S ART OF FROSTING

When your cake or cake layer is ready to frost, place on a large cake dish and brush off any crumbs from the top and sides with a pastry brush.

For a single-layer cake, spoon a generous amount of frosting onto the center of the top of the cake and, using an icing spatula (available in kitchen supply shops) or a plain silver or metal knife, spread the frosting as evenly as possible toward the edges of the cake. Add more frosting to the top and, always spreading from the center to the edges, frost down the sides slowly, evenly, and smoothly. Repeat till all the frosting is used up.

For a layer cake, frost the top of the first layer in the above manner, then place a second layer on top of the frosted one, frost it, and continue stacking and frosting the tops, frosting the tops evenly but saving enough frosting for the sides. Use the remaining frosting to frost the sides, spreading it evenly and smoothly.

For a tube or Bundt cake, spoon the frosting all around the top and gradually spread it evenly and smoothly over the top and down the sides.

For cupcakes, place the individual cakes on a large platter, spoon equal amounts of frosting onto the tops, and spread the frosting evenly and smoothly over the tops and, if desired, partway down the sides.

To simply glaze a regular cake, pour the hot frosting very slowly over the top and let it drip down the sides. To glaze a sheet cake still in the pan, pour the hot frosting slowly over the top and let stand till cooled before cutting into squares, wedges, et cetera.

Before serving any frosted cake, allow the frosting to stand for about 1 hour to set.

(Note: If frostings made with confectioners' sugar are not quite stiff enough to spread easily, gradually stir in a little more sifted confectioners' sugar till the frosting is firm. If the frosting is too thick, stir in a little milk or cream till a nice spreading consistency is attained.)

FROSTING YIELDS

Top and sides of one single-layer 9-inch cake: 1 to 1¼ cups

Top and sides of one 2-layer 9-inch cake: 2 to 2⅔ cups

Top and sides of one 3-layer 9-inch cake: 2½ to 3 cups

Top and sides of one medium (9½ × 5½ × 3-inch) loaf cake:
   1 to 1½ cups

Top and sides of one large (16 × 5 × 4-inch) loaf cake: 2 to 2½ cups

Top and sides of one 9- or 10-inch tube or Bundt cake: 3 cups

Tops of 16 large or 24 small cupcakes: 2 to 2¼ cups

Glazing one single-layer 9- or 10-inch cake: 1 cup

Glazing one 10 × 15-inch sheet cake: 1⅓ cups

Martha's Sweet Note

I generally use wooden spoons to mix batters, frostings, glazes, and fillings by hand, since they seem gentler on the ingredients and the long handles are easier to manipulate. To test the consistency of mixtures by seeing if they coat the back of a spoon, however, the surface of a silver spoon is much better than that of a wooden one.

CHOCOLATE-MARSHMALLOW FROSTING

*M*other's spectacular Satan Chocolate Pound Cake (page 86) just wouldn't be the same without this frosting inspired by her chocoholic sister, Jane Theiling (my Aunt Dee). It's also superb spread over regular Pound Cake (page 238), Sponge Cake (page 239), and, for really delectable overkill, Baptism Marble Chocolate Cheesecake (page 110). And, of course, it can turn ordinary cupcakes into marvels of rich extravagance.

2 cups granulated sugar
One 5-ounce can evaporated milk
10 large marshmallows
½ cup (1 stick) butter
One 6-ounce bag (1 cup) semisweet chocolate chips
1 teaspoon pure vanilla extract

*I*n a large, heavy saucepan, combine the sugar, evaporated milk, and marshmallows, bring to a boil over moderate heat, and cook for 6 minutes, stirring. Remove the pan from the heat, add the butter, chocolate chips, and vanilla, and beat with a wooden spoon till the frosting is thick and smooth, about 10 minutes.

YIELD About 3 cups frosting; enough for the top and sides of a 10-inch tube cake or a 3-layer 9-inch cake, or for about 2 dozen cupcakes

SEVEN-MINUTE FROSTING

*T*his feathery-white vanilla frosting was conceived to complement Mother's inimitable Snowflake Coconut Cake (page 106), but it also works equally well on Butter Pecan Cake (page 138), Resolution Cranberry-Orange Spice Cake (page 12), and the squares of Easter Moravian Sugar Cake (page 46). The frosting is really very elemental, so experiment with it on any number of your favorite cakes.

5 large egg whites
2½ cups granulated sugar
½ cup water
½ teaspoon pure vanilla extract

*I*n the top of a double boiler, combine the egg whites, sugar, and water and beat slowly with an electric mixer till well blended. Over boiling water, beat the mixture briskly till stiff peaks form, about 7 minutes. Remove the pan from the heat and beat in the vanilla. Continue beating till the frosting is thick and smooth, then use immediately.

YIELD About 3 cups frosting; enough for the top and sides of a 3-layer 9- or 10-inch cake

CARAMEL FROSTING

There is, in my jaded opinion, simply no frosting on earth quite like this simple buttery one that gilds the lily on the sumptuous Caramel Cake (page 108) that Mother always made for her daddy's birthday and that she still surprises me with from time to time. The frosting is also superb on 1-2-3-4 Cake (page 237) and Pound Cake (page 238), as well as on plain cupcakes.

½ cup (1 stick) butter
1½ cups firmly packed dark brown sugar
½ cup milk
4 cups confectioners' sugar, sifted

In a large, heavy saucepan, melt the butter over low heat. Add the brown sugar and milk and, stirring, bring the mixture to a boil. Remove from the heat and let cool, then gradually add the confectioners' sugar and stir till well blended and very smooth.

YIELD About 3 cups frosting; enough for the top and sides of a 3-layer 9-inch cake or for about 2 dozen cupcakes

ORANGE BUTTER FROSTING

This zesty frosting is a sensation on any chocolate cake, and Mother has even substituted it with nice success for the regular chocolate frosting on The Great $100 Chocolate Cake (page 42). It's great on Chocolate-Orange Cupcakes (page 111) and transforms any gingerbread or shortbread into a truly stunning and unusual dessert. I've also frosted Mother's Raisin Rum Cake (page 56) with this mixture, and guests have raved with delight.

One 1-pound box confectioners' sugar, sifted
¾ cup (1½ sticks) butter, softened
2 teaspoons grated orange rind
1 teaspoon grated lemon rind
¼ cup fresh orange juice
1 tablespoon fresh lemon juice

*I*n a large mixing bowl, cream the sugar and butter together with an electric mixer till fluffy and smooth. Add the citrus rinds and juices and beat till the frosting is very smooth.

YIELD 2 cups frosting; enough for the top and sides of a 10-inch tube cake or a 2-layer 8- or 9-inch cake, or for a dozen cupcakes

CHOCOLATE SAUCE

Mother uses this all-purpose sauce primarily to adorn scoops of her Classic Vanilla (page 214) and Crunchy Peanut Butter (page 215) Ice Creams, but she also thinks nothing of spooning a little of the rich sauce over her Chocolate Bread Pudding (page 141) and simple slices of Angel Food Cake (page 240). And if you really want something rather elegant and unusual, drop a dollop or two of the sauce on Polished Poached Oranges (page 204).

8 ounces unsweetened baking chocolate
2 cups granulated sugar
One 12-ounce can evaporated milk
1 teaspoon pure vanilla extract
¼ cup (½ stick) butter

In a large, heavy saucepan, melt the chocolate over low heat. Add the sugar and stir till well blended. Increase the heat to moderate, gradually add the evaporated milk, and cook, stirring constantly, till the mixture thickens, about 10 minutes. Remove the pan from the heat, immediately add the vanilla and butter, and stir till the butter melts. Serve the sauce hot or cold. (Keeps in a tightly covered container in the refrigerator for up to 1 week.)

YIELD 3 cups

LEMON SAUCE

I think this must be Mother's favorite dessert sauce, since she serves it on everything from Buttermilk Gingerbread (page 225) to Brownie Pudding (page 130) to Blackberry Fool (page 183). I also love it on her Secession Brown Betty (page 159) and am convinced that it heightens the flavors in Cranberry-Apple Cobbler (page 94).

½ cup granulated sugar
4 teaspoons cornstarch
⅛ teaspoon salt
1 cup water
2 large egg yolks, beaten
2 tablespoons butter
½ teaspoon grated lemon rind
2 tablespoons fresh lemon juice

In a medium-size, heavy saucepan, combine the sugar, cornstarch, and salt, mix well, and gradually stir in the water. Cook the mixture over low heat till bubbly and thick, stirring constantly. In a small bowl, beat the egg yolks till frothy, then, stirring constantly, add a few tablespoons of the hot sugar mixture to the yolks. Stirring constantly, pour the egg mixture into the hot sugar mixture and continue to cook, stirring, for 1 minute. Remove the pan from the heat, add the butter and lemon rind and juice, and stir till well blended. Serve the sauce hot or cold. (Keeps in a tightly covered container in the refrigerator for up to 1 week.)

YIELD **2 cups**

BUTTERSCOTCH SAUCE

Since it's so incredibly rich, Mother makes this sauce in small amounts to be served discreetly over ice cream, any type of Brown Betty, and Apple Dumplings (page 114). The sauce is also awfully good drizzled on Buttermilk Cupcakes (page 241) and any firm chocolate confection. Just remember not to oversauce.

1 large egg yolk, beaten
¼ cup (½ stick) butter, cut into pieces
¼ cup water
⅔ cup firmly packed light brown sugar
⅓ cup corn syrup

In a medium-size, heavy saucepan, combine the egg yolk, butter, water, brown sugar, and corn syrup and cook over low heat till thick, about 10 minutes, stirring constantly. Stir the sauce well before serving. (Keeps in a tightly covered container in the refrigerator for up to 1 week.)

YIELD About 1¼ cups

MOCHA SAUCE

This is probably the most subtle dessert sauce in Mother's repertory, a highly versatile blend that goes as well over Crunchy Peanut Butter Ice Cream (page 215) as over Good-Luck Brownie Pudding (page 130) and Orange Bavarian Surprise (page 35). If you really want something mind-bogglingly good, try substituting this sauce for the brown sugar glaze on Banana Caramel Pound Cake (page 155).

8 ounces unsweetened baking chocolate
2 cups granulated sugar
One 12-ounce can evaporated milk
¾ teaspoon instant coffee granules
2 tablespoons boiling water
1 teaspoon pure vanilla extract
¼ cup (½ stick) butter, cut into pieces

In a large, heavy saucepan, melt the chocolate over low heat, then add the sugar and stir till well blended. Increase the heat to moderate, gradually add the evaporated milk, and cook till thickened, about 10 minutes, stirring constantly. In a cup, dissolve the coffee granules in the boiling water and stir into the chocolate mixture. Remove the pan from the heat, add the vanilla and butter, and stir till the butter melts and the sauce is very smooth. Serve the sauce hot or at room temperature. (Keeps in a tightly covered container in the refrigerator for up to 1 week.)

YIELD 3½ cups

CARAMEL SAUCE

Like most Southerners, everyone in our family has always loved caramel in any shape or form, not the least of which is this luscious sauce of Mother's, often spooned over certain ice creams, Banana and Georgia Kiss Puddings (pages 171 and 34), and her crisp Apple-Bourbon Fritters (page 37). I also relish the sauce cold over just a slice of slightly undercooked Pound Cake (page 238).

1 cup granulated sugar
2 level tablespoons cornstarch
¼ cup cold water
1 cup boiling water
¾ teaspoon pure vanilla extract
1 teaspoon corn syrup

In a medium-size, heavy saucepan, combine the sugar and cornstarch and stir till well blended. Moisten the mixture with the cold water and stir. Cook the mixture over low heat till it turns light brown, about 10 minutes. Add the boiling water and, stirring constantly, cook till the mixture is clear, about 5 minutes. Add the vanilla and corn syrup and stir till the sauce is well blended and smooth. Serve hot or cold. (Keeps in a tightly covered container in the refrigerator for up to 1 week.)

YIELD About 1½ cups

HARD SAUCE

*M*other learned to make this classic dessert sauce as a child at the knees of her mother's black maid, Essie, and today she still serves it on everything from bread puddings to Apple Dumplings (page 114) to various fruit cobblers, crisps, and crumbles. Personally, I love it over gingerbread. Note that, if desired, one tablespoon of rum, bourbon, or brandy can be substituted for the vanilla extract for an interesting variation.

½ cup (1 stick) butter, softened
2 cups confectioners' sugar, sifted
⅛ teaspoon salt
1 teaspoon pure vanilla extract
¼ cup heavy cream

*I*n a medium-size mixing bowl, combine the butter and sugar and beat with an electric mixer till light and fluffy. Add the salt and vanilla and beat well, then add the cream and beat till the sauce is smooth. (Do not chill this sauce for any length of time, or the texture will be adversely affected.)

YIELD 1 cup

BRANDY SAUCE

*T*his sauce is a natural for almost any apple dessert (Brown Bettys, baked apples, apple fritters, etc.) and, more particularly, try it on Mother's Stone Fence Applesauce Cake (page 154), her Orange-Cranberry Tea Bread (page 198), or, instead of the traditional bourbon sauce, on Sam's Bread Pudding (page 62).

¼ cup (½ stick) butter, softened
1 cup confectioners' sugar, sifted
1 teaspoon boiling water
2 tablespoons brandy
Dash of salt

*I*n a small mixing bowl, combine the butter and sugar and beat with an electric mixer till light and fluffy. Add the water, brandy, and salt and beat till the sauce is smooth. (Keeps in a tightly covered container in the refrigerator for up to 1 week.)

YIELD 1 cup

SWEET WINE SAUCE

No sauce is so uniquely Southern as this simple warm combination of butter, sugar, and any good sweet wine used to enhance Persimmon Pudding (page 97), any mixed berry crumble or cobbler, and, yes, even Mother's Coffee Cake Muffins (page 113). And if ordinary "Get Well" Baked Custard (page 143) and Prune Whip (page 145) sound too bland for your taste, serve them with a little of this sauce spooned over the top.

¼ cup (½ stick) butter, softened
⅓ cup granulated sugar
1 cup sweet wine (sherry, Madeira, or port)

*I*n a medium-size mixing bowl, combine the butter and sugar, beat with an electric mixer till light and fluffy, and set aside.

*I*n a small saucepan, warm the wine over low heat, add to the butter mixture, and beat till the sauce is creamy and smooth. Serve hot. (Keeps in a tightly covered container in the refrigerator for up to 1 week.)

YIELD About 1¼ cups

CUSTARD SAUCE

*G*ingerbread with custard sauce seems to be one of those gustatory marriages made in heaven, but Mother also serves the velvety sauce with her Bereavement Chocolate Bread Pudding (page 141), various other puddings, and virtually any fruit crisp, slump, flummery, or fool.

4 large egg yolks, beaten
⅛ teaspoon salt
¼ cup granulated sugar
2 cups milk, scalded (See Sweet Note on page 18) and cooled slightly
1 teaspoon pure vanilla extract

*I*n a medium-size, heavy saucepan, combine the egg yolks, salt, and sugar and stir, then gradually add the scalded milk, stirring constantly. Cook the mixture over low heat, stirring constantly, till it thickens slightly and coats the back of a spoon. Remove the pan from the heat, place in a larger pan of cold water, and stir for 2 minutes. Add the vanilla, stir till well blended, and chill the sauce for about 1 hour before using. (Do not keep this sauce.)

YIELD About 2 cups

SOUR CREAM SAUCE

*D*ollops of this tangy cold sauce can virtually transform fruit pies, tarts, and crisps, as well as other desserts like Damson Plum Roll (page 162) and Chocolate-Almond Charlotte Rousse (page 64), but, mostly, Mother makes it to spoon over cobblers and any simple compote of fresh berries. Notice that the sauce must thicken in the refrigerator for at least four hours for the right consistency.

1½ cups sour cream
½ cup heavy cream
¼ cup granulated sugar
1 teaspoon pure vanilla extract
Pinch of freshly grated nutmeg

*I*n a medium-size mixing bowl, combine the two creams and whisk together till very soft. Add the sugar, vanilla, and nutmeg and whisk till the mixture begins to thicken. Cover with plastic wrap and chill till quite thick, about 4 hours.

YIELD **2 cups**

Index

...A'S WHITE FRUITCAKE

...ter
...gar
... unbeaten
... all-purpose flour
...rum
...poon baking powder
... " vanilla
... " almond extract
... " lemon extract
... lb. crystalized pineapple
... lb.   Cherries
... lb. chopped nuts.

Cream butter & sugar, add eggs one at a time
well. Sift flour, baking powder together.
2 cups flour to coat fruit and nuts. Add rem...
flour alternately with rum to other mixture, b...
well. Add flavorings. Finally add fruit & nut...
Spoon into individual baking cups for individual
cakes or into desired size well greased pans.
Bake at 275 degrees 30 to 45 minutes for individu...
cakes and larger ones until done when tested with a
straw. Remove from oven and pour small amount of ru...
over hot cakes. Store in airtight tins.

Use some of unchopped fruit and nuts to decorate
cakes before baking

English Toffee

1 cup butter—1/2 ch.
1 " sugar—brown
1 egg yolk—add—hot heat—
2 Tbl vanilla—add—heat
2 cups all purpose flour—add—heat
1 cup chopped nuts—add—heat
Spread in teflon or a ... 10 X 15 pan.
... egg white
... 300° for 25...
slightly ... ...
cut th... ...

Coffee cake

Base: 1 cup shortening,
Dissolve 1/2 " sugar in
1 " boiling water
   mixture until lukewarm
1 pkg yeast in
   warm water, a
sug + sugar add
... add
... with
... powder...

TOWN & COUNTRY 1700 BROADWAY, NEW YORK, N.Y. 10019   Jim Villas

Peanut Butter Cookies

1 cup butter
1 cup sugar   } cream
1 " d brown sugar
1 tsp vanilla
3 eggs, beaten — add
... cup peanut butter   stir in
          flour
     add meal
     ts soda

---

2 eggs—lightly beaten
1 cup scalded milk
Add yeast mixture +
Gradually beat in
3 1/2 to 4 cups flour (enough ...
1/2 hr. — lightly beaten
Butter top dough (enough ...
1 cup currants or raisins
1 1/2 hr. or double. Punch down dough + cu...
off pieces large enough to shape into balls
about 2 in. in diameter. Arrange balls on
buttered baking sheet so they touch on
another + let rise covered in warm place
45 min. or until double. Brush each ball on
buns with egg white lightly beaten
mark each bun with cross + brush
Bake in 350° oven for 20-25 min...
golden — Remove + rock—

...375. In sm...
...la. In large bo...
...la.; beat until
...mixture; mix we...
...s. Drop by teasp...
Bake 8-10 minutes.

SUGERED PEANUTS.

peanuts.
...gar and water th...
On low heat, sti...
up adhers to the
...for 30 minutes